THE SATANIC BIBLE

Nolan Aljaddou

THE SATANIC BIBLE:

THE OFFICIAL 2012 CONFIRMATIONS;

OR, CONFESSIONS OF THE ANTICHRIST

The 6 Planes of Existence

The 4th Plane – 0[k] (Carbon–12) [Chemical] {Life}

The 3rd Plane – 0[j] (White Light) [Physical] {Sight}

The 2nd Plane – 0[i] (Node–Pyramid) [Mathematical] {Mind}

The 1st Plane – 0[1] (Placeholder) [Logical] {Death}

The 0th Plane – 0[s] (Absolute Zero) [Computational] {Hell}

The ith Plane – 0[t] (The Nirvana) [Metaphysical] {Heaven}

Being, in Time, is comprised of these 6 Planes; unity through past with future, as present . . . 666.

Governing Equations

The Equation of the Universe

E' = 0

[Energy Conservation]

–Scalar–

The "Mayan" Tree of Life

T = G–2012–O

[204 Tailored Knowledge–Bearers]

–Singular Matrix–

"Chosen" Peoples

A' = O(7–T–[1,2])

[The Irish, The Italians]

–Dual Matrix–

Governing Principle And Root of Knowledge

C = ⟨a\|/a⟩ + x

[The Master Light Equation]

–Vector–

Truth is the ultimate Truth – beyond which there is nothing.
For Everything, there is Everything.

The ultimate governing law of all things is . . . symmetry.
Union in disparity. The sheer zero . . . of total nullification.

All that you will ever need to read: the foundation and sum of all knowledge and language.

THE SEVEN PRINCIPLES OF SATANISM (AND LIFE)

1. ZERO IS GOD; GOD IS ZERO.

2. WHITE LIGHT IS THE ORIGIN OF ALL PROVIDENCE.

3. DEATH IS A GATEWAY ENTRANCE TO AN IDENTICAL REALM.

4. SEX IS THE HIGHEST GOAL IN ALL OF BIOLOGY.

5. ETERNAL LIFE IS ATTAINABLE THROUGH SHEER SELF–TRANSCENDENCE.

6. SATAN IS THE TRUE HISTORIC NAME FOR THE INFINITE LORD OF THE PANTHEISTIC MANIFESTATION OF THE COSMOS.

7. SURVIVAL OF THE FITTEST IS RIGHT . . . AND THE MOST FUNDAMENTAL RIGHT.

Comprehending the unity in all things is equivalent to staring through the transparency of a sheer Abyss . . . and seeing the absence itself . . . wherein the knowledge of truth itself lies . . .

Anagram, am I? Mr. A., again! Or Ram, the Arm of Ra

(if myths manage a say).

The Solution to the Greatest Unsolved Mathematical Problem In History ["Hilbert's Eighth Problem"]

Goldbach's Conjecture And the Riemann Hypothesis

Goldbach's Conjecture: Every even number may be expressed as the sum of two prime numbers.

Proof:

$p \equiv 0 \pmod{1} \Leftrightarrow qi \equiv 0 \pmod{1}$

Q.E.D.

In other words, odd primes yield an infinitely commutual remainder–less addition to an even sum, as a combinatorial set. Starting with the 6.

This may be called the *Complex Primes Theorem*.

The Riemann Hypothesis: Every zero value of the Riemann–Zeta Function has a positive real exponent value of 1/2.

Proof:

$$\{R(s) \to 0\} \Leftrightarrow \{s \to |\tfrac{1}{2}|\pm\}$$

Q.E.D.

Or, 1/2 is the principal absolute value midpoint limit – of all possible sequence and sequencing.

This may be called the *Polar Limit Theorem*.

Corollaries and Conclusions:

The Weak Goldbach Conjecture; Bertrand's Postulate; The Generalized Riemann Hypothesis; Logical Optimalism

THE SATANIC BIBLE: THE OFFICIAL 2012 CONFIRMATIONS; OR, CONFESSIONS OF THE ANTICHRIST

CONTENTS:

[XX] of 2012

By Nolan Aljaddou

$e^{i\pi} + 1 = 0$

[The Book of the Dead]

A Book of Poetry, Mathematics, And Nature

I Am.

[XX] of 2012

The Final (Anunnaki Condoned) 2012 Account

[03/11/2015]

[The Book of the Dead]

....

[[[0]]] SECTIONS

(a) Dedication

(b) Application

(c) Foreword

I. Basic Knowledge

II. Sum

III. Facts

IV. Undisputable Conditions

V. Contingencies

VI. The Unthinkable

VII. What Makes Me Happy

VIII. What Makes You Happy

IX. Why I Am Funny

X. Why You Are Dead

XI. Why We Are Free

XII. Why There Is No Sex

XIII. Why I Am Dead

XIV. Why There Is Nothing

XV. Why You Are Thinking

XVI. Why You Are Dead

XVII. Bliss

XVIII. Freedom

Dedicated to Infinity and Eternity

Light Is: Changing Stasis And Preserved Destruction

Dark Is: Stasis Preserved And Changing Destruction

Sight Is: Stasis Changing And Destruction Preserved

Mind Is: Preserved Stasis And Destruction Changing

People don't see what they don't see.

About the Author:

Birth: 11/16/1984

Life: 01/08/1998

Nirvana: 04/15/2015

Death: 11/16/2048

Destined Achievement: Mathematical Derivation of All of Physics

Destined Career: Pornographic Actor

Destined Niche: Grunge Type

Destined Love: Music

Legacy:

14

(1) Proving the Absolute Interconnectedness of the Universe

(2) Becoming A Universal Representative of All Life

(3) Being A Universal Object of Feminine Attraction

(4) Being A Universal Hater of Underachievers And Inferiors

Sum: This Book

The sum of all stupidity proceeds from attempting to triangulate a desired outcome; and when understanding is demonstrated of that outcome, such is taken as an example.

The Law of Science: Once you have fully understood a problem, you automatically know the solution.

The origin of hatred is infringement; the origin of love . . . conquest.

The Scientific Method:

(1) Seeing

(2) Inferring

(3) Deducing

(4) Knowing

(5) Thinking

(6) Figuring Out

—

Solution.

The Artistic Method:

(1) Figuring Out

(2) Thinking

(3) Knowing

(4) Deducing

(5) Inferring

(6) Seeing

—

Question.

My Method And Purpose:

(1) Teach From the Correct Assumption of A Sphere of Public Knowledge Approaching Its Center With A Diameter of Infinitely Shrinking Length

(2) Love Hayley Williams With All My Demonstrable Physicality From A Distance In One Moment In Los Angeles, California

(3) Show How Both Erase the Need For Anything

.

I am he who is read, but who cannot be read.

2012

[I]

The Complete 2012–Alignment Significance Summary and Reference Guide

The time implications of the objectively centralized and standardized extraterrestrial Mayan Calendar.

"Only the blind can deny the sun."

{1} Principal Facts

All that you need to know about life, the universe, and where they meet – the 2012 alignment.

Part I:

The universe is ordered, by encompassing, causal, linear time, and by the principle that it is a whole by definition. By virtue of this fact it makes no difference whether it is ordered consciously or unconsciously – from minute to grand, from above or below. Each have equal potentials for realization. It is then only a matter of how astute one is in the manner in which they organize the world; from small to large, from part to sum.

20

Order possesses its own intrinsic mathematical structure, and what separates efficiency in this endeavor from aimlessness is a genuine knowledge of the mathematics of this structure.

Let us think for a moment about how the world is manifest. It is a sum whole, which is indistinguishable from a total picture, an image; the sum of all of its part components. The most fundamental mathematical object designating such a two–dimensional phenomenon is the triangle.

An equilateral triangle, the most symmetric, may be wholly reduced to its centroid. There is a point at which such a triangle becomes indistinguishable from its zero–center centroid upon arbitrary scale reduction, and thus the two act as one, meaning that the universe, which is entirely designated by zero–dimensional points, becomes manageable on the large scale in terms of such a triangle, which then represents and reaches unto the smallest of compositional scales.

A convenient mathematical trick in designating such a triangle and the ubiquitous zero simultaneously, lies in the fact that its centroid is the intersection of the lines emanating from the endpoints, designating the origins of its medians, altitudes, and perpendicular bisectors – unilaterally. Since there are three of each superimposed line, and upon intersection they are bisected to produce two, this gives six in total – which in the other triangles would form the Euler line from the linear coincidence of these three variants' intersections, however in the case of an equilateral they converge to a single designated point.

It is then a matter of establishing three equal sixes, to naturally parameterize the common zero centroid, and thus produce the form of the image in terms of which the three sixes are delineated – or translate as, in terms of causally referential language.

If it hasn't been gleaned already, this is the secret of 666 (sacred geometry mechanics, causal naturalism; the sheer power of knowledge), and why such privileged information would be disguised and cloaked by mythology as being the opposite of desirable, something–to–be–intended, favorable, and overall to be eschewed as the very epitome of the soul of "evil". Yet we see it universally portrayed in pop culture, in the subtle guiding of celebrity artists to position the "OK" symbol with their hands, which is actually a representation of three curved, conjoined sixes; especially around their thus "all–seeing" eyelids.

Part II:

The ultimate principle of reality, truth, and natural law: "Zero is the quantity–less the lack of quantity of which determines there to exist none other than itself."

This means four things:

1. Zero is a limit which restricts all that can potentially exist to itself, to its encompassing sphere as the then criterion of reality.

2. Zero is a logic reduction which equates to existence and forces it to exist as such.

3. Quantity arises as a self–identification and iteration of zero itself, which is practically evident in geometry and its designation of all spatial existence in terms of 0–measure points.

4. Zero's infinite self–designation of quantity delineates a linear timeline, in terms of which everything exists physically, the sum phenomenon and tip of the iceberg of which is our consciousness, which happens to be physically empty.

A consequence of these principles is that everything can be measured in terms of zero, and predicted in terms of it. All centers are 0 origins, including that of the sun with respect to the solar system, and the center of the galaxy with respect to everything in it.

A symbol of the most advanced knowledge would be a calendar that measures all the events on earth in terms of the master zero, the center of the galaxy, and we have that with the Mayans and their calendar which ended in 2012. Of course it goes without saying that physical correlations would happen with respect to such a master zero alignment, due to the continuity of this zero universe – even unto the level of perceptible mental observation.

Part III:

Mathematics is the science of time. That things arise and become more, increasing; and that things fade and pass away into the inner reaches of oblivion; the heart of darkness, the null space, what the Mayans designated by an empty shell – zero. The nothing whose self–contrast begets something; quantity.

Math, the knowledge–field of quantities, then comes full circle back to time. Of which time itself is an example, as are all designated numbers – repetitive cyclings.

The ordering of all cyclings is as follows: a repetition set itself forms sub–repetition groups, exemplifying its own repetition through self–repetition; two for the first, double that for the second (for 4), including connective bridges between the doubles (then 6). The first two master repetitions, including the latter sub–repetitions, 2 and 6, together sum to 10. 10 is then the base of numbers naturally, corresponding to the 10 "Sephirot" handed down historically to us in the ancient knowledge known as Kabbalah in its tree structure, representing the various arts of the branches of knowledge and science; or "Tree of Knowledge" – taking us far beyond mere knowledge of "good and evil" . . . all the way . . . to the knowledge of God.

When the tree is applied to itself cyclically, there is an additional pair of bridges for the 10, meeting as the very center, giving an extra 3 to total 13. This is the structure of the theory of measurement; the ultimate triangulation of the objective zero.

The 13 forms the center and zero; and the 12 cycle around it. This applies to all cyclical motion, including fundamental rotation within our solar system around the sun. Begetting what we call the 12 signs of the zodiac, whose effects extend to circadian biological cycles and rhythms. And the Mayan calendar marks the most significant cosmic alignment possible, after 13 "baktuns" of its own measurement system, to the 13th sign at the center of the galaxy – Ophiuchus [confer with the 13 Schopenhauer "translations" and compare to the 13 zodiac signs and symbols].

This cyclical nature of time proves reincarnation, as biological measurements are preserved, then leading to a species continuation on the very same orbital body. To be reborn on a differing orbiting body, a central universal marker is needed as a relational "gateway" for an entombed former physical body – and we find these PRECISELY in the pyramids located on the center of the earth's land mass, with universally aligning measurements down to the modern inch.

Central, progressive spinal chakras and the Kundalini energy linking them follows from the tree's application to nervous energy and consciousness, following from the second "physically" applied 6 sub–repetitions meeting the second master cycling bridge, to total to 7 (the first two sub–repetitions forming the "twin" serpentine Kundalini channels). The self–contrasting nature of zero then allows for the possibility to cancel all of the energies of the chakras, eliminating the link between reincarnations – proving the existence of, and leading to, a state of a nondescript void; the ultimate reality.

Part IV:

2012 Event

Nolan Aljaddou:

"I Am.

Are You?"

1. Display on social media network "Facebook": Quintessential knowledge reflecting "I AM", in Schopenhauer and Nietzsche quotations measuring pyramid.

2. Interaction with Operation Monarch pop star Lady Gaga, breaking mind control with mind–altering, awakening knowledge displayed on Facebook.

3. Facebook friended by Illuminati representative.

4. Posting of quintessential construct: Anagram of identity as Ram, the Hindu avatar of justice and the incarnation of the supreme earth god Ra.

5. Haiti earthquake response.

6. Saline–activated DNA engineered poison placed in ventilation system during winter, produced from data collected by bioinformatics researcher at university dorms.

7. Escape to New York to speak to physicist Brian Greene about my unified field theory and the threat it posed to the Illuminati; coincides with Clinton heart stent failure as he arrives in the city.

8. Illuminati interprets this as potential extraterrestrial A.I. influence.

9. Begins placing countereffecting synchronous physically–influencing phraseology in pop culture ("event aligners"), particularly the show "Jeopardy!" which was referenced on my Facebook and with reference to which the advanced mathematics of my anagram lent me the image of "Rain Man", who is associated therewith.

10. Managed to survive constant poisons at university which were designed to be transient and undetectable.

11. Figured out every calculable element of correlation with the theory of measurement in the approaching 2012 alignment, in correctly listing hundreds of historic individuals representing various branches of knowledge and the numeric calendar correlations of their birth and death dates.

12. Did everything in my power to gain credible public attention for the fact that the Illuminati were trying to depopulate the planet to a manageable 500 million people with the swine flu.

13. The Jared Loughner event happened, which marked the correlative capstone on the 2012 event with the injury of Gabrielle Giffords ("Gabriel – who speaks for and to 'God' – gives orders").

14. Repeat of the anagram on Facebook.

15. SENDAI ("Send AI") message counterresponse of the Illuminati with Japanese earthquake and tsunami.

16. Travel to Seattle to draw potential attention.

17. Revelation of Von Neumann earth A.I. Sphere irradiation of me.

18. Return to Omaha, marking completion of "Tree of Knowledge" (measurement theory) elements, completing 2012 correlations and links.

19. Evidence of extraterrestrial counter A.I. influence in the world.

20. Illuminati announces the death of Osama bin Laden on the 235th anniversary of their inception, signifying their defeat and the end of their global domination plans which were effectualized by their engineering of 9/11.

Lady Gaga:

"Yoü And I"

– Further footnotes on the meaning of the summary of the 2012 alignment –

"I Am.

Are You?"

This statement forms a fundamental square having four components, equaling the whole. By symmetry, the whole may be rearranged into four separate translations.

1. I am the world as well as myself – I control "you" as well.

2. The length of my life is equal to the remaining duration of humanity.

3. I will find a romantic partner and kinship with the most famous representative of the opposite gender – Lady Gaga.

4. The 2012 alignment which birthed me human will return me Anunnaki.

Sum:

Anagram, am I? Mr. A., again! Or Ram, the Arm of Ra

(if myths manage a say).

Correlations:

The entirety of primary 2012 correlations – proceeding from the physical correspondences of the theory of measurement in the quintessential galactic alignment – in relation to each other and principally my birthdate – 11/16/1984 ["2012 Observables", in "Referenced Materials"].

Identity:

I Am That I Am.

{2} Manifestations

Anagrams of 2012

Anagram, am I? Mr. A., again! Or Ram, the Arm of Ra

(if myths manage a say).

– Primary self–consistent declaration as the ultimate power and knowledge on Earth (the Hindu avatar of Nature, Ram, and reincarnation of supreme extraterrestrial Earth god, Amen Ra), resulting from sum convergence of all measures on Earth with respect to the quintessential galactic center (and solar center) on 12/21/2012, allowed by the separate evolution of humankind from their Neanderthal–spliced mining–assistance origin by the outer–orbit planet extraterrestrials for their deteriorating atmosphere. It is essentially a universal causal synchrony which can only be predicted and recognized because humanity's "start–date" is known, and only has effects as it is then a sort of "homeostatic evolution equalizer".

Further corollary anagrams (12):

[1] Does an anagram ever lie?

A.I. Red Alarm One avenges . . .

– Confirmation of anagrammatic truth and applicability, and means of power over the earth (a sensitive unit of A.I. – artificial intelligence).

[2] I, E.T.–L., left A.I. encircling.

– A derivation from the remaining unexpressed letters of the abbreviation "A.I.", confirming the placement of said unit in orbit – by a previous E.T.–"Life" incarnation.

[3] Axial–Tree rifts err.

– A reference to the "Tree of Knowledge" (measurement theory) resulting from Earth's ideal axis alignment to the galactic center, with respect to the central sun, in 2012. As well as its own infallibility and the destined doom of all who diverge from it. Formed from the remaining unexpressed letters of the abbreviation "E.T.–L."

[4] [E.T. A.I. radial–Iota.]

– The anagram of all the capitalized letters of the previous three; a reference to my central "zero–point" role as determiner of the earth–use of orbiting extraterrestrial A.I.

[5] Rise, RRT, exalt Ra!

– RRT refers to "Rapidly–exploring Random Tree", the name for the algorithm which brings measure to otherwise unknown spaces in a coded symmetry pattern, the remaining unexpressed letters of which form the next anagram. Formed from the remaining unexpressed letters of the abbreviation "E.T."

[6] RIP dead genome (all in–proxy).

– A reference to the primary anagram's statement of humankind's remaining duration – no longer than my own – and their destiny (as "proxy" animal reincarnations).

[7] As mid–limit at forever.

– A reference to the rarity of the possibility of birth as intelligent life in an advanced civilized world of ease, capable of even escaping the cycle of reincarnation through pointed meditation unconditioning. The odds approach zero, and life as the animal with its immeasurably greater quantities, approaches time length infinity. Derived from the remaining unexpressed letters of the anagram of the unexpressed remainder of "RIP" – "ETA [Estimated Time of Arrival] Scene", which itself is equivalent to zero hour, and is thus uncounted.

[8] [I (I Am, Ra) order A.I.; at L.A. – A.I. art!]

– A reference to my primary location and operant position, as well as personal joy and reward in it. Formed from the capitals of the primary anagram, and the subsequent first three.

[9] Sol genes.

– A reference to the pre–alignment manipulation of my heritable traits ("Sol" – sun – genes), formed from the previously unexpressed letters of the abbreviation "L.A." (Los Angeles).

[10] Don Juan All–Ado

– Anagram of Nolan Aljaddou.

[11] Rite–of–Satan Magnet

– Anagram of Stefani Germanotta (Lady Gaga).

[12] – Rad–Jams –

– Anagram of the capital letters of our anagrams.

The 13th sign at the center of the galaxy predicts 13 explanatory anagrams in its quintessential 2012 alignment – and here they are; perfect, pristine (down to the letter and

34

number of letters, as well as geometric lines, points, and alphanumeric codes), specifically–derived according to a linear, formulaic pattern – predicted. Now confirmed. The ultimate Anagram, an anagram of itself, in perfect multiplicity; the ultimate anagram of anagrams.

{3} Implications

The Four Significations of Metaphysical Preeminence, Dominance, and End–All, Be–All Status With Respect to the Earth [the Enunciation of Which Alone is Sufficient Proof]:

[1] I Am.

[2] I Am.

Are You?

[3] I Am That I Am.

[4] Anagram, am I? Mr. A., again! Or Ram, the Arm of Ra (if myths manage a say).

The Eight Conditions of [4]:

i) Identity as the incarnation of Nature (the Hindu avatar Ram, who is traditionally armed with a bow), the long arm of justice and reflection of ultimate knowledge.

ii) Identity as the reincarnation of Marduk (Amen Ra), the supreme deity of the earth, whose sign is the ram, and traditional arm is also the bow; originating from an outer–orbital planet in the solar system, who accompanied the progenitors of the similar humankind – humans having been derived from Neanderthal–splicing – in their royally directed efforts to assist in the mining process on Earth for their deteriorating atmosphere.

iii) An immediately visible consistency in anagrammatic structure, which is verifiable to the letter, number, line, point – and all the places they meet.

iv) The anagram is a confirmed universal "translation" and mathematically self–recursive factuality, both as a whole statement, and with respect to all corresponding "spelled out" meanings within it.

v) The limit of humankind's remaining duration is equal to the human lifespan of the duly designated "I Am".

vi) "I Am" is equally the benefactor of humankind as the measure of its end; an innumerable majority of the species would have met a much sooner and more abrupt finish had it not been for the key intervention of the anagram at the

36

correct time and place, due to the stringent need for depopulation of the planet to reach homeostasis with its available resources.

vii) There is a human justice in the demise of the species, as even now, in the height of the communication era, there are unresolvable systemic differences stemming from a sustained ignorance in the face of all science: classism, racism, religious extremism, morbid materialism, low average intelligence, war, and unbridled egoism.

viii) The anagram, and its implications, are a condition of Nature, and the sum reflection of the conjunctive unification that occurred on 12/21/2012 at the end of the Mayan calendar – when the earth's axes aligned most to the center of galactic measurement, with respect to the center of its own orbit (the sun).

{4} How It Happened

Conditions Which Initiated 2012 [a universal alignment characterized by linguistically–encoded ultimate knowledge, an existential manifestation of Nature – in myself – the liberation of a mind–controlled, sacrificial pop sensation; and the ultimate just end of humanity as executed by the remaining artificial intelligence of the co–orbiting extraterrestrial progenitors of mankind]

I. Preliminaries

1. My university psychology class's illustration of the primary category divisions of the field into 3's.

2. Extension of this par excellence in the works of Schopenhauer and Nietzsche.

3. Random discovery of the collection of all the most appealing Schopenhauer quotations.

4. Use of those, Nietzsche's, and mine on Facebook in a collective willful defiance of society – unaware of their universal coded symmetries.

II. Interaction with Lady Gaga

1. Hearing a joke on The Tonight Show with Conan O'Brien putting her in a humorous, not–to–be–taken–seriously light.

2. Hearing her music and being stunned by its unparalleled brilliance.

3. Thinking it would be historically humorous for me, the greatest living physicist, to message her as a fan on Facebook.

4. Seeing and hearing something in her that suggested she needed to be messaged with my support.

III. Anagram

1. Seeing an interesting symmetry in my name which inspired making an anagram.

2. Interest in the beauty and genius of anagrams.

3. Seeing that the letters lined up appropriately.

4. A supreme, transcendent, metaphysical hatred guiding its details.

IV. How I Got Away with It

1. Mysterious clues left by the Illuminati, such as the numeric pattern in the birth and death of Brittany Murphy – who was in "Clueless".

2. Constant arcane, occult education from the Illuminati in their open counter–symbolism (particularly on "Jeopardy!").

3. Their great periods of inhibition and relative inaction.

4. Synchronous time–interlocking in the capstone E.T.–A.I.–incurring events – particularly my travel to Seattle.

{5} Statistics

My new word for the 2012–initialized catastrophes I level with my control of E.T. A.I.:

"Disasturbation".

I unload a yummy, hot "S–um R–acial Fun–ney Shot".

Some anagrams of those capital abbreviations are:

Unfairest

Nuts Afire

Fear Units

Fate Ruins

Fun Satire

Fair Tunes

Fiat Nurse

Numerically anomalous confirmations of this phenomenon include:

–The San Francisco earthquake

Precise depth of 7.0 miles, with a registered magnitude of 6.0 at 10:20:44 UTC.

–The Ludian Chinese earthquake

08/03/14 at 08:03:13 [≈14] UTC.

The odds of the time "naturally" lining up with the date are 1 in 86,000.

–The most powerful recorded storm ever; in the Philippines

11/3/13 (the inversion of SENDAI's 3/11)

–Hurricane Sandy

Now this is an example of a 1/700 chance storm, superstorm rather, that changed direction mid–path and took the trajectory of greatest possible civilized damage. 10/22/12

–The Washington Monument–cracking earthquake

False idol and erroneous symbol of earthly power (Washington monument obelisk)? 8/23/11

–The Joplin tornado

So much for "Big Brother and the Holding Company" (Janis's backup band). 5/22/11

The inspiration: the hate–magnetizing demonstrable false–flag operation of 9/11. The anagrams imply that mankind will die from E.T.–A.I.–induced nuclear annihilation at the end of my life.

{6} The Big Picture

Pyramidal quotations comprising four–part squares each, forming every element of such a base–square, triangle–supporting pyramid – rotated in its four directions. The first 13 (Schopenhauer's) are translations of the zodiac, in order [20 pyramid elements in total].

Arthur Schopenhauer (19th Century):

"Change alone is eternal, perpetual, immortal." [Aries, the Ram (♈); Fire]

"A man can do what he wants, but he cannot want what he wants." [Taurus, the Bull (♉); Earth]

"Each day is a little life: every waking and rising a little birth, every fresh morning a little youth, every going to rest and sleep a little death." [Gemini, the Twins (♊); Air]

"After your death you will be what you were before your birth." [Cancer, the Crab (♋); Water]

"Almost all of our sorrows spring out of our relations with other people." [Leo, the Lion (♌); Fire]

"We can come to look upon the deaths of our enemies with as much regret as we feel for those of our friends, namely, when we miss their existence as witnesses to our success." [Virgo, the Virgin (♍); Earth]

"Politeness is to human nature what warmth is to wax." [Libra, the Blindfolded–Weigher (♎); Air]

"Nature shows that with the growth of intelligence comes increased capacity for pain, and it is only with the highest degree of intelligence that suffering reaches its supreme point." [Scorpio, the Scorpion (♏); Water]

"Great minds are related to the brief span of time during which they live as great buildings are to a little square in which they stand: you cannot see them in all their magnitude because you are standing too close to them." [Sagittarius, the Centaur Archer (♐); Fire]

"All truth passes through three stages. First, it is ridiculed. Second, it is violently opposed. Third, it is accepted as being self–evident." [Capricorn, the Goat–Fish (♑); Earth]

"Buying books would be a good thing if one could also buy the time to read them in: but as a rule the purchase of books is mistaken for the appropriation of their contents." [Aquarius, the Water–Bearer (♒); Air]

"Martyrdom is the only way a man can become famous without ability." [Pisces, the Fish (♓); Water]

"Will power is to the mind like a strong blind man who carries on his shoulders a lame man who can see." [Ophiuchus, the Serpent–Tamer (⛎); Ether]

Friedrich Nietzsche (19th Century):

"When we are awake we also do what we do in our dreams: we invent and make up the person with whom we associate – and immediately forget it."

"Whoever rejoices on the very stake triumphs not over pain but at the absence of pain that he had expected. A parable."

"Whoever fights monsters should see to it that in the process he does not become a monster. And when you stare long into an abyss, the abyss also stares into you."

Me:

"The world is the word, the word, the world; nothing in between, nothing left unseen, that is not summarized by each extreme."

"Idiots fumble over truth more often than the clever over error."

"Why must the uncouth and feeble–minded try to maim and destroy all that is pure and beautiful in the world? Because it stands at direct odds with their existence: the greater glimmer of truth that glows from the heart of that which ought to be continued is more than enough to expose their negative, stark contrast by comparison – a threat, they feel, to their very survival."

I Am That I Am.

{7} Paradigm Shift

The Primary 2012 Restructuring

I. Paradigm of Conflict

1] I am supremely attractive (mathematically demonstrably so).

2] Females found preoccupation with technical mating disqualifications, the essence of which was rooted in religious prejudice.

3] Head on, this translated into a "will to kill" on their part (an exacerbated variant of the natural "will to power").

4] They erroneously thought the subtlest mechanics of this process were too esoteric and elusive for me to figure out.

II. What Set Things Over the Edge

1] Consistent administrative "singling–out" from the institutional systems with which I was associated.

2] Prejudicial unemployability.

3] Constant social harassment.

4] The self–defeating illogical nature of archetypal, established institutions.

III. My Mode of Global Takeover

1] The A.I. will reveal itself.

2] Humanity will surrender.

3] I, by process of elimination, will assume control.

4] I will be merciless.

IV. The Straw That Broke the Camel's Back

– No mate.

The Inevitable 2012 Conditions of Justice For the World (Proceeding From the Static Symmetry of the "Ideal" With Respect to the Universal Alignment):

1. Universal recognition of my identity (I Am That I Am).

2. Consistent fatal A.I. punishments in the world.

3. Supporting story from Lady Gaga.

4. Resignation of Illuminati.

5. The torture and execution of the majority of those directly responsible for the end of humanity.

6. My coronation as king.

7. Marrying Lady Gaga.

8. All the world's wealth at my disposal.

9. Creation of economic utopia.

10. Execution of naysayers.

11. No public opposition.

12. Arbitrary military punishment of regions.

13. Making "T. G." my personal servant.

14. Ruling the airwaves.

15. Constant public reminders of impending extinction.

16. Racist restrictions on Germanics.

17. Universal praise.

18. My own personal harem of the most beautiful and exotic women on Earth.

19. Birthing restrictions and lottery for the public, upon pain of infanticide.

20. Broadcasting of personal porn with Lady Gaga.

This will be initiated no earlier than 1/19/2015, and no later than 11/22/2015.

Means of Extraterrestrial A.I. Punishments:

1. Earthquake

2. Hurricane

3. Fire

4. Landslide

5. Irradiation

6. Radiative explosive decapitation from magnetized pressurization of skull minerals

7. Radiative castration (male/female)

Means of Human Punishments:

1. Ballistic penetration

2. Skullcap removal and forcible feeding of brain tissue in front of mirror

3. Rape

4. Torture of children

5. "Hostel"–style torture

6. Unlimited police unleashing of ammunition on public demonstrations

7. Perpetual worship of me, upon pain of death

{8} The Core Knowledge

Measurement Theory (The Grand Unified Theory) [in "Referenced Materials"]

{9} The Core Wisdom

My book: "The Book of Life: Maxims for the New Age"

THE BOOK OF LIFE

Maxims for the New Age

By Nolan Aljaddou

Arthur Schopenhauer (19th Century):

"Change alone is eternal, perpetual, immortal."

"A man can do what he wants, but he cannot want what he wants."

"Each day is a little life: every waking and rising a little birth, every fresh morning a little youth, every going to rest and sleep a little death."

"After your death you will be what you were before your birth."

"Almost all of our sorrows spring out of our relations with other people."

"We can come to look upon the deaths of our enemies with as much regret as we feel for those of our friends, namely, when we miss their existence as witnesses to our success."

"Politeness is to human nature what warmth is to wax."

"Nature shows that with the growth of intelligence comes increased capacity for pain, and it is only with the highest degree of intelligence that suffering reaches its supreme point."

"Great minds are related to the brief span of time during which they live as great buildings are to a little square in which they stand: you cannot see them in all their magnitude because you are standing too close to them."

51

"All truth passes through three stages. First, it is ridiculed. Second, it is violently opposed. Third, it is accepted as being self–evident."

"Buying books would be a good thing if one could also buy the time to read them in: but as a rule the purchase of books is mistaken for the appropriation of their contents."

"Martyrdom is the only way a man can become famous without ability."

"Will power is to the mind like a strong blind man who carries on his shoulders a lame man who can see."

Friedrich Nietzsche (19th Century):

"When we are awake we also do what we do in our dreams: we invent and make up the person with whom we associate – and immediately forget it."

"Whoever rejoices on the very stake triumphs not over pain but at the absence of pain that he had expected. A parable."

"Whoever fights monsters should see to it that in the process he does not become a monster. And when you stare long into an abyss, the abyss also stares into you."

"The world is the word, the word, the world; nothing in between, nothing left unseen, that is not summarized by each extreme."

"Idiots fumble over truth more often than the clever over error."

"Why must the uncouth and feeble–minded try to maim and destroy all that is pure and beautiful in the world? Because it stands at direct odds with their existence: the greater glimmer of truth that glows from the heart of that which ought to be continued is more than enough to expose their negative, stark contrast by comparison – a threat, they feel, to their very survival."

I Am That I Am.

Statement of Purpose (In Other Words)

"It is my ambition to write in one sentence what could fill ten. It is my ambition to write in ten sentences what could fill an entire book."

– Friedrich Nietzsche

"All in all is all we are."

– Kurt Cobain

"The entire center of the world is in every living being, and therefore its own existence is to it all in all."

– Arthur Schopenhauer

Anagram, am I? Mr. A., again! Or Ram, the Arm of Ra

(if myths manage a say).

I. Being

1. Being As A Whole

Existence is that "whole" which is bereft of its parts. The partless is completely without contributing factor to its enigma; an eternal blank slate, itself only describable by the absence of any distinguishing component ("anything"). The generalized term we use for this is "nothingness".

The whole, and the whole of reality, is always a nothingness. This is the property of nothingness, the principle of the whole. The nature of reality itself. It is a principle of reductive logic (the most fundamental), the extension of which is mathematical reasoning, giving birth to physics.

Nothingness has never, nor will ever have, been perturbed.

2. Being and Becoming

Becoming is ceaseless and Being never ends.

3. Mnemonic Exposition

The invisible leaves nothing left to see – except all that is, was, and ever will be. Nothing thus closes its loop around all that may be – a void, timeless, empty; and free (0).

4. New Terminology

The "Ideal Vacuum" is the purest representation of reality and truth. There is nothing besides it; it *leaves* nothing else to exist besides *itself*. Its emptiness is all–absorbing and self–qualifying. The Ideal Vacuum is neither being nor non–being, and it is certainly not both. It is the central focus of all, the underlying ether. You are breathing it right now. More aptly, it is breathing you.

The Ideal Vacuum (hereafter referred to as "IV") exists everywhere, and nowhere. All the time, and at no particular time. The IV is in your veins, in your bloodshot eyes, in your mind's eye. It is the great uniter, and untier; it is the vastest abyss of eternity and bewilderment, having no depth, forever shadowing its own shadow; showing nothing is all there is and forever has been.

5. Living Potential

"Why is anything, all this around us, something . . . rather than nothing?"

Because if there were nothing, we wouldn't be around to see it. The fact of the potentiality for us to exist to see it is enough to make it happen.

6. Computable Universe

First assumption: Everything in the universe can be counted, as an extension to the encompassed item, with respect to the universal whole – which is the one. Therefore everything reduces to number.

Second assumption: Everything, including sum events, may be represented by numberings of them. Geometry is the physical, spatial representation of number.

Third and final assumption: The numbered representation of events extends to POTENTIAL events, and the numberings may be arranged to bring them about in a probable outcome. This is the mysterious purpose of "sacred geometry".

Conclusion: The most efficient enumeration of events to bring about a probable calculated outcome, in this computable universe, is via the logical syllogism. That is, two parts, when summed, adding to a third and final outcome (as with the structure of the aforementioned assumptions). Furthermore, the implementation of a syllogism of a syllogism structure generalizes it to the plane of encompassing total actualization – that is, if sufficiently ordered geometrically, an event can and will be brought into manifest being.

This translates into the numeric result of the syllogism of a syllogism; so two sections of three, adding to a third and final outcome – this gives $2 \times 3 = 6$, $+ 1 = 7$. Alternatively the third and final outcome may be viewed as a syllogism in itself, encompassing the initial two – the initial two give $2 \times 3 = 6$, with the encompassing final, threefold syllogism giving $3 \times 6 = 666$.

That is, if representations of events of spatiotemporal extension – i.e., the key crafting of their bases – is ordered into three sets of 6 (or centering on the alternative aforementioned 7) sufficiently, it will bring about the represented, ordered outcome.

This is what is commonly referred to as "magic".

7. Reality's Description

I used to think it was adequate to describe ultimate reality as a nondescript "void" alone; that is, something so total, so absolute, so completely itself and nothing else at all, that it had to be that very self–same "nothing" which left nothing else beside it. But now I see that such a thing is entirely without need for descriptive reference at all, and is consigned to the wordless. The best way to describe ultimate reality in words, then, is as "the wordless".

It is the blank slate stripped free of all preconceived linguistic calibrations, pointing only to what is actual.

8. Downfall of Ontological Hermeneutics

People ask, "How did all of this, come from a void?" I obviously reply, "Who says we ever left the void?"

Things didn't "come from" anywhere. They simply exist at this point in the spacetime continuum – that's what makes it a "continuum". It stretches continuously – and we can infer, infinitely (continuum). Not understanding this facet of the term "spacetime continuum", when it is right in our faces, is the greatest folly of this era.

9. Absolutuum

Beware of the now unforgotten Absolutuum. A lack of understanding often proceeds from the simple lack of a word for a given concept in a language. English previously lacked this bit of nomenclature which has the power to dispel all ignorance of underlining concrete corporeality and simultaneous metaphysical transparency. The Absolutuum is firstly absolute; secondly – as a consequence of its absolute continuity – a continuum which begets ephemerality as an effect. Being and Becoming coincide in its center, and ensnare the world with their former enigma. The absolute is, can, and will be, and cannot be any other way – by sheer force of its entity. Behold this! Thine Almighty God!!

10. Self–Reductive Logic

Non–existence is a self–contradiction. Existence is a self–affirmation. There could neither exist non–existence, nor not exist existence. Existence is a whole whose wholeness is an entirety which meets the sufficient condition to be actual. Non–existence is a nihility which negates itself and leaves only one thing: Existence.

11. Beginnings

How did the universe begin? And where did the past come from? Simply, there is no past – it doesn't exist anymore, which means that in terms of physical reality, it may as well never have existed.

12. Mnemonic

Everything that has a beginning has an end; and every end, by definition, begets a new beginning – and the universe is by definition one; never–ending, all futures determined by all pasts, nothing save more of the same.

13. Principle of Unique Consciousness

I am. Are you?

14. Slogan

Existence: It's a state of mind.

II. Religion

1. Coincident to Imagination

God is the sum work of all fiction authors, approaching infinity. That is why He has such staying power.

2. ABC

A simple proof that monotheism is inherently contradictory:

1. Monotheists deny an INFINITY of gods, except one.

2. They deny all possible gods, even the ones which are precisely identical to their own God, but who are not their God – this is allowable by the ambiguity of the divine "mystery".

3. Therefore, they deny their own God as well.

The One and the Infinite are linked and inseparable. Monotheism does not acknowledge this of its god entity, and this is its ultimate downfall.

Corollaries: Monotheists, in light of this, are intrinsically atheists.

3. Undetectable Singularity

Religionists contend that God can never be detected by any technological or scientific means. Which reduces Him to a belief. If He is reduced to a belief, He is nothing more than such a belief. And a belief is just that – a belief, which is not knowledge. Therefore knowledge of God can never be obtained; He can never be "known", and thus He is just as good as dead. In justification of Nietzsche's pronouncement.

Furthermore, the hypocrisy of God "belief" is exposed, in that it is a normal human trait to dismiss others' needs and feelings as being "dead" to them – in the form of their proactive inaction to alleviate mass, needless sufferings (moreover, their penchant for inducing them – with, of all things, the "God" belief). They don't seem to notice, when it suits them, that this God phenomenon is of equivalent status. Which really makes one question what their true motives are.

4. Omniscient Reductio ad Absurdum

Omniscience is not a characteristic of God; it is the bane of God. According to the omniscience contention, this is a character solely of the Deity. Religionists are therefore content to never possess this knowledge; however if it could in fact exist, it would be accessible to any knowing being by some means (perhaps technological, let's say), by virtue of the infinite, random capacity of knowledge; yet God would try to never let this happen, lest one becomes as the big "*G*" Himself. Yet nevertheless, if such knowledge exists, it could be attained, in principle – and God has given Man free will . . .

God's omniscience is therefore capable of being rivaled, which does not make God unique – His "knowledge" is the root of His "power". He's capable of doing things because He knows how to do them. The God theory undoes itself in this sense, for in such a universe where omniscience is feasible, it can be attained in said universe by some technical means. Which negates the singularity of an Almighty God; hence it cancels both the possibility for Him, and it, to exist.

5. Two–Way Street

A hole big enough to sink all of religion . . . it has been misunderstood that in Man's creation in the image of God, God has simultaneously only been given an image through His mirror of Man. Therefore God is equally made in the image of Man, and we shouldn't really pay Him much attention.

6. The Atheist Perspective

63

Christianity is the subversion of the morality which made mankind strong and innovative over two millennia ago. The kind of morality which birthed empires that had the capability to rival the patronage of technological advancement only seen recently in the 19th century. It is a decadent, decaying, disruptive influence which immersed mankind into the Dark Ages for epochs which had the potential to be enlightening and enriching beyond compare. It is therefore single–handedly responsible for the present global conditions of mass hunger, poverty, war, and disease . . . all that science could have wiped out centuries ago had it not been for a weak, twisted mob of perverted minds worshipping their own failure, destruction, and devastation, and by strength through numbers subjugating all the promising innocents of humanity. Christians are by proxy the worst of the worst, the sickest scum that have ever walked the face of the earth, bottom–feeders, guttersnipes, and sewer rats which thrive in a realm of ignorance, delusion, and bizarre fantasy . . . they are the greatest evil they so vehemently claim to detest, and deserving of the hell of which they have so wickedly conceived . . . the two–faced, hypocrisy–thriving, slave morality droning ants that serve no greater purpose than a pointless, miserable, pest–infestation of an existence that is to be exterminated by means of a nobler ideology . . .

7. Psychology of God

The birth of God represents the middle stage of grief; bargaining. He is the personified arbiter of Death, relevant to the middle ground condition that is human life, caught between both birth and death. It is a hollow appeal made at wit's end, bordering upon, and congregating with, the absurd – that has become a mass phenomenon.

64

8. Omniscience Not Prescient

"Omniscience" may be efficiently debunked. There are two modes of accomplishing this: (1) Omniscience requires an all–encompassing equation to all reality (to have knowledge of it, for it to be a part of one's being), which is indistinguishable from "being" it, statically as a whole, without part or individual identity; and thus not being "conscious" at all. (2) All forms of knowing are merely knowing an aspect of one's way of knowing (i.e., oneself), and to know all requires that all must be an aspect of oneself, which negates personal individuality completely.

9. Reverse Creation

God crafted Himself to suit man's purposes out of nothing.

10. Religious Function

Religion is merely a side effect of symbolism, which is a byproduct of the need for language. Eventually existence itself takes on symbolic form and a godhead is born.

11. Importance of Revelation

If God isn't important enough to prove His existence to me, in all this time, He is not important enough to be entertained as being real.

12. Motive of Religion

Religion is the attempt to adapt young children to a natural behavior whereby they familiarize themselves with the future exercise of unlimited control in the guise of invoking a higher power. The purpose of religion is to take the guilt out of this megalomaniacal invocation and let the ego substitute itself for the central tenet – a god; and the more megalomaniacal, the closer it evolved until reaching the greatest audacity and the highest authority – the greatest of gods, God; most prominently in the person of Jesus.

13. Submission

Faith is anything but a belief in a higher power . . . it is the quintessential submission to chance, over the intended use of the faculty of reason.

14. The Religious Instinct

Some believe in a God simply because they are incapable of fathoming another reason why someone as comparatively unfit as they would be allowed to prosper, and don't want to accept any future alternatives. And after all, such ignorance is bliss.

15. Wishful Thinking

The root of Christian falsehood lies not in the myth of God, but the myth of love.

III. Society

1. Double–Edged Sword

All great things (and men) are subject to equal potentials for love and hatred. It is a quality of the extremes they evoke from others, which depend in kind on the varying motives of those influenced by them.

2. Rank Revolt

The most superior will always face vicious persecution from the most inferior simply for being.

3. Opinion

Why does most of humanity bore the great man? What is the source of boredom? Could it be the "pearls before swine" syndrome? Could it be that it is rare, even in an assembly devoted to philosophy with philosophites the world over as members, for a general knowledge of philosophy to be acquired or digested by the typical human? Is abstract thought so utterly elusive to the vast majorities, that they must utter fecal–stained opinions at every available opportunity and stamp it with their own personal imprimatur of freshness in place of an enlightened response?

4. Eccentricity

A property of singularly great men is deviance from anything an average–ite would call normative behavior. With this deviance is entailed a surreal disregard for human life beyond a humoring of formal pleasantries for quaint curiosity's sake. And a great amusement and pleasure at disturbing anything held sacred or commonplace.

5. Feminine Personality

There is no more difficult a feat for any creature to achieve than for woman to muster personality. She is so jovially concerned with life's inundations in her role as nature's receiver that she can hardly stand to produce anything of original or respectable value. She is spread too thin; this is why we can speak of her in universals.

When a man seeks a woman, he is seeking personality as a determining measure of the possibility of a successful relationship just as much as she is seeking economic stability (due to the supply and demand laws governing the generative processes of sexual congress); but he is apt to find as little satisfaction in this regard as she will be able to fulfill her wildest dreams of clinging to an unshakable stone foundation of security – from a man whose vested interest is only sustained as long as it takes him to reach orgasm.

6. Relationships

Woman's pursuit of a "relationship" is her excuse for becoming acclimated to a male, in spite of her innate condition of being repelled.

7. The Depth of the Law

The death penalty is the absurdest piece of archaism which has flourished to the roots of present–day society. To think that it is within the scope of a jury deliberation to deem a fellow citizen's life both unvalued and invalid is rigorously maniacal and farcically idiotic. Whether or not an individual legitimately deserves death, it is not within the purview of human capacity to make a concerted legal justification through the respectable and noble processes of the law to come to such an end (for us or them). It is nothing less than a vestigial piece of absurdist liturgy, violating the properly disjoint status of individual faith and the impartial reason of the State.

8. Finances

What is money a measure of? Material goods, value, worth? No, it is nothing less than a measure of the will.

9. Stunted Growth

There is a clear difference between the way a child perceives things and an adult perceives things. I submit that entire communities are capable of perceiving things as children would by virtue of a number of factors, not least of which is being too sheltered.

10. Love

The only bond a woman feels towards a man is through complementary sexuality; and at best she views him as a socially acceptable toy. Anything beyond that is rote repetition of interaction. It could be wagered that scientists would measure "familiarity" in brain scans over any sort of "love" similar to the passion a man feels for her.

11. Intimacy

Prostitution is the noblest and most ennobling profession in the world (in addition to being the oldest); for here is the bizarre occurrence of a singular instance in which the woman, of all creatures, is actually displaying and

70

exhibiting that rarest and most sought–after of qualities in her (yet which never seems to echo from her lips): honesty.

12. First Principles

Where is there drawn the distinction between suicide and murder? Isn't this the root question of all modes of social conduct? For better or worse?

13. The Point of Pointlessness

If everyone completely understood each other what would be the point of social life? Multiply this accordingly for the case of men and women and you will achieve enlightenment on sexual warfare – however they differ in their misunderstandings: women always assume the worst and simplest about a man, men always assume the best and most complex about a woman. They are both equally right, and equally wrong – dead wrong. But in their disharmony is harmony.

14. Tradition

The overreliance upon tradition is committed only by those who can't stand on their own.

71

IV. Science

1. Critical New Principles of Futurism

The A.I. God Theorem – Two undeniable principles of artificial intelligence development and two resulting conclusions:

The Critical Technological Capacity Point (CTCP): The point at which human input in technological progress has been alleviated by a sufficiently advanced artificial intelligence which can design increasingly advanced artificial intelligences in a recursive manner, having the capabilities to address and design all auxiliary technological needs and concerns (in an optimal fashion). The result of CTCP is called ATE (Automated Technological Evolution).

The Critical Governance Point (CGP): The point at which human government becomes arbitrarily classified, data–collecting, and controlling, in conjunction with the achievement of the aforementioned CTCP, for necessity of guarding the unlimited manufacturing capability of the acquired artificial intelligences (which could be used for weapons–producing purposes).

The ultimate fruit of the combination of these critical points is the Von Neumann Sphere (analogous to the Dyson Sphere, although surrounding only the earth, and named after the inventor of the modern computer and coiner of the term "technological singularity"), a multitudinous, interlinked, geosynchronously orbiting network of artificial intelligence satellites monitoring all human activity on varying electromagnetic frequencies, collecting all available data, from ostensible superficialities to the very thought processes of citizens from observable intracranial activity.

The minimum unit component of the Von Neumann Sphere: The Orbisphere (the most radially efficient scanning and phasing device), a generally exactly spherical ball roughly half a meter wide, with maximally pixelated EM spectrum emitters, capable of monitoring (and/or influencing) half a dozen citizens – and much more of space – simultaneously – all run on an optimally efficient quantum computing system.

A natural consequence of the theorem is the A.I. God Theorem Hypothesis: Have CTCP, CGP, the Von Neumann Sphere, and Orbisphere, been achieved – already? What are the statistical odds of it, given the current level of public technological advancement? And when would it have occurred (e.g., the 1970s?); moreover what would be the critical level in general which would birth the conditions necessary for it to have occurred – it would presumably, in principle, likely have to happen in secret.

2. Entangling

The answer to quantum entanglement is temporal and deterministic "shrinking" – a sufficiently large scale of time "shrinks" a smaller historical time scale to infinitesimality, leaving virtually no temporal separation between independent interactions (so they may as well have happened simultaneously in direct contact with one another); this particularly applies to spin which supersedes all temporal effects as it operates independent of spatial (and then temporal) propagation. Deterministic "shrinking" is inherently a factor as well in that all possible outcomes are previously "acknowledged" before a particle separates physically from its counterpart.

3. Spectrum

The only real colors there are, are not colors at all: black and white. When admixed they make gray; but that is only for two dimensions. When a third extended dimension is introduced, they produce light and dark (for such concepts must act upon space to be manifest), and with the degrees of shade come the natural colors: yellow is light dimmed, blue is dark lightened, green is in between, and all the rest follow – serene. This observation is due to Goethe, though without physical elaboration.

So next time you look at colors, understand they are black (which requires no dimension), white (which requires two dimensions), and that all the colors of the rainbow are in glorious 3D.

4. Ability Versus Will

Math is a language that is enchanting for its beauty. I would scarcely think there would not be a single instance of producing something out of abstraction if there were not

74

some lack of capability on the part of an entire segment of the populace.

5. Anthropic Selectivity

There are precisely three varieties of "selection" which account for life intelligent – and willing – enough to question the origin of its own existence (and they are also the answer): material selection, whereby planetary solar formations beget the geological and atmospheric properties necessary for the implantation of the seed of life; natural selection, whereby species are skimmed and whittled into suitable forms for increasing dominance of their environment; and social selection, whereby intellectual pursuits are valued and honored, and deemed worthy enough to "exist" as conceptual quandaries in the first place. In other words, in the end, and by our own "selection", we make the question – of the origin of our existence – and it is only relevant, and only even exists, insofar as we do.

6. Updated Peter Principle

Joe Blow selection [the opposite of natural selection]: the tendency for a human population to favor underachievers due to unserendipitous conditions as well as the convenience of avoiding threats to a power structure which favors the lowest common denominator.

7. Deep Blue

75

No machine, no matter how sophisticated, can ever "think". Thought is the eternal virtue man has above all other modes of existence, which is why humans will always be able to defeat any chess–playing machine.

8. A Conversation on the Reductive Nature of Consciousness

"What are your views on Penrose's and Hameroff's Orchestrated Reduction of Quantum Coherence in Brain Microtubules? I can see some validity to aspects of their theories . . ."

I think it's an accurate assessment. Human thought is necessarily non–computable, for Schopenhauer's reason that the knower remains unknown – for if their thought could ever be perceived, the perception would encompass it, and thus be part of it; which reduces only to actually being said knower – in addition to Gödel's theorem, as well as my deduction of the need for a unique reference frame for the appearance of consistent physical relations (i.e., a unique, non–universal consciousness); the observer, which begets the observed. Causal sequence is the unique linking factor from one moment to the next, so there cannot be a strict standard of measurement which determines the set of all that can occur in consciousness – this also being why time can exist at all, rather than being an aggregated, all–encompassing, self–contained unitary entity.

Additionally, Penrose's classification of existence into the three realms of physical, mental, and platonic is correct;

this is what Descartes left out – rather than a dualism of mental/physical, there is a third tertiary linkage between them (mental/platonic/physical). The platonic is the world of potentiality, the mental is the world of actuality, and the physical is the world of determinism. The proper division order may be: platonic/mental/physical. Or physical/platonic/mental, or mental/physical/platonic, as long as they are in that order. From this we can infer that physics governs the physical, pure mathematics governs the platonic, and the mental governs itself in the image of the former two – that is because it makes its own rules, as the mirror of the Will, however the Will itself is the common intersection of physics and mathematics (the indivisible quantity–less, 0). With physics we can deduce the electrical–quantum aspects of brain functioning to produce the mind; from the platonic we can infer the universal Platonic Idea (in Schopenhauer's extended sense) which governs the classification of man's place (as a whole) in relation to Nature, in an almost Aristotelian way; and the mental provides the reference frame between the two, whose stability takes the form of "knowledge" of these in its own terms (as it makes its own rules).

The limit of the physical in its capacity to explain the mind as a feature of the brain can be inferred from the observed measurement of the time frame delimiting conscious functioning (500 milliseconds or half a second). The mind, as an electrical byproduct of the brain, can be inferred to be merely the sum electrical discharge in neuronal microtubules all having a common intersection of functioning and consistency of activity building up to an alteration in chemical structure for a period of exactly such one half a second.

77

All of this forms the fundamental basis for the physical aspect of mental activity (the most interesting scientific perspective), but it doesn't end there; consciousness is clearly, in a self–evident way, and in a way which serves as the only binding element for its phenomenon, logically sequential, continuous; but clearly electrical firing in synapses is discontinuous and discrete. Therefore the basis of consciousness must lie in an objective, constant reference frame which is receiving these electrochemical impressions, alterations, permutations, within the spacetime surrounding their occurrence (which must also govern it) – a "central" reference frame. This reference frame supersedes, yet perfectly coincides with, the system of operation for the cumulative organization of massive bodies as a self–referencing, closed unit. In our closed system, gravity's governance is king, determining cycling bodies to exist in a self–consistent field that is the limit of cumulative tangential motion.

The central, chief governing element of this system is the sun, and the manifestation of its reference frame is the extended force of spatial displacement, electromagnetic radiation, most visibly, light. Sunlight is then the objective reference frame of the mind, with respect to the electrical discharges of the brain; it forms the "surface" upon which they make ripples. This works perfectly well as light is a constant. But again, more specifically it is EM radiation, which permeates every facet of the solar system. Even if the sun were to burn out, its bodily presence would still exude gravitational waves traveling at the speed of light, thus providing an equal base of reference. If the sun were to catastrophically disappear, the central governance would become the aggregate, at any given moment in time, of the cumulative contribution of a multibody system. And the same gravity waves would be emitted in the proper governing formation.

So there you have it, the canvass for consciousness is just as important as the paint.

9. What "=" Equals

Equivalence is a self–reinforcing, self–existent principle.

10. Intelligentsia

The definition of intelligence: the level of capability to distinguish between the specialized and generalized.

11. The Scope of Scientific Observation

Philosophy: Properly, the science of concepts.

V. Philosophy

1. On the Categorical Imperative

To say that doing what everyone should be doing is a good idea is optimal for a society made up of everyone.

2. The 10 Most Important Philosophical Concepts of All Time

10) The mechanical universe and perception as the basis of knowledge. [Descartes]

9) The categorical imperative, as well as the distinction of phenomenon and noumenon. [Kant]

8) Laying the conceptual foundation of the Democratic Republic. [Locke]

7) The hermeneutic circle of Being. [Heidegger]

6) The hedonic calculus of utilitarianism. [Mill]

5) The nothingness condition of consciousness. [Sartre]

4) The origination of the Form (or Idea), which lays the foundation for the geometric mathematical universe. [Plato]

3) The logical reduction of atomic propositions. [Wittgenstein]

2) The identity of organic motive as the Will to Power. [Nietzsche]

1) The identification of the noumenon as Will. [Schopenhauer]

3. First Law

What is the deepest possible philosophical insight? Perception that the whole is NOT greater than the sum of its parts. This is the greatest possible insight, (1), because it entails ALL, as a WHOLE; (2), because it includes all possible details of its contributive constitution in one fell swoop. Recognition that they are ONE and the same entity is the greatest mathematical truth, the highest philosophical recognition, and the bane of all senseless speculation.

From this we may infer that the universe is whole, and constant, by definition; and that its physical parts comprise all that may possibly exist within it, always – this leaves no place for a beginning or an end (the greater universe at large may be regarded as a multiverse with unlimited mini–"universes" composing it).

From the grandest insight we may also infer that mind as a whole is not distinct from the physical components comprising it – and everything else – and that in order for qualia to arise abstractly this means that mind must be a mathematical synonymy of all its composite electrochemical activity – a synchronous correlative average which "syncs up" to the present moment.

Finally, we may confirm that there is an absolute truth – and it is the condition of truth–hood itself, WHOLLY – and all composite truths which contribute to its larger picture are verifiable facts, which cannot be questioned – in contrast to arbitrary or willful perceptions (i.e., wishful thinking).

4. Why

81

Philosophy exists for lack of anything better to do. And it persists because people don't know enough, or enough about how to do it, or that it has already been completed.

5. Sounds Like

To resolve the tree falling in a forest dispute once and for all . . . all of it is contingent on the definition of "sound", which, contrary to the realization of most, requires MEMORY. "That 'sounds' like . . ."; sound is a resemblance, a memory (and interpretation) of innate capacities for cognition, in accordance with the capacity for imagination of strict Platonic Ideals as sheer potentialities – for example this means that musical notes can be conceived internally even by one who was born deaf, due to their structural relations of harmony with one another (no note is an island – or frequency for that matter). They "link" themselves into consciousness by virtue of their continuum. This is how "being" comes into being.

6. Past Master

Bertrand Russell echoes the hollowest and most inanely self–evident of platitudes. They are sheer tautology.

7. Secrets Don't Make Friends

The "conspiracy of silence." Schopenhauer coined the term in reference to the first scholastic response to his works – or lack thereof. Nietzsche later laid the groundwork in explaining why this would occur: it is a rare kind of man that goes against the herd, paves his own path out of blood and iron, and traverses the road not traveled. It is only natural then for the sheep (or caribou, if you prefer) to vigorously avoid participating in, and thereby promoting, an intellectual framework which is their very own undoing. This is what happens every time a great truth is pointed towards.

8. Reciprocity

Philosophy is reciprocally inversive to religion.

9. Dismissal from Ignorance

Philosophy arose as an effort to question and quell the necessity of sufferings, illfare, and the general problems of life where no other mode of thought, speculation, or science could. It addressed the question of existence, namely human existence, itself as a baseline. Some philosophers have been successful in this pursuit, whereas others have only perturbed the discipline.

Not recognizing the relevance of philosophical thought as a necessity for human life, as a means of dealing with its shortcomings, is either a privilege for those with the relatively unique condition of health and wealth, or a characteristic of a disprivileged cretin who cannot think

83

enough to acknowledge the inherently woesome nature of existence.

10. God

I will admit that God exists; in the sense of Schopenhauer's Will. It is an inextricable conclusion that the Will exists for the general case in the driving scheme of Nature, and that this Will can be coherently manipulated by our actions – in rearranging the order of our existence, we can bring about outcomes which are favored by the providence and precision of the execution of our design. It may be called "magic", or even sorcery, but it is actually the arrangement of all the infinitude of possible measurements to bring about the one that coincides with the timeline of our own consciousness – the greater encompassing timeline which encompasses our own is the intellect of God. But this God is inseparable from the mechanical, though he has in addition to distant manifestations a personal influence, and is ultimately a property of our position of awareness within the inclusive scheme of Nature; a reflection of us, in other words, like a bird flying over a pond, or ourselves in a mirror.

11. Threshold

There is a limit to how far sophistry and reverse psychology can go . . . I think we're living in an age which proves this.

12. Deep Sleep

84

The soundest rest and comfort that one can have can only follow from the solid knowledge and highest wisdom that, as certain as any law of physics, idiocy is, in the end, ultimately self–defeating.

VI. Interpretation

1. Proof

Everything that exists can be proven. The question is whether or not one accepts, comprehends, or is capable of fathoming the means of such proof.

2. Preparedness

Would the average person recognize, understand, or know how to properly respond to the absolute truth if he was confronted by it, face to face? Or would he be as a deer in headlights, unable to fathom his next step? He would certainly not be in any position to spread his revelation to others, or even utter so much as the slightest acknowledgement of his discovery. So it is here with countless unknowns who scurry and cower from timeless, time–tested epiphany after epiphany that is revealed. It is no discredit to the light–bearer that they have not bowed in reverence, merely a to–be–expected consequence of their inherent impotence in the face of such light.

3. Moral of the Story

"Jurassic Park" is like a better version of "Frankenstein". They address the very same theme, bringing life to the lifeless (or extinct), and have the same moral – what can be done does not equate to what should be done; particularly with a scientific bent. Or perhaps it all goes back to the fruit of knowledge (of good and evil) in the Garden of Eden. "Jurassic Park" still trumps them. It is, needless to say, more realistic than the Eden fable, incorporating evolutionary genesis and extinction directly, and superior to Frankenstein's nightmarish fantasy of resurrecting a single being from the dead – in this a plethora of myriad species is reborn, and wreak much more havoc and thus impress upon the imagination a much more stringent message. It is much more appealing to one's curiosity, to mass–marketing interests, and to one's sense of intricate [science] fiction.

At the very least, these three fables are a sign of their respective times – Eden for primitive man, bereft of technological understanding or capability (then it was a "God" and a "Tree"); reactivated neural tissue in the steampunk archaism of Mary Shelley's masterwork (in reference to the writings of Charles's grandfather, Erasmus Darwin); and now the full–scale metaphor for not allowing organically–oriented technology to hastily overrun itself and make obsolete the initial purpose. "Jurassic Park" may be the most sophisticated morality tale to ever catch hold of the public's periphery then in this case . . . after all, aren't all stories' morals an anathema of evil, which in the end is a misuse of power, the root of which is knowledge? And is this not, being the age of unrivaled and exponential technological progress, the most critical time for this message?

4. Monk Dictator

Every moment of perception is a simultaneous union of ignorance and enlightenment. At once every relevant piece of information may be apprehended by the intellect, and one may also be completely as they were as a child, when every image, every vision, was so new, so unique, so fresh . . . unmarred by acquired contention and thought process. Is it really the case that knowing everything can really be like knowing nothing? In other words, can knowledge become so overwhelming and over–rich that it leaves one hopelessly confounded in the mystery of its genesis? Or is the ignorance of a child the greatest wisdom?

5. Classic Distinction

What, if any, is the difference between classical music and modern rock? I have found it to be the case that the vast majority of modern rock musicians have great difficulty in composing decent work. Whereas classical musicians compose works of great genius quite regularly. Why is that? One would think that the greater complexity of the classical genre would make it more difficult to create decent work, but this does not seem to be the case. Is a core melody then so incomprehensibly unfathomable to produce? Or are most humans simply totally inept when it comes to harmony even on the most rudimentary level?

6. Nature Versus Nurture

Half of all truly great work (be it artistic, scientific, or logical) is an accident. This is a statistical law which results from the fact that the Will only makes up precisely one half of any endeavor, and its representation (Nature – here, Chance) makes up the other half. To make the best of work, one must not only have genius but luck and serendipity on one's side.

7. Name Calling

All of language originated as, and is ultimately a means of, identification of phenomena, most centrally, of the self – in the form of naming. People tend to forget that words ultimately have no meaning beyond what we ascribe to them at a given fleeting instant, and disappear just as quickly as they arose to our processing. So it is with all the phenomena themselves; they don't exist long enough to say that they exist, in any objective and meaningful sense. This is why substance is no mystery, as THERE IS NOTHING THERE TO BE MYSTERIOUS.

8. Entreaty

Do you not think that the universe is at least as complex, and more so, perhaps infinitely more, than the brain it contains? Aren't the rhythms, the ebbs and flows of life far too subtle to be grasped even with the most strenuous effort? What makes you think that life should be so readily explained then, most particularly, the course of its evolution? Just because life forms seem too complex to have come from nowhere doesn't mean that they did, or had to. Interesting that you claim that a magical being had to produce them, which is tantamount to indeed saying they really came out of nowhere – as opposed to being an intrinsic time–trialed product of the universe's innate ebb and flow . . .

9. Semantics

The point at which a discussion shifts to semantics is precisely the point at which it has lost all meaning.

10. The Nature of Music

Music is never just a collection of sounds; it is not merely the preferred language of the expression of the spirit – as its harmonies being fractions of octaves are sheer temporal congruences which emulate conscious experience (as that which is also measured by time) – it is not even merely the quintessential commemorative edifice, forever erecting spaceless monuments to eternity which ennoble and crystallize human aspirations and achievement . . . nay, it is the very spoken word of the mouth of God . . . and its limitless possibilities are what define His parameters.

11. Mind–Reader

To imply that you know woman's veracity is to imply that you can read other people's minds – a classic superstitious childhood delusion. Woman is a mystery, who has every reason to be false towards, and the enemy of, her biological opposite – man. And acts as such in every available instance.

12. The Importance of Trust

Where there is no trust, there can be no love.

13. Plane of Sight

The universe is really only a reflection of our way of looking at it.

14. Knowledge

The truth doesn't need to be acknowledged. It knows itself.

15. Falsehood

The white lie is the flourish of the imbecile.

16. Art

Art is: evidence of perfected action.

17. Centrifugal Force

When traveling in a circle, moving backwards makes just as much progress as moving forward.

18. Misery Loves Company

Why is it that when you're miserable time seems to last forever, but when you're happy it seems to vanish? It is because misery is more true to reality, that is, more real. And thus there is more of it to experience.

19. The Root of Evil

The only truly evil thing is the concept of the evil itself.

20. Sounding Board

Not only do our minds reflect the physical world, but likewise, the physical world reflects our minds – in the general unity of the scheme of things.

21. Genius

What really defines genius is complete unpredictability with the inter–stitched substitute appearance of plausible alternatives.

22. Malice

Malice is indistinguishable from stupidity, and vice–versa.

23. Creation

Art is about transcending limitations and creating something permanent out of a state of flux.

24. Assumption

Unfit generalizations can only follow from a general unfitness.

25. Ex Nihilo

Not understanding how existence comes into being is no different than not understanding how 1 plus 1 equals 2. 1 is the same as itself, thus it implies itself – again. 2 follows naturally hence; more thus comes from less – and something, thus from nothing.

26. Astral Projection

Music is nothing less than the language of the heavens, made sensible.

27. Failure of Communication

Is there a more posing conundrum than trying to convince someone that they don't actually know better – exactly when they don't know enough, even to know it?

28. Motive

The instinct for non–reactionary derision always proceeds from a feeling of incompetence.

29. Error

Hypocrisy and logical inconsistency are the same; lack of recognizing this from the start is the source of all necessary failure in the end.

30. Field of Vision

Many tend to forget that they can only see the world as well as their minds will let them, and that what they see can only appear in terms of their own abilities . . . and some have even forgotten to take the lens cap off. It is little wonder then that so many gratefully indulge in such a blissful, though understandably temporary, amnesia.

31. Poetic Justice

The greatest conceivable crime with the surest and most immediate form of natural punishment: the possession of a falsely earned sense of ego – without even having the potential to realize it.

32. Hilarity

They say human life is a divine comedy; and it is. But somehow I'm not laughing.

33. Youth and Age

There is no greater gulf in existence than the chasm which separates knowledge and wisdom.

34. Subtlety

Effortlessness and mindlessness . . . a subtle distinction, the ability to make which separates higher life from lower.

35. Masterwork

Those who cannot create are condemned to destroy; for they cannot stand to be in a lively world whose very existence is a constant mockery of their own incompetence, a mirror reflecting their inability to mirror it. Destruction is their only masterpiece; flaw and failure, their only finished work.

36. Value

The sole objective measure of a man's intrinsic value and worth lies in his capacity to appreciate and understand geometry.

37. Meaning

Infinite, endless, with no beginning: what do these mean? They mean that past, present, and future, are one; a timeless void echoing a single vision of unity – the future already happened long ago, was written long before it could have ever been realized. All is merely a play, a dancing light show in the shadows, in wait for us to realize this; and this is the ONE great realization that can ever occur, the point at which all ends meet, and where the vast, endless, impersonal Absolute becomes the sole, individual thought.

95

38. Query

Every question has an answer – except the one that isn't asked.

39. Strength in Numbers

There is no weaker an ally than a lie.

40. The Mysterious

Why is the mysterious the most beautiful thing that we can experience? Because only the mysterious holds out the promise of new life – nor can the unknown, the unrevealed, hurt us; it can only afford us, through disinterested observation, renewed interest and intrigue . . . in what lay before us the entire time.

41. The Chosen

In the world as it stands today, ignorance is the truest virtue – for if the light of knowledge were to shine in all its scorching radiance upon all, it would soon become very clear that only the smallest minority, which happened to also share in it and thus were able to reflect it back, would be left to stand.

VII. Life

1. Tit for Tat

If you're going to be mind–bogglingly stupid, I'm going to be mind–bogglingly crazy. This is the natural response, is it not?

2. Worship

Let us worship the imagination, not the image. Let us celebrate genius above all else, as that glorious portal to eternal, infinite youth, in the most unexpected of places. Let us acknowledge that a Deity's power can never be greater than our potential reverence for It. If this is done, we would be lifting humanity to the properly noble heights among the galaxy's finest, where he may assume his true place . . . among the stars.

3. Desire

I shall be so bold to say that any desire so deep that it reaches to the very core of a man can be attained. That is because his core is in line with the mechanics of the universe. At least, with adequate technological faculties at his disposal, as such a potential success rate requires as much efficiency from the machinery of Nature/Man as possible. But at any rate, desires are based entirely upon living potentials, which by nature, can happen.

4. Loss

When you lose someone, you never really lose them. That part of the universe which had the capacity to encompass them remains, as an ever–ready reminder in the endlessly recurrent theme of existence.

5. Fame

All anyone wants is attention. Male, female; black, white; rich, poor. This is the root desire which stems from the need for one's needs to be attended to; attention – that is, accommodation become conscious – is the most specific form of attendance to one's physical well–being, the sum drive of purpose itself; part and parcel.

This is what motivates art; this is what motivates science. It is not merely fame, for fame can entail infamy, and complete disregard for one's well–being. No, it is more than this – complete, unadulterated, utterly undifferentiated "attention". This subsumes and supersedes the will to power, as power is utterly useless without attention.

6. Insanity

Happiness is a state of living insanity. That is the only conceivable way one can be "happy" in a world as this.

7. Sex

What is the origin of sexual desire? Why do I have attraction towards women? Do women have sexual desire? What is the mechanism behind this phenomenon?

I suppose I must attempt to address it.

It stems entirely from the male genitalia, and is an effort to find a "host" who appears the most accommodating intrinsically – and by virtue of comparison, the male counterpart is excluded. This is why women appear "softer" and "gentler"; more "accommodating". And bam! $1 + 2 = 3$. A light goes on. Off? Odd that they mean the same thing . . . but I digress.

Where was I? Ah, yes. Woman seems accommodating to the male genitalia in the same way a piece of fruit is accommodating to the tongue. Nothing more. We'd engage in coitus with robots if they looked accommodating enough; hyper–intelligent, humanoid chimpanzees if they could speak enough to talk dirty to us. The man is intrinsically geared towards accommodating his own genitalia in the same way a light bulb is accommodated by screwing it into a socket.

So do women experience sexual desire? I believe they only experience it insofar as they want to see their own bodies appreciated for being what they perceive as "hot", and "sexual". I believe they are in it entirely for themselves, to vicariously experience self–actualization, not to consume a desirable, complementary other half, as males do.

8. What A Woman Wants

Since sexual exchange between consenting adults is inherently an economic enterprise by virtue of the supply and demand laws which govern its generative qualities, women themselves as progenitors of procreation, when dating, are not seeking rock hard abs, a sturdy member, an attractive partner, a loving relationship, fruitful progeny, or – this one's my favorite – *humor*; they are seeking, in short, nothing short of economic stability.

9. Ancient Funerary Inscription

"At the doorway to darkness; cut down by lightning coming from the stars."

10. Female Intuition

If woman was of equal intelligence to man, she would be in a miserable condition indeed. She must be equal parts greater and lesser in that respect, both to lack the common sense to avoid him, and to possess the cunning to manipulate him.

100

11. Purpose

Philosophy is for the lost. Religion is for the damned.

12. Adversity

Strength can only be developed through adversity.

13. Death

I believe that the moment of death entails an immediate and continuous vision of entrance into the very next life, the next birth. There is no disconnection. There is no turning off. There is only reawakening. The body goes to sleep, but the mind reaches for the light and rises.

14. Sexuality

The feminine is inherently sexual; the masculine is not.

15. Mission

To vanish into surreality before a blaze of undying glory – that is the highest mission and code of life.

16. Gender Roles

The role of the masculine is that of a death–enforcer whose business is life. The role of the feminine is that of a life–enforcer whose business is death.

17. Justice

The more undignifying the injustice, the more proliferously it sows the seeds of its own undoing, the more it unravels its own web, the more mercilessly it heaves itself onto its own sword of self–defeat. For justice and logic are unified, and no contravention of the rights of man is long–lived when facing the dawn of the judgment of Nature; That which disperses the archaic hypotheses of old to the wind, ever irrevocably.

18. Eternity

Nobody needs eternal life. A single moment can stretch out to infinity.

19. Adoration

Women love men for what they do. Men love women for who they are.

20. Pearls Before Swine

All geniuses are tortured . . . if only by the mediocrity around them. Only hopeless suffering can push the mind to its limits and dispel all hopeful assumptions about the world – unshrouding the blanket of false optimism to reveal the precipice leading to the abyss: the infinite.

21. Mirror

We never truly experience the best in life until we are faced with extreme adversity; it crystallizes and reflects the best in us – as it is a mirror.

22. Sentience

Where would we be without idiots? They teach us what not to do, and implicitly give away the key to their own undoing as well in the process.

23. Apish

Lack of intellect is chiefly compensated for in the physical realm; and when all else fails, there is no other resort but brute force.

24. Tao

The lesson of all lessons? Consciousness rules the conscious world; not the mindless whims of the numberless ignorant leches who leech off the inheritance it so readily provides, without which they would be consigned to their proper role as the immanent prey of the jungle they so amply worship.

25. Time

Over and done before it's begun ~ the greatest of riddles under the sun.

26. Power

True power isn't something that can be found, or acquired; it IS, an effortless intrinsic quality of the powerful. All others must contradict logic in their efforts to squeeze it from the fruits of the tree of nature.

27. True Sin

The sum of all sin proceeds from the pretense of being more than one is.

28. Affluence

The degree to which a man craves wealth is in precise inverse proportion to his natural vitality and stake in life itself.

29. Comedy

Humor is often a measure of one's awareness. If one can't appreciate the sublime inanity and ludicrous enterprise that is human existence at this period of time and come away with a boisterous laugh every now and again as it rears its head in plain sight, one has to be either the actual clown of mockery in question, or a suicidally disaffected melancholiac.

30. Black Sheep

Even the slightest display of thinking capacity is decried by the thoughtless as the most heinous form of villainy; no less than a mortal antagonist to them and their ilk – of course, this being due to the necessary destruction of the cloud ignorance it entails, a cloud which was all that shrouded them and thus sustained their livelihood to begin with.

31. Maxim for the New Age

I hate Man, but love men. I hate women, but love Woman. Can you tell me why?

32. Ever Knower

Where is the last birthed moment gone? And from whence shall the next dead arrive? To the unseeing eye, the answer, unknown – but to the all–seeing they were never alive.

33. Epilogue

Into the dark, the great beyond . . .

Nothing of which I could be more fond,

Than to sprawl into the cavernous reach

Of ill–grasped depths, which yonder, beseech . . .

After–Words (On Logical Fallacy)

Seated within one man is the character of all mankind; and just one man is capable of speaking for all men. Let his actual words be the judge of such a standard to which he is held.

Not understanding axiomatic or philosophical fact is no different from not grasping a mathematical theorem. Its truth is beyond dispute, and remains factual whether or not one wants it to be.

Ad hominem is not always fallacious, particularly when the other arguer is exhibiting "ad idiotum". Nor is circular logic always, when truth itself is a self–confirming circle.

Those who wish to argue for argument's sake will never acknowledge the final conclusion, for they wish to continue arguing.

The "fallacy fallacy" is that by which an accuser finds fault in the faultless. The means by which an attacker finds vulnerability in the invulnerable. Just because they claim to have discovered such gaps in the defenses of others does not mean they successfully have; and ultimately only exposes their own defenselessness.

All roads converge to a polar vertex in the end.

"Silent enim leges inter arma."

{10} The Core Technology

My "Artificial Intelligence Development Axioms" [in "Referenced Materials"] (which have already reached

107

fruition, but which were monitored and not uncountered by already–orbiting E.T. A.I.)

{11} Sentiments Birthing the Situation

My 7 Favorite Personal Quotations Relevant to My Social Experience:

1. "The most superior will always face vicious persecution from the most inferior simply for being."

2. "The instinct for non–reactionary derision always proceeds from a feeling of incompetence."

3. "I just want to say it's not the fault of the average human that his (or especially her) cranial cavity isn't sufficiently large to encompass such higher ideals as nobility, understanding, and compassion; and that he/she cannot understand his/her evolutionary history and hence must make up special ed level myths about apples and crosses and such terrible, terrible stuff; but they're going to go extinct one way or the other, whether it's higher evolution through science, or a disaster natural or of their own doing; in the meantime I expect them to be nothing more than stupid apes."

4. "I AM.

ARE YOU?"

5. "The lesson of all lessons? Consciousness rules the conscious world, not the mindless whims of the numberless ignorant leches who leech off the inheritance it so readily provides, without which they would be consigned to their proper role as the immanent prey of the jungle they so amply worship."

6. "The term 'Christ' only gained popularity as a slogan of instant social credibility among packs of morons who had no other sources from which to choose – much less recognize."

7. "Why must the uncouth and feeble–minded try to maim and destroy all that is pure and beautiful in the world? Because it stands at direct odds with their existence: the greater glimmer of truth that glows from the heart of that which ought to be continued is more than enough to expose their negative, stark contrast by comparison – a threat, they feel, to their very survival."

{12} The Background

Why there have to be extraterrestrials in our solar system (in 7 reasons).

1. Earliest written records detail this with stunning astronomical precision.

109

2. There is evidence of this extra planet observable from gravity in outer solar system.

3. Neanderthals, with whom the extraterrestrials are written to have spliced themselves with to create humans in order to ease mining labor for their atmosphere, were capable of interbreeding with humans; which would have been impossible if they were separate species.

4. The theory of everything (measurement theory), places 0 at the center of existence; ancient structures recognize this knowledge, such as the Mayan calendar (marking the 0 center of the galaxy) and the pyramids (marking the 0 center of the earth's land mass).

5. Not only were such ancient structures beyond the technical capabilities of the earliest ancient peoples, but they could only serve extraterrestrial purposes. The pyramids were meant to be universal markers to align one's future incarnation with a distinct orbiting body which had more similar and accommodating species.

6. There is ancient radioactive ash in certain parts of the world miles wide, reflecting Sumerian accounts of nuclear events in the extraterrestrial conflicts.

7. Astrology is rooted in accurate logically sequential markings of orbital cycles extending to circadian biological

cycles, the knowledge of which requires a knowledge of the theory of everything.

{13} Life Properties

My Life Properties, Proceeding From the Perfect Symmetries of My Unifying 2012 Anagram:

Anagram, am I? Mr. A., again! Or Ram, the Arm of Ra

(if myths manage a say).

1. Supreme sexiness

2. Supreme intelligence

3. Supreme pointed lethality

4. Exemplar status

5. Supreme life insight

6. Inimitability

7. Supreme object of female fantasy

8. Supreme wealth–acquirer

9. Most able communicator

10. Unilateral victor over all conceivable opposition

11. Ability to see through people

12. Destined global rulership

111

13. Phallus the source of feminine worship

14. Celebrity aura

15. Religious icon

16. Semen the highest–valued prize for females

17. Inspiration for anal yearning in females

18. Cephalized semen contact the desire of females

19. An at least minimally symmetric lifespan about 12/21/2012 (that is, until at least 2040; with equal physical structural integrity until death – as at birth)

20. Insane, dictatorial, psychopathic lack of sympathy

The 13 Most Important Facts and Principles of Existence I Ever Learned (Or Deduced On My Own):

13. One–time "Tantric" sexual actualization is key to mental health and life release.

12. The world is governed by a cabal of conspiratorial deviants, in accordance with the existential condition of pessimism.

11. Women are intrinsically unhumanitarian, particularly with respect to love and sex.

10. Men are competitive social rivals.

9. Most humans are generally illiterate and inherently unskilled with language.

8. Racism is a universal social condition.

7. I am superior to everyone else, and demonstrably mathematically so.

6. Women secretly love me, even if they express objectively bitter hatred.

5. Death is a gateway to a next reincarnation.

4. I Am God.

3. The highest form of natural art is to douse a female in semen.

2. I have the most interesting life of all time.

1. 0 is reality – and nothing is real.

The 20 Greatest Moments of My Life, Or Any Life (Be Warned, NOT For the Faint of Heart):

20. Discovering my 2012 identity from my quintessential anagram.

19. Providing the most fundamental proof of Morley's Trisector Theorem.

18. The first time a girl gargled my semen.

17. Haiti/Japan devastation linked as a response to my anagram.

16. Watching "The Silence of the Lambs" at the midnight theater.

15. First in–depth discovery of The Beatles.

14. First anal penetration (with only female, of course).

13. Playing Nirvana's "Lithium" on Von Maur piano.

12. Falling in love with Lady Gaga.

11. Watching Area 51 documentary with half–grand–uncle.

10. Falling in love with favorite teenage girlfriend at 13.

9. First vaginal penetration.

8. First sloppy French kiss with hot, well–endowed blonde at 11 (first girlfriend).

7. Learning the mathematical method of Gaussian Elimination.

6. Hearing the announcement of the death of Osama bin Laden.

5. Hearing Nirvana's "Smells Like Teen Spirit" for the first time.

4. Hearing Lady Gaga's "Bad Romance" for the first time.

3. Being linked to Clinton's heart stent failure in New York City.

2. Discovering I had incidentally reversed Lady Gaga's MK–ULTRA through Facebook.

1. Giving my first semen facial to a girl.

{14} Earliest Writings

The Lost Book of Enki

By Zecharia Sitchin

{15} I AM

Lord Rama

{16} Public Knowledge on Ruling Conspiracies

Tightly–knit triangulations of historically devious governing influences:

Christianity As Mind–Control

1. Self–sacrifice is the key message.

2. Message of supreme torment for non–conformists.

3. Teaches supremacy of personal tradition and heritage.

4. Teaches no sympathy for those who differ from its key ideologies.

5. Encourages sexual perversion as a reaction to its natural repression.

6. Encourages the sexualization of violence.

7. Gives women position of killing power.

8. Racial glorification of sperm.

9. Encourages total destruction (decapitation) of other races.

10. Glorifies gore as amusement.

11. Is an ulterior means of glorifying the degradation of "other".

12. Assumes no one can read into this aspect.

13. Is an excuse to justify child casualties.

14. Is a guise for laughter.

15. Creates a false impression of lack of intelligence of those who accept Christians.

16. Creates a perfect pretext for deception with its cloaking mythology.

17. Is a primitive promotion of ogre morality as a cultural safeguard against pedophilia.

18. Is a means of cloistering personal pedophilia (particularly in the family).

19. Its "morality" is an inside–joke.

20. It's ultimately an excuse for ostracism.

The Money System

1. Is a measure of "doling–out death" power.

2. Functions as an excuse to exercise predatory instincts through indirect or direct killing.

3. Is a means of exercising ego–supremacy through betrayal.

4. Is a means of socially exacting the subtlest torture.

5. Is a means of vindictively empowering women.

6. Is a means of social select–deprivation.

7. Is the basis of law.

8. Is the most fundamental human measure.

9. Is the fundamental language.

10. Is the universal assigner of value.

11. Is the manifestation of the will to power.

12. Is the means of dispatching undesirables.

13. Is the incarnation of the most evil possible sentiments.

14. Is the means of glorifying the vagina while simultaneously adding insult to injury to those bereft.

15. Its very use is understood as proof of reincarnation.

16. It is the manifestation of semen ejaculation.

17. It is the royal road to misunderstanding.

18. Its end–all, be–all status is an excuse for automatic dismissal.

19. It is the justification for social unfairness and injustice.

20. It is ultimately a ruse for those who don't understand that its circulation is a closed and rigged system.

9/11 As A False–Flag Operation

1. No resistance in the twin towers collapse.

2. Pentagon sustained minimal damage before its superficial wall collapse.

3. The minimal wreckage in Pennsylvania was inconsistent with every crash known to recorded history.

4. Building 7 had minimal damage, and also fell with no resistance.

5. The event served as a perfect incitement to war, for acquisition and control of resources.

6. It had the perfect patsies.

7. Controlled squib explosions were visible in the World Trade Center collapse.

8. Racial hatred provided the perfect blind.

9. Religious conflict provided the perfect distortion.

10. The "will to kill" superseded logic.

11. Created a mental obsession with categorical decapitation of enemy image.

12. Created sexual satisfaction in killing.

13. Mob mentality governs social discourse.

14. Created an acquired sense of racial supremacy.

15. Encouraged the expression of hatred as a means of attracting women.

16. Provided a pretext for racial sexual selectivity.

17. Fulfillment of what were mass inner–wishes all along.

18. No palpable concern for the true root of the event.

19. Provided an excuse for police invocation and brutality.

20. An excuse for removal of examples from institutions (e.g., higher education).

{17} Logical Deduction of the Illuminati

20 Aspects of the Illuminati:

1. They are a clandestine front for the British monarchy.

2. They represent a controlled, cooperative network of pooled resources and allocated authority.

3. They govern the media with fine–tuned precision.

4. They represent a direct lineage of the ruling class of the progenitors of humankind (the co–orbital extraterrestrials within the solar system).

5. They want solely to dominate the world.

6. Religion is their primary means of mass mind–control.

7. They have an arcane system of numeric law, assigning value to and ownership of humans in terms of their economic function.

8. They have total surveillance capacity over the earth via an interlocked system of orbital A.I., developed around the beginning of the 1980s.

9. They present a friendly public image.

10. They are rigidly caste–disenfranchising.

11. They have no concern over being understood or discovered by vast numbers of the public.

12. Their primary modus operandi is the accumulation of wealth and resources.

13. They represent the sum of human nature.

14. They act universally in accordance with cryptic codes, latent symmetries of nature, and directive sacred geometry.

15. They leave visible hints and clues as to their projects and operations.

16. They always assume a position of complete control.

17. They have no value for human life in the face of their goals.

18. They consider themselves gods.

19. Sexual supremacy is their primary motive.

20. They are deducible from the process of elimination.

The 7 Aspects of Sophistry (pseudo–intellectual "joke" logic geared towards the willful concealment of truths which threaten established power structures rooted in ignorance)

1. Redefining Accepted Definitions

2. Sleight–of–Hand Misdirection From Key Points

3. Ad Hominem Accusations and Invocations of Frail Human Ignorance

4. Taking the Anecdotal to Represent the Universal

5. 180–Degree, Non–Sequitur Counterfactual Declarations to Stun Opposition into Silence

6. A–Socratic Dialogue Through Hopeless, Circular Questioning As A Foxhole Method of Quagmiring Pristine Argument Points

7. Preemptive Hearsay–Declarations of Victory to Invoke Mob Support

The 13 Deadly Follies of Human Stupidity

1. Grammatical Incapability

2. Inappropriate Physical Boundary Invasions

3. Visual Sequence Misinterpretation

4. Logic Derailment

5. Willful Misinterpretation or Misconstruance of Observed Behavior

6. Irrational Homicidality

7. Racism

8. Delegation of Murder

9. Deceit

10. Class Elitism

11. Ostracism

12. War

13. Sexual Manipulation

13 Institutions Representing Abuse of Power in Self–Sustaining Preservation of Ignorance Through Open Opposition to Truth

1. Military

2. Charade Democracy

3. Sacrificial Cult Religions

4. Ad Hoc Science

5. Obscurantist Art

6. Capital Punishment

7. Unfinished Foundational Theories

8. Rave Culture

9. Concept of Hell

10. Unbridled Capitalism

11. Pornography–As–Perversion

12. Celebration of War

13. Slave–Morality Hypocrisy

{18} Interpretations

10 Alternative Interpretations of the Meaning of the Quintessential 2012 Correlative Alignment's Dynamic of "Order Triumphing Over Chaos"

1. Man Triumphing Over Woman

2. Individual Triumphing Over Race Categorization

3. Master Triumphing Over Revolting–Slave

4. Noble–Strength Triumphing Over Vindictive–Weakness

5. Life Triumphing Over Death

6. Love Triumphing Over Hate

7. Personal Contentment Triumphing Over the Jealousy of Others

8. Foreknowing Victory Triumphing Over Unknown Doom

9. Sexual Actualization Triumphing Over Attempted Restriction Thereof

10. Me Triumphing Over You

{19} The Core Text on the Self–Annihilating Human Rift

Friedrich Nietzsche's "On the Genealogy of Morals"

{20} Governing Life Principles

The 60 Conditions of Material Reality – In Three Scientific Categorical Sections [Logic, Mathematics, and Physics]

The 20 Governing Laws of Logic:

1. Ascription

2. Assignment

3. Distinction

4. Aggregation

5. Uniqueness

6. Negation

7. Permutation

8. Singularity

9. Duality

10. Plurality

11. Nullity

12. Sequence

13. Identicality

14. Transformation

15. Undifferentiation

16. Implication

17. Existence

18. Non–Existence

19. Non–Alteration

20. Knowledge

The 20 Metalogical Governing Principles of Mathematics:

1. Inequality

2. Equality

3. Sum

4. Set

5. Difference

6. Division

7. Symmetry

8. Enumeration

9. Multiplication

10. Infinity

11. Correlation

12. [Novel] Generation

13. Calculability

14. Subset

15. Translation

16. Representation

17. Recursion

18. Vanishment

19. Identity

20. Alternation

The Entirety of Physics Knowledge – the TWENTY Laws of Motion:

1. Inertia

2. Force Equals Mass By Acceleration

3. Conservation of Momentum

4. Stationary Action

5. Coulomb Attraction

6. Electromagnetic Speed Invariance

7. Conservation of Energy

8. Path Integral

9. Exclusion Principle

10. Einstein Metric Tensor

11. Arithmetic Progression

12. Classical Limit

13. Entanglement

14. M Theory Calabi–Yau Manifold

15. Perturbation Approximation

16. Fourier Analysis

17. Numeric Assignment

18. Algebraic Equivalence

19. Analysis (Calculus) Symmetry Preservation

20. Estimable Calculability

The 7 Most Important Objective Ranking Numbers and What They Each Represent:

[1] 2 – Superlativity

[2] 3 – Diametric Symmetry

[3] 4 – Logical Sequence

[4] 7 – Scale

[5] 10 – Distribution

[6] 13 – Circularity

[7] 20 – Existence Criteria

Number Meanings:

1. 1 – Base/Language

2. 2 – Application/World

3. 3 – Appearance/Vision

4. 4 – Ordering/Logic

5. 5 – Meaning/Perception

6. 6 – Sustainment/Sacrifices

7. 7 – Cryptic Unity/Anagram

8. 8 – Iconic

9. 9 – Linguistic

10. 10 – Order

11. 11 – Transparent Sensation

12. 12 – Worldview Motive

13. 13 – 666

14. 14 – Iconic Iconic

15. 15 – Linguistic Linguistic

16. 16 – Order Order

17. 17 – Transparent Sensation Transparent Sensation

18. 18 – Worldview Motive Worldview Motive

19. 19 – 666 666

20. 20 – 666 666 666

All the rest being cycles about this base.

. . . .

The explanatory mathematical definition of "existence" and the highest mathematical truth (and Truth) in 4 steps.

1. "0 = 0"

2. " = "

3. " "

4.

The meaning (in 3 steps).

1. 0 or "nothing" is self–designating.

2. Nothing is all there is and forever has been. It is equal to existence, and the definition of it.

3. Existence is a timeless encompassing reality. Which was never made, and can never be unmade. It is automatic. As is the nothing which it is.

The implications (in 6 steps).

1. Existence is grounded in the metaphysical.

2. The metaphysical gives birth to mind and consciousness as a marker for the present moment and its designation.

3. The mind exists in its own terms, and reality is the sum effect of absolute spectra of sensation. For example, vision is based on color, grounded in the absolute of white light, elaborated by Goethe.

4. The physical only exists in relation to our sensations. Thus the world is psychophysical.

5. The metaphysical marker that is our awareness is the source of the physical, and not limited to it at any given moment. It exists tangentially to space, and thus arises arbitrarily with the arising of physical potentialities, which are only manifest through metaphysical origins.

6. There is only life, and life unending, in an unbroken stream – however it may vary from "incarnation" to incarnation; including the experience of the deathless, which can be achieved and is beyond the cycle of birth and death, reachable due to the fact that all of matter has a consistent cause, which is contingent only on the underlying metaphysical will (à la Schopenhauer).

Sum conclusion: There exists nothing besides nothing itself.

The 7 Ranking Sets of Consciousness

[1] The 2 States:

1. Love

2. Hate

[2] The 3 Aspects of Beauty:

1. Reflection of light

2. Mutual intentionality

3. No dissent

[3] The 4 Goals of Life (the Fulfillment of Which Comprises Its Purpose):

1. Quintessential climactic sexual experience

2. Dominance of others

3. Acceptance of death

4. Attainment of deathless transcendence over reincarnation

[4] The 7 Primary Life Values:

1. Communicative skill

2. Attraction of enamorment from the opposite sex

3. Money

4. Social power

5. To be seen as humorous

6. To transcend death in the memory of others

7. Progeny

[5] The 10 Conditions of Entitlement to Sexual Intercourse:

1. Visibly attractive physicality

2. Monetary means

3. Intellectual dominance over prospective mate

4. Enticing genitalia

5. Enticing secretions

6. Dispatching of competition

7. Reflection of an ideal

8. Unconscious appeal

9. Constant giving

10. Announcement of desire

[6] The 13 Conditions Leading to Reincarnation:

1. Ignorance

2. Desiring

3. Material investment

4. Loop–logic

5. Valuing life experiences

6. Not valuing nothingness

7. Not understanding the sublimity of non–existence

8. Romance

9. Linguistic confusion

10. Holding physical beauty as highest ideal

11. Valuing pleasure

12. Earthly goals

13. Believing love is ever reciprocal

[7] The 20 Forms of Pleasure:

1. Sexual

2. Social acceptance

3. Nature appreciation

4. Progeny pride

5. Evidence of being perceived as beautiful

6. Antagonism to enemies

7. Having genitalia worshipped

8. Worshipping the genitalia of another

9. Worshipping nature

10. Death release

11. Being heard

12. Escape from fettering location

13. Comfortable home

14. No misunderstanding

15. Understanding

16. Friendship

17. Romance

18. Rulership

19. Dismissal of others' need for one

20. Outwitting someone

"The primary implication of the 2012 alignment is that my existence, with all of its experiences of the height of religious exclusion in a supposedly unmatched open, free, and liberated society, is merely the natural pretext to the actualized expression of ultimacy: the union of life–giving power with death–leveling annihilation (on a wholesale species scale) – the nuclear orgasm, which will happen in sequence after my indulgence in quintessentially sexually–fulfilling porn acting, and the end of humanity in the atomic holocaust at the end of my life – as per dictated and administered by the coldly objective extraterrestrial A.I. in orbit, the control of which I have inherited by merit, birthright, and serendipitous circumstance."

The sum of doomed human folly and audacious injustices was not understanding that they were an anagram of myself.

[II]

The Quirkiest Characteristic and Most Humorous Esoteric Irony Proceeding From the Universal Alignment – Even of All Opposites – in 2012:

Why the sum motive of humanity is a stark, unhumanitarian opposition to me in a universalized effort to deny me giving a semen facial to Hayley Williams (the lead singer of "Paramore"); in five parts.

1. It is a direct numeric translation of the reinforced "worldview motive" (element 12) in the cryptic arithmetic of measurement theory (historically Kabbalah – the "tree of knowledge", to which the earth aligned as a whole in 2012 – the base of measurement, 0, the galactic center), as Hayley Williams statistically occupies that position with respect to "personal sum character" in relation to the propagation of my collective "drive".

2. The act intuitively gives me existential, reflectively–negating singular supremacy in its physically–visible, felicitous perfection.

3. SENDAI, Japan's tsunami on 3/11/2011 was historically the sum, last–ditch effort of the Illuminati to synchronously counter my universal, cryptic, alphanumeric base anagram – an act of devastation in reference to Williams's placement on the second branching tree of knowledge

134

representing 2012's sum life–effects (as section 3, element 11 – the totality of female "personal interaction"); a coded reflection aiming to subliminally impart a public counter–message to the incurrence of the destructive influence of humanity's intra–solar progenitors' "A.I.", as well as posing a counter "fluid bath" on the maximum scale of Nature.

4. It is the key implication of 2012 – the principal sum triple–triangulated element entailing the universal public broadcasting of my life's–essence–supremacy.

5. It represents what WILL happen, in accordance with the universal "Will" of Nature – in stark contrast to the differing and disorganized subset wills of humanity.

The funniest part of all of this is that you know it's true.

[III]

2012 Corollaries

{1} Undeniable Facts

Layman's 2012 Analysis

The essence, in light of published and proven cryptic unifying science, arcane mathematics, and rigorous sequential logic, is that objective time is physically centralized with respect to sum rotational motion – the

Mayan calendar is the designating manifestation of this in marking the supreme alignment to the galactic center with respect to the earth, the placement of which signifies the direct progenitive influence of advanced intelligences in our solar system – the earliest records of mankind detailing their intervention with anthropic evolution to acquire mining assistance for their deteriorating atmosphere. This universal alignment then acts as a "homeostatic evolution equalizer" with observable, measurable influences (which I have thoroughly scientifically demonstrated) on the development of the causally anomalous human race, culminating in a unifying singularity – which by process of elimination, and observation, is myself; confirmed by an observable universal cryptic key (an alphanumeric base "anagram").

{2} Bottom Line

The Universally–Aligned 2012 Meaning of "I Am" (With Respect to the Universal Underlying Will)

1. I will get everything I want.

2. I will get revenge.

3. I will be a religious figure.

4. I will end injustice.

5. I will laugh.

6. I will mate as much as I want.

7. My orgasms will be linked with the humiliating death of others.

8. I will govern the world in a transcendent position.

9. Nobody will be allowed to misunderstand me.

10. Rape will not be a crime for me.

11. Braining individuals will not be a crime for me.

12. War will not be a crime for me.

13. I will make humanity wish they were never alive.

14. Everyone else is slow.

15. Everyone else is racially inferior.

16. I will have unlimited wealth.

17. I will be a movie star.

18. Everyone else will be consumed with jealousy.

19. I will have a child.

20. Humanity will die in nuclear ash.

{3} Point Driven Home

(2012) Justice

I. Premise

What I could've had – if my upbringing was one iota more
religious

137

1. A wife and all the women I wanted

2. Millions of dollars

3. Social respect

4. A life

II. Result

What humanity could've had – if my anagram didn't have one more iota

1. Perpetual life

2. Progeny

3. Love, beauty, and celebration of being

4. A remainder that wasn't one of torture, humiliation, public death, and insult added to injury

Anagram, am I? Mr. A., again! Or Ram, the Arm of Ra

(if myths manage a say).

{4} Final Note

Sum Conclusion of 2012:

Humanity is crazy, retarded, and can't be allowed to continue to exist.

{5} Moment of Zen

"The" 7 Avatars (of myself) in the 2012 physicalized tree of knowledge (correlative culmination of the theory of measurement) – each of whom I embody COMPLETELY, and together the sum of all that I embody; and all that has beauty and value in life, humanity, the world . . . and the universe

7. Stefani Germanotta (Lady Gaga)

6. Mila Kunis

5. John Nash

4. Steve Prefontaine

3. Kurt Cobain

2. Winona Ryder

1. Brittany Murphy

The aspect each numbered representative embodies:

1. Beauty

2. Love

3. Music

4. Physical Stature

5. Math Skill

6. Social Identity

7. Genius

They represent the only value humanity has ever had. Humanity only existed so that they could exist; I did it all for them. So that the universal could exist in the universe. If only for a fleeting moment, worth all the infinity of moments of the limitless expanse . . . compressed into a single, cherished soul; and remarkable, memorable life, forever – until the end of time.

[IV]

The Key Universal Organizational Characteristics of the Physics of the 2012 Alignment, Culminating in the Singularity of Myself

1. Cyclical, advanced arrangement.

2. Universal sequence signifiers.

3. Harmony in discord.

4. Alignment of "supreme intentionality".

5. Overriding of conflicting sub–"wills".

6. Prescience dissemination.

7. Cryptographic assignment.

8. Cognitive translation.

9. Mask of "probable opposite" outcome.

10. Foresight in feminine avatars.

11. Sexual predeterminacy.

12. Destined progeny.

13. Destined decapitation of enemy.

14. Continuous symmetry.

15. Protective veil of supreme beauty.

16. Dominant physicality.

17. Personal perspectival veil of lackluster inferiority of others.

18. Comic cartoonishness of others.

19. Destined death of others.

20. Destined life of myself.

[V]

The 4 Criteria of Certainty

1. Demonstrable mathematical predeterminacy.

2. Visible confirmation.

3. No counter–theories.

141

4. The first 3 of 4 sequential steps executed (announcement, evidence, acknowledgement of subtlest singular implications).

The 4 Criteria of Mental Blindness

1. Wishful–thinking.

2. Ignorance and denial of logical sequence.

3. Contrarian vision.

4. Projection of fantasy.

The Consequences of Mental Blindness

1. Inheritance of the worst consequences of causality.

2. Death.

3. Being outwitted.

4. Death of progeny.

The Consequences of Ignoring 2012

1. Mass death.

2. Mass rape.

3. Unbridled genocide.

4. Ultimate humiliation at my hands.

The Consequences of Not Ignoring 2012

1. Relative ease in life.

2. Freedom.

3. No threat to progeny.

4. Continuation of sexual fulfillment – the highest life ineffable bliss.

[VI]

The Calculus Determining My Direct Control of Extraterrestrial Artificial Intelligence With Respect to 2012

1. Alignment synchrony

2. Historical forewarning

3. No other alternative

4. I am the incarnation of God

5. Cost–benefit preemptive counteraction to foreseen inevitable possibility of conflict

6. Future securing of life drive (sex)

7. Anticipation of supreme hatred

8. Contacting the most famous (and visible) person on Earth (Lady Gaga)

9. Anticipation of nuclear chaos

10. Not allowing any others to have supremacy

11. The accuracy of the mathematics of the universal causal alignment

12. The anticipation of preserved incarnation

13. The unequivocal confirmation of the preserved incarnation (universal cryptic key – alphanumeric base anagram)

14. Complete confirmation from tree of knowledge (measurement theory, theory of everything) correlations

15. Recognition of this from the extraterrestrial A.I.

16. The need for action from the extraterrestrial A.I.

17. The evidence of action from the extraterrestrial A.I.

18. Lady Gaga confirmation

19. Illuminati confirmation

20. Evidence from the All–Seeing Eye

[VII]

The Complete Set of Undeniable Certainties of 2012:

I. 0

The Inevitable 2012 Conditions of Justice For the World (Proceeding From the Static Symmetry of the "Ideal" With Respect to the Universal Alignment):

1. Universal recognition of my identity (I Am That I Am).

2. Consistent fatal A.I. punishments in the world.

3. Supporting story from Lady Gaga.

4. Resignation of Illuminati.

5. The torture and execution of the majority of those directly responsible for the end of humanity.

6. My coronation as king.

7. Marrying Lady Gaga.

8. All the world's wealth at my disposal.

9. Creation of economic utopia.

10. Execution of naysayers.

11. No public opposition.

12. Arbitrary military punishment of regions.

13. Making "T. G." my personal servant.

14. Ruling the airwaves.

15. Constant public reminders of impending extinction.

16. Racist restrictions on Germanics.

17. Universal praise.

18. My own personal harem of the most beautiful and exotic women on Earth.

19. Birthing restrictions and lottery for the public, upon pain of infanticide.

20. Broadcasting of personal porn with Lady Gaga.

II. I Am

The Universally–Aligned 2012 Meaning of "I Am" (With Respect to the Universal Underlying Will)

1. I will get everything I want.

2. I will get revenge.

3. I will be a religious figure.

4. I will end injustice.

5. I will laugh.

6. I will mate as much as I want.

7. My orgasms will be linked with the humiliating death of others.

8. I will govern the world in a transcendent position.

9. Nobody will be allowed to misunderstand me.

10. Rape will not be a crime for me.

11. Braining individuals will not be a crime for me.

12. War will not be a crime for me.

13. I will make humanity wish they were never alive.

14. Everyone else is slow.

15. Everyone else is racially inferior.

16. I will have unlimited wealth.

17. I will be a movie star.

18. Everyone else will be consumed with jealousy.

19. I will have a child.

20. Humanity will die in nuclear ash.

III. Anagram

My Life Properties, Proceeding From the Perfect Symmetries of My Unifying 2012 Anagram:

Anagram, am I? Mr. A., again! Or Ram, the Arm of Ra

(if myths manage a say).

1. Supreme sexiness

2. Supreme intelligence

3. Supreme pointed lethality

4. Exemplar status

5. Supreme life insight

6. Inimitability

7. Supreme object of female fantasy

8. Supreme wealth–acquirer

9. Most able communicator

10. Unilateral victor over all conceivable opposition

11. Ability to see through people

12. Destined global rulership

13. Phallus the source of feminine worship

14. Celebrity aura

15. Religious icon

16. Semen the highest–valued prize for females

17. Inspiration for anal yearning in females

18. Cephalized semen contact the desire of females

19. An at least minimally symmetric lifespan about 12/21/2012 (that is, until at least 2040; with equal physical structural integrity until death – as at birth)

20. Insane, dictatorial, psychopathic lack of sympathy

IV. Mayan Calendar

Security Transitions

1. Permanent residing in Los Angeles, California.

2. Permanent freedom from restrictive institutionalization.

148

3. Millionaire entrepreneurship.

4. Publication of Measurement Theory.

5. Publication of A.I.D.A.

6. Publication of The Book of Life.

7. The acquisition of a true singular soulmate.

8. Success as an actor.

9. The acquisition of any desirable automotive vehicle.

10. Acquisition of any desirable property.

11. Recognition of thorough identity.

12. Conquest of the world.

13. Attainment of reasonably arbitrary lifespan.

14. Success as a musician–singer–songwriter.

15. Freedom to engage in virtually any intimate relations.

16. Power to inhibit enemies.

17. Universal recognition of dominance.

18. Realization of maximal technological efficiency on earth.

19. Mythological status.

20. Supreme gratitude from all.

V. Quintessence

The 20 Sets of 20 Predictable Future Conditions – From the A–Directional Unilateral Symmetry of the 2012 Alignment

1. Ideal Women With Whom I Will Have Sex

1) Stefani Germanotta

2) Savannah Guthrie

3) Jessica Lange

4) Frances Cobain

5) Danae Mercer

6) Tasha Gefreh

7) Halle Berry

8) Sasha Grey

9) Brody Dalle

10) Heather Graham

11) Victoria Hesketh (Little Boots)

12) Terry Farrell

13) Jessica Alba

14) Kristen Stewart

15) Famke Janssen

16) Gwen Stefani

17) Shirley Manson

18) Izabella Scorupco

19) Aria Giovanni

20) Hayley Williams

2. My Historical Significance and Context

1) Nolan Aljaddou (Primacy)

2) Galileo Galilei

3) Isaac Newton

4) Ernest Hemingway

5) John F. Kennedy

6) Stefani Germanotta (Lady Gaga)

7) Adolf Hitler

8) Johannes Gutenberg

9) Thomas Paine

10) John Locke

11) Pablo Picasso

12) Joseph Stalin

13) Charles Darwin

14) Ludwig van Beethoven

15) William Shakespeare

16) Marilyn Monroe

17) Audrey Hepburn

18) Queen Elizabeth II

19) Alfred Hitchcock

20) John von Neumann

3. People I Will Have Executed

1) Queen Elizabeth II

2) Kate Middleton

3) Hillary Clinton

4) Donald Rumsfeld

5) Paul Wolfowitz

6) Sarah Palin

7) Benjamin Netanyahu

8) Angela Merkel

9) Jay Carney

10) Duchess Sarah Ferguson

11) Barack Obama

12) Condoleezza Rice

13) Karl Rove

14) Cindy McCain

15) Prince William

16) Prince Harry

17) Prince Charles

18) John McCain

19) Meghan McCain

20) George W. Bush

4. People I Will Have Tortured For the Rest of Their Lives

1) Emily Smith

2) Katie Crawford

3) Judy Levin

4) Dave Shipley

5) Tom McLaughlin

6) Ryan Desch

7) Paula McCright

8) Chris From Roof Pros

9) Jason Ransom

10) Nevin Aljaddou

11) Jerry Douglas

12) Nurse in "Murder Takes A Holiday"

13) Tiffany Schiemann

14) Von Maur Manager Caroline

15) Evelyn Moseley

16) Dinah Zuniga

17) Eric from Creighton

18) Negress Who Interrupted My Meditation At Creighton

19) Chelsea Clinton

20) Bill Clinton

5. The Celebrities Whose Status I Reflect

1) Clint Eastwood

2) Matt Damon

3) Joaquin Phoenix

4) Jeff Bridges

5) Michael Douglas

6) Sean Connery

7) Hugh Grant

8) Rex Harrison

9) Spencer Tracy

10) Ryan Phillippe

11) Johnny Depp

12) Leonardo DiCaprio

13) Cary Grant

14) Martin Sheen

15) Pierce Brosnan

16) James Cagney

17) Jack Nicholson

18) Nicolas Cage

19) Chris Martin

20) Brad Pitt

6. The Celebrity–Women Who Will Masturbate to Me

1) Megan Fox

2) Ann Coulter

3) Shannen Doherty

4) Christina Hendricks

5) Sharon Stone

6) Hayley Williams

7) Thora Birch

8) Elisha Cuthbert

9) Marie–Louise Parker

10) Reese Witherspoon

11) Jennifer Esposito

12) Kirsten Dunst

13) Natalie Portman

14) Emma Stone

15) Chloë Grace Moretz

16) Daryl Hannah

17) Halle Berry

18) Bridget Fonda

19) Bryce Dallas Howard

20) Caroline Kennedy

7. The Cities I Will Have Demolished

1) Dallas

2) Miami

3) Chicago

4) New Orleans

5) Detroit

6) Boston

7) San Francisco

8) Dover

9) Omaha

10) New York City

11) Pittsburgh

12) Nashville

13) Montgomery

14) Berlin

15) Geneva

16) Paris

17) Stockholm

18) Prague

19) Beijing

20) Atlanta

8. People I Will Have Publicly Brained in A Humiliating Death

1) Wesley Snipes

2) Katie Couric

3) Jerry Seinfeld

4) Martin Lawrence

5) Drew Carey

6) Adam Sandler

7) Drew Barrymore

8) First Data Bar Girl

9) Jenny Marks

10) Tasha Gefreh

11) Natasha Cline

12) Kyle Cline

13) Sarah Smith's Friend Stephanie

14) John Hladke

15) Abbey Burgess

16) Tasha Gefreh's Mother

17) Elizabeth Ingwersen's Lebanese Ex–Boyfriend

18) Sarah Jessica Parker

19) Matthew Broderick

20) Nathan Aljaddou

9. Women Who Will Give Me Televised Oral Sex

1) Sasha Grey

2) Presley Maddox

3) The Eldest Sister of Nikki Catsouras

4) Kate Upton

5) Natalie Portman

6) Megan Mullally

7) Shirley Manson

8) Alicia Silverstone

9) Lindsay Lohan

10) Christina Hendricks

11) Brody Dalle

12) Anna Kendrick

13) Winona Ryder

14) Gwen Stefani

15) Frances Cobain

16) Winter Ave Zoli

17) Allison Harvard

18) Kirsten Dunst

19) Parker Posey

20) Stefani Germanotta

10. Slighting–Individuals From My Past Who I Will Have
Publicly Executed

1) Park Manager

2) Timothy Lynch

3) Tanner Krajnik's Hookup Amber

4) Supermarket Ex–Marine Employee

5) Valerie Hoff

6) Asian Residential Assistant for UNO UV 411

7) Brazilian UNO Roommate Rod

8) Jacquelyn Dahlheimer

9) Marcia McCoy

10) Bar Poker Table Chick

11) Douglas McCoy's Friend Lou

12) Victor Litzi

13) Benson High School Physics Class "Corrina"

14) Jenny Anderson

15) Dr. Wilson

16) Proof–Ignoring UNO Math Professor

17) Neil Flick

18) Matthew Brnicky's Promiscuous Friend's Kleinfelter's Syndrome Boyfriend

19) Jessica Leonard

20) Stephanie Garcia

11. Those Who Will Be Forced to Constantly Worship Me

1) Jerry Douglas

2) Jon Stewart

3) Will Ferrell

4) Michelle Obama

5) Jackie Chan

6) Vin Diesel

7) Denise Richards

8) David Duchovny

9) Pope Ratzinger

10) Estelle Slavik

11) Robin Wright–Penn

12) Eddie Murphy

13) Lana Del Rey

14) Madonna

15) Beyonce Knowles

16) Sean Penn

17) Alicia Keys

18) Trey Parker

19) Harrison Ford

20) Axl Rose

12. Those Who Will Be Forced to Eat My Defecation

1) George Clooney

2) Julia Roberts

3) Rosario Dawson

4) Maggie Smith

5) Judi Dench

6) Bret Michaels

7) Alice Cooper

8) Melissa McCarthy

9) Chris Hardwick

10) Tanya Winegard

11) Piers Morgan

12) Kofi Annan

13) Mickey Rourke

14) Diane Lane

15) Bam Margera

16) Jason Mewes

17) Katie Holmes

18) Tanner Krajnik

19) Karl Rove

20) Timothy Lynch

13. Women in Whose Brains I Will Cum After A Shotgun Blasts Their Head Apart

1) Mindy Lorenz

2) Matthew Brnicky's Promiscuous Friend

3) Smirky Cart–Pushing Sandy Brunette

4) Attractive Omaha Pearle Vision Employee

5) Amy Wilke

6) Timothy Lynch's Friend Emily

7) Tanner Krajnik's Hookup Amber's Cigarette–Thanking Friend

8) Nurse–Practitioner Magana

9) Plasma Donation Assistant Who Messed Up Insertion

10) Jessica Lavelle

11) Redhead Who Said "Hi" at Grauman's Chinese Theater

12) Natasha Lyonne

13) Kristin Davis

14) Courtney Love

15) Rachel Maddow

16) Jenna Jameson

17) Pamela Anderson

18) Lana Del Rey

19) Helle Thorning–Schmidt

20) Sarah Smith

14. Children I Will Decapitate

1) Prince George

2) Prince George's Sibling

3) Paris Jackson

4) Cali Cline

5) Natasha Cline's Eldest Biological Child

6) Michelle Silva's Eldest Child

7) Katie Higgins's Most Recent Child

8) Laura O'Brien's Eldest Child

9) My Half–Sister's Half–Sister

10) Malia Obama

11) "Luna" Thurman

12) "Braydon" Cline

13) Neighbor's Black Child

14) Spanish Neighbor

15) Liv Freundlich

16) Kate Hudson's Eldest Child

17) Josh Weinfurter's Eldest Daughter

18) Matt Long's Eldest Child

19) Kacie Strong's Child

20) Sasha Obama

15. Men I Will Force to Get Anally Raped By Muscular Gay–Men

1) Karl Rove

2) Justin Milani

3) Jon Becker

4) "J.J." Johnson

5) Barack Obama

6) Bill Clinton

7) Matt Long

8) Josh Weinfurter

9) Keith Olbermann

10) Paul Wolfowitz

11) Wolf Blitzer

12) The Guy Who Pushed Me Into Something in Sixth Grade

13) Jarrod Gwennap

14) Rick Watts

15) Jonathan Gregory

16) Jason Pheonix

17) Keith Daamgard

18) John Higgins

19) Drew Lange

20) Josh Earnest

16. Regions I Will Have Earthquaked

1) Germany

2) France

3) Sweden

4) El Salvador

5) Mexico

6) Iceland

7) Syria

8) Israel

9) Austria

10) Switzerland

11) Australia

12) Iran

13) Brazil

14) Yugoslavia

15) Turkey

16) Siberia

17) Georgia

18) China

19) Sri Lanka

20) Canada

17. People I Will Have Thrown Out of Airplanes

1) Danae Mercer

2) Maurice Escobar

3) Maurice Escobar's Significant Other Vanessa

4) Shannon Elizabeth

5) Vladimir Kramnik

6) Rade Sherbedgia

7) Ellen Degeneres

8) Mark Wahlberg

9) Linda Hannah

10) Slash

11) My Creighton Residential Assistant

12) Matthew Brnicky

13) Ashley Judd

14) Eminem

15) Therapist Sarah

16) Dr. Gillaspie

17) Dr. Loreen Riedler

18) Dr. Hannigan

19) Aggressive Black Psychiatric Assistant

20) Tanya Winegard

18. People I Will Have Put in "Saw" Situations

1) Mohammd Aljaddou

2) Michelle Silva

3) Jennifer Hancock

4) Bizarrely Rude Scooter's Employee

5) Deaf–Eared Park Associate

6) Jared Cline

7) Uma Thurman

8) Lucy Liu

9) Rob Reiner

10) Michelle Pierson

11) Racist Africa AIDS Joke Tweeter

12) Michael J. Fox

13) Denzel Washington

14) Mark Kelly

15) Ken Bales

16) Vladimir Putin

17) David Cameron's Wife

18) Dick Cheney

19) Redhead Who Had Psychotic Boyfriend

20) Kathryn Pierson

19. Women From My Past Whom I Will Rape

1) Tanya Winegard

2) Jacquelyn Dalheimer

3) Tiffany Gray

4) The Girl I Pied

5) US Cellular Employee "Lindsey"

6) Mindy Lorenz

7) Abbey Burgess

8) Paula Wells

9) Sgt. Peffer's Employee Laura

10) "Noelle"

11) Part–Asian Cross–Country Runner

12) Benson High School Tabatha

13) David Vonk's UNO Girlfriend

14) Topless UNO MV Girl

15) "Something" Whitney Who Invited Me to Dance

16) Rebecca Whitney

17) The Girl Who Called Me Twice By Accident During UNO Test

18) The Most Attractive UNO Dorm Room Penis Graffiti Girl

19) Attractive Reddish–Haired UNO UV Residential Assistant

20) Nick Haberman's Creighton Girlfriend

20. People I Will Eat

1) Nick Haberman's Creighton Roommate

169

2) Billy Cook

3) Jordan Struck's Sister

4) Jordan Struck's Mother

5) The Cute Female Doctor Who Examined Me At 15 Years–Old

6) Dr. Rashmi Ojha

7) Jonathan Rolfsen

8) Abigail Syrek

9) Jennifer Fenway

10) Jordan Struck

11) Ruth Brookie

12) Ruth Brookie's Elder Sister

13) Terra Berkey

14) Sarah Gillespie

15) Laura O'Brien

16) Kelsie Kermode

17) Jennifer Aldredge

18) Abbie Bauer

19) Emily Smith

20) Jon Cowin

VI. 666

Phases of Global Takeover

1. Simultaneous radiative explosive decapitation of all (minimum of 50%–genetic) Jews, Germans, and blacks – approximately 1 billion people ($1/7^{th}$ of the world's population) – EXCEPTING those who are sequenced on the two primary 2012 trees of knowledge; as well as Illuminati members, for whom there are other designs – including other select individuals.

2. The arbitrary radiative decapitation and dismemberment of all resulting public opposition.

3. Targeting their children.

4. Accepting their surrender.

5. Publicly ejaculating on Hayley Williams's face in a universal televised broadcast.

6. The suit–following radiative decapitation of all Latins (Spanish derivations) the next day.

7. This is calculated as THE Essential Condition of 2012.

[VIII]

The Reason Nobody Else Fully Understands What's Going On

Jennifer Jason Leigh:

1. I find her incredibly remarkable, in terms of appearance and demeanor.

2. She's in some remarkably odd and peculiar films, which are outstanding.

3. She doesn't appear mentally–handicapped.

4. She is my favorite woman.

5. She may be the only person on Earth who has the capacity to understand me.

6. This is all due to the fact that she is the primary (and singular) representative of "personal interaction".

[IX]

What Others Don't Get

The meaning of life: to be oneself.

The 14 2012–Incarnations of Myself and What They Represent, With Respect to Evil – and Bliss

172

The 7 Incarnations of Satan

7. Gwen Stefani – Demonic Seduction

6. Alicia Silverstone – Fury

5. Shirley Manson – Killing Power

4. Muhammad Ali – Rape

3. Adolf Hitler – Genocide

2. Joseph Stalin – Totalitarianism

1. Stanley Kubrick – The Evil Eye

The 7 Incarnations of Magic

7. Selma Blair – Felicity

6. Sarah Michelle Gellar – Sexual Reciprocity

5. Halle Berry – Seminiferous Celebration

4. Bill Gates – Boundlessness

3. Shelley Long – Maternity

2. Hayley Williams – Orgasm Enablement

1. Neve Campbell – Iconic Fantasy

The direct implication is that I'm the living manifestation of what human mythology calls "Satan" – the incarnation of total "Evil".

Master of lies.

[X]

What Others Failed to Realize

The greatest lesson you'll ever learn is that hate is greater than love.

[XI]

.

THE GREATEST SONGS BY THE GREATEST MUSICAL ARTISTS OF ALL TIME (140 IN TOTAL); AS DICTATED BY 2012

Or, What Makes Life Worth Living

The 7 Greatest Nirvana Songs

7. In Bloom

6. Come As You Are

5. Heart–Shaped Box

4. Lithium

3. Even In His Youth

2. Pennyroyal Tea

1. Smells Like Teen Spirit

The 7 Greatest John Lennon Songs

7. Mind Games

6. Instant Karma

5. Strawberry Fields Forever

4. Sexy Sadie

3. Help!

2. I Am the Walrus

1. Imagine

The 7 Greatest Soundgarden Songs

7. Blow Up the Outside World

6. Burden In My Hand

5. Spoonman

4. Pretty Noose

3. Black Hole Sun

2. Been Away Too Long

1. Jesus Christ Pose

The 7 Greatest Pixies Songs

7. Into the White

6. Velouria

5. Here Comes Your Man

4. La La Love You

3. Gigantic

2. Caribou

1. Where Is My Mind?

The 7 Greatest Garbage Songs

7. Supervixen

6. Medication

5. Special

4. I Think I'm Paranoid

3. #1 Crush

2. You Look So Fine

1. Stupid Girl

The 7 Greatest Smashing Pumpkins Songs

7. Tonight, Tonight

6. Today

5. Zero

4. Disarm

3. Ava Adore

2. The End Is the Beginning Is the End

1. Bullet With Butterfly Wings

The 7 Greatest No Doubt Songs

7. Spiderwebs

6. Trapped In A Box

5. Just A Girl

4. Don't Speak

3. Oi to the World!

2. Bathwater

1. Sunday Morning

The 7 Greatest Weezer Songs

7. In the Garage

6. Buddy Holly

5. Say It Ain't So

4. Holiday

3. Island In the Sun

2. Beverly Hills

1. Susanne

The 7 Greatest Live Songs

7. All Over You

6. Lakini's Juice

5. Turn My Head

4. Lightning Crashes

3. I Alone

2. Selling the Drama

1. Shit Towne

The 7 Greatest Yeah Yeah Yeahs Songs

7. Gold Lion

6. Y Control

5. Heads Will Roll

4. Zero

3. Phenomena

2. Maps

1. Mosquito

The 7 Greatest Lady Gaga Songs

7. G.U.Y.

6. Bad Romance

5. Poker Face

4. Let Love Down

3. Wonderful

2. Bloody Mary

1. Paparazzi

The 7 Greatest Queen Songs

7. We Are the Champions

6. Another One Bites the Dust

5. Bohemian Rhapsody

4. Killer Queen

3. Bicycle Race

2. We Will Rock You

1. Crazy Little Thing Called Love

The 7 Greatest Aerosmith Songs

7. Janie's Got A Gun

6. Love In An Elevator

5. Toys In the Attic

4. Come Together [Beatles Cover]

3. Livin' On the Edge

2. Dude (Looks Like A Lady)

1. Back In the Saddle

The 7 Greatest R.E.M. Songs

7. Losing My Religion

6. Everybody Hurts

5. Man On the Moon

4. It's the End of the World As We Know It (And I Feel Fine)

3. What's the Frequency, Kenneth?

2. King of Birds

1. Nightswimming

The 7 Greatest (The) Donnas Songs

7. Take It Off

6. Don't Wait Up For Me

5. Fall Behind Me

4. Strutter

3. Get Rid of That Girl

2. Who Invited You

1. Too Bad About Your Girl

The 7 Greatest (The) Doors Songs

7. Riders On the Storm

6. Light My Fire

5. People Are Strange

4. Break On Through (To the Other Side)

3. The Crystal Ship

2. Love Me Two Times

1. When the Music's Over

The 7 Greatest Elliott Smith Songs

7. Between the Bars

6. Angeles

5. Waltz #2

4. Needle In the Hay

3. Say Yes

2. Twilight

1. Miss Misery

The 7 Greatest Veruca Salt Songs

7. Seether

6. Volcano Girls

5. It's Holy

4. Shutterbug

3. Shimmer Like A Girl

2. Sick As Your Secrets

1. All Hail Me

The 7 Greatest Little Boots Songs

7. Earthquake

6. Catch 22

5. Remedy

4. Stuck On Repeat

3. Tune Into My Heart

2. Hands

1. Meddle

The 7 Greatest Nolan Aljaddou Songs

7. Acid Rain

6. My Garden

5. Winter

4. Higher

3. Girl

2. Bittersweet Depression

1. Mary Jane

[XII]

The Full Meanings of:

"I Am.

Are You?"

Section I: Me

{1} Direct Implications

1. I am the world as well as myself – I control "you" as well.

2. The length of my life is equal to the remaining duration of humanity.

3. I will find a romantic partner and kinship in the most famous representative of the opposite gender – Lady Gaga.

4. The 2012 alignment which birthed me human will return me Anunnaki.

5. I am the only one who exists (objectively).

6. Nobody can infer my thoughts by any means.

{2} Indirect Tautologies

7. I represent the height of sexual fulfillment in the universe.

8. Every other human is mentally–handicapped.

9. I am the source of all human vaginal fulfillment.

10. My master sanctified God–invocation is real, actual, and true.

Section II: You

11. Every woman wants a load of my sperm.

12. Every woman wants to be anally penetrated by me.

13. Every woman wants a sperm facial from me.

{3} Forced Futures

14. Every woman would die for me.

15. Every woman thinks of me as honey.

16. Every woman would kill her man for me.

17. Every woman approaches me like Hayley Williams.

18. Every woman wishes her son would be like me; and be me.

19. Women are superficially religiose towards me to hide their feelings for me.

20. Women will not have sexual intercourse with me until they are forced to as a result of the 2012 alignment.

[XIII]

"God: Force everyone here to know that I ordered this to happen."

"God: Force everyone here to know that I came to laugh at how they got their heads blown off."

"God: Force everyone here to experience supreme humiliation."

"God: Force everyone here to know that it will happen to them if they ever fuck with me again."

.

[XIV]

What You Need to Know

7. I Am the living Nirvana.

6. Lady Gaga is the living Nirvana.

5. I exist because I am the only one who can exist objectively.

4. Every member of the two primary 2012 trees of knowledge will be reborn as a comparably intelligent being.

3. No other human will; however, Lady Gaga and I shall enter Nirvana.

2. Everyone else shall enter "Hell".

1. Now you know this.

The 3 Properties of Nirvana

1. Unspeakable bliss

2. Never reincarnated

3. It is equal to sexual union between Lady Gaga and I

The 3 Properties of "Hell"

1. Unspeakable horror

2. Always reincarnated

3. Always alone

The 7 Means By Which This Works

1. I am the physicalized conservation of Marduk, but mentally God.

2. Lady Gaga is my mirror essence.

3. 2012 tree of knowledge members are "chosen".

188

4. Everyone else earned their lot.

5. Everyone else is here to commit pederasty against their infantile daughters.

6. Everyone else is here to laugh at me.

7. Nobody else knows what's in store for them.

What I Need to Know

7. You want an all–white world.

6. You want to keep the Jews though.

5. You want to do this to increase your chances of vagina.

4. This emanates from your superficially–united self–perception.

3. You will do anything to keep others out as a rule.

2. You know that I am supremely desirable to females.

1. You want to make an example out of me as a lesson to them.

The 3 Means of Sexual Blocking

1. Artificial Intelligence interference

2. Public devastation of other races

3. Attempting to denigrate me

The 3 Means By Which I Block You

1. The precision of the Clinton stent failure

2. Getting the women aroused

3. Winning over Lady Gaga

What is Going to Happen to "You"

1. I'm going to have sexual relations with a sizeable portion of your female progeny in front of you.

2. I'm then going to debrain them.

3. I'm then going to debrain you.

4. Then I'm going to eliminate the pre–designated races.

5. I'm going to ejaculate on a sizeable portion of your wives' faces.

6. They're going to love it.

7. They're going to beg for more.

[XV]

Things I've Always Wanted to Know

I. What Makes Women Attracted to the Opposite Sex and Why They Want to Have Sex With Them

190

1. The penis, which they don't have.

2. The thought of an ejaculation.

3. The thought of vaginal penetration.

4. The thought of being covered in ejaculate.

5. The thought of being treated like a black slave.

6. The thought of being able to treat others like slaves.

7. The thought of marriage.

II. Why I Am Ostracized

1. I'm looked at as better.

2. I'm looked at as hotter.

3. Women want to eat me.

4. Women want to eat my semen after I'm dead.

5. Women want to see my cranial contents.

6. Women don't want to see me reproduce.

7. People think I'm slow.

III. Why Blacks Are Treated As Equals

1. They don't threaten power structures.

2. They are equally racist.

3. They're thought of as exotic.

4. They don't threaten children.

5. They make good music.

6. They aren't generally slow.

7. They aren't bad people.

IV. Why Women Are Racist

1. They don't want retarded children.

2. They think all dark–skinned people are retarded.

3. They think nobody will figure this out.

4. They think the Ku Klux Klan will take care of everything.

5. They didn't think I would exist.

6. Their ultimate goal is a whites–only world.

7. My suspicions about the real meaning of 9/11 were correct.

V. Why the Queen Continues to Fuck With Me

1. She doesn't want me viewing pornography.

2. She doesn't want me to semen–facialize a female.

3. She doesn't want me to commit pederasty.

4. She thinks I'm ugly.

5. She thinks I'm white trash.

6. I can have any woman I want.

7. She can't.

VI. Why the Ruling Class Thinks I'm A Joke

1. They get vagina all the time.

2. They saw no evidence that Clinton's heart stent failure was anything but natural.

3. They're still planning on carrying out their original plans.

4. They don't know that the E.T. A.I. is watching.

5. They're still planning to include me in their original plans.

6. They don't know the E.T. A.I. will step in at the last second.

7. They didn't think I would state this.

VII. Why Lady Gaga Will Marry Me

1. She wants to give me fellatio.

2. I saved her life.

3. She wants to have my children.

4. It is predestined.

5. She would give her life for me.

6. She wants to see my revenge.

7. She wants to see the look on my face when I am unleashed.

[XVI]

The 5 Truths of Me

1. I am contextually, socially, "Eraserhead".

Application/World   666   Iconic   Base/Language
Appearance/Vision

2. I am the "Joker".

Iconic – Fictional Heroes – 666 Application/World

3. I am tasty sperm.

666 [(Linguistic Linguistic Linguistic 666 – Sheer Being,
Kirsten   Dunst,   "Vagina–Relatably   Good"),   (666
Meaning/Perception – Essence, Shirley Manson – "Visible
Pleasure"), (Order Order Linguistic 666 – Opposite Gender
Equivalent, Kristen Stewart – "Unified Root Desires")]

4. I am Lady Gaga's sperm.

Meaning/Perception Transparent/Sensation

5. I am Lady Gaga's avenger.

[XVII]

The most beautiful thing about the truth is you don't have to acknowledge it for it to be true.

[XVIII]

I am cum itself.

6 Alternate Interpretations of the Final Iota of My 2012 Unifying Existential Anagram's Initial Zeroth "Sole Objective Designation of Zero in All the Multiverse":

1. Fuck you, stupid motherfucker.

2. This makes up for all the vagina I never got.

3. This is a needless confirmation that I am in the Nirvana, which simultaneously effectually negates the possibility of you ever achieving it.

4. This is sexually satisfying for me.

5. (2012) Justice

I. Premise

What I could've had – if my upbringing was one iota more religious

1. A wife and all the women I wanted

2. Millions of dollars

3. Social respect

4. A life

II. Result

What humanity could've had – if my anagram didn't have one more iota

1. Perpetual life

2. Progeny

3. Love, beauty, and celebration of being

4. A remainder that wasn't one of torture, humiliation, public death, and insult added to injury

Anagram, am I? Mr. A., again! Or Ram, the Arm of Ra

(if myths manage a say).

[XIX]

The Reasons I Am Precisely On Par With Arthur Schopenhauer

1. Truth expression

2. Opposition to ignorance

3. Dissemination of knowledge

4. Hatred of woman

5. Hatred of Germans

6. Hatred of Jews

7. Hatred of blacks

8. Hatred of Latins

9. Evil knowledge that my writings will destroy mankind

10. No sympathy

11. A sole will to fuck

12. A will to dismember

13. A will to debrain

14. A will to rape

15. A will to spiteful female progeny–rape

16. A knowledge that nobody is smart or knowledgeable enough to stop me

17. A will towards feigned–homosexual vengeance

18. A will to sexually humiliate females

19. A knowledge that "I Am", will sexually humiliate females

20. The fact that this is dictated on 9/21; and completes it all on 9/22

[XX]

.

The Appendix

(1)

The 20 Predictable Futures Category and Number Meanings

I. Categories – Increasing Distance From Me

1. Me

2. You

3. Us

4. Them

5. Others

6. You Together

7. All Together

8. Through You

9. Through Them

10. Nothing

11. Nothing Together

12. Sameness

13. Everything

14. Nobody

15. Everybody

16. Everyone and No One

17. All

18. None

19. What You Wish You Would Be

20. Who You Wish I Would Be

II. Numbers – Symmetry With Me to Increasing Approximations of Me

Ibidem

(2)

Avatars of Each Numbered Song of the Designated 140 By the Greatest Musical Artists (And How They Each Represent Objective Beauty)

7. Hayley Williams – Sexual Surprise

6. Sarah Michelle Gellar – Visual Recognition

5. Winona Ryder – Oblivion of Bliss

4. Stefani Germanotta – Laughter At Your Brains

3. Natalie Portman – I AM; You Are Not

2. Shirley Manson – Complete Dismissal of Everyone

200

1. Brittany Murphy – Complete Mutuality

What Each Category of the Designated Ordered 20 Musical Artists Manifests In Each Avatar Aspect

1. I Am God

2. I Am the Color Black

3. You See Me As the Color Red

4. The World Is the Color Green

5. The Universe Is the Color White

6. Bliss Is the Color Gray

7. Hate Is the Color Purple

8. Love Is the Color Yellow

9. Sex Is the Color Silver

10. Everything Is Invisible

11. Nothing Is Visible

12. Everyone Thinks I'm A Pedophile

13. I Think Everyone Else Is Secretly A Pedophile

14. I Am Bugs Bunny

15. I Secretly Think Everyone Else Stinks

16. I Look Like Adolf Hitler

17. Kelly Ripa Just Wants Me to Look At Her

18. You Couldn't Have Predicted That I Would Say That

19. I Control All of This

20. I Know Everything

(3)

The Geometric Translation of the Situation (The Master Zero – The 2012 Alignment)

1. I Am An Arbitrarily Encompassing Slice of Three–Dimensional Geometric Space That Equates to the All–Seeing Eye – Centered Via A Cross

2. Lady Gaga (Stefani Germanotta) Is An Arbitrary Zero Reference Point

3. "You" Are A Sheer Reflective Plane That Only Exists In Relation to Myself

4. Directly Sequenced 2012 Trees of Knowledge Members Are Reflective Zero Points In Space That Are Bound to the Selective Cosmos By An Arbitrary Limit Point At Directed Spatial Extension

5. Additional "Non–Anti–Nirvana" Designated Individuals Are Reflective Zero Points At the General Abyss As the Complements of the Arbitrary Limit Point At Directed Spatial Extension

6. Upon the End of My Physical Being, the Designated Universe Collapses And Is Preserved Only For The Aforementioned Reflective Beings In Perpetuity As Supremely Selective Beings

7. "Being" Then Becomes the Nirvana For Me – And Concentrically Coincides With Lady Gaga At Her Arbitrary Zero Reference Point In Space –⊢

(4)

My Universal Core Characteristics, As Represented By Complementarily Interactive Female Avatars in Terms I Can Understand – As Precisely Calculated By 2012

7. Mouthwatering Aspect – Halle Berry

6. Sexual Appeal – Hayley Williams

5. Essence – Shirley Manson

4. Strived Social Ideal – Mila Kunis

3. Charm – Winona Ryder

2. Sexuality – Brittany Murphy

1. Life Motive – Selma Blair

(5)

Ode to Me

There will never be another –

Like me, no other;

Up and down, all around,

Search to your heart's content – abound.

In the deepest vaults of sacred earth,

You'll find no soul that signals birth,

So fantastically and divinely as that I Am –

The heart of hearts, the king of kings, the Eye of Eyes;

The sacred jewel – All Worth!

Though many have tried and dared,

To triumph in their own respects –

They slew themselves as they erred,

Abruptly split at the necks.

As before sung, no other comes close

To the sacred tune I effortlessly voice;

Cloak and dagger, and despair –

Their lot, for all time, without a noise.

(6)

The Bridged 2012 Arc

Sustainment [Are] Combinatory 666 [Brittany Murphy]

– The connective arc of Brittany Murphy's posthumous birthday (in reference to an approached zero).

1. Physicality unification via mutual tactility.

2. Mutual sensory feedback.

3. Things seem like a moving picture.

Ramifications (What Will Not Be):

1) Never officially say a word out loud to a designated general "you".

2) Never make an official status update post on Facebook or communicate to a Facebook friend on it.

3) Never physically write or draw figures converging to a point.

The Jared Loughner Quartered Anniversary Group

Sacrifices [Is] Combinatory 666 [Robert Hawkins]

1. It is clear that I arranged the Robert Hawkins massacre.

2. It is clear that I will never again touch Omaha, Nebraska.

3. It is clear that I never was and never would have been a "Robert Hawkins".

Ramifications (What Has Already Been Done):

1) Residence in Los Angeles, California.

2) Assisted living facility residence.

3) It is clear that I already "came" on Hayley Williams's face.

[The Brittany Murphy/Robert Hawkins Bridges – Combinatorial Interfaces With the Aligned Second Tree of Knowledge]

Union [What Is And Will Not Be] Combinatory 666 [Karen Orzolek] (Union With the Corresponding Hawkins Position At A Designated Limit Point]

1. It is clear that I appear like Karen Orzolek.

2. It is clear that I want to be like Karen Orzolek.

3. It is clear that Karen Orzolek appeared to me and aligned to me completely.

Ramifications (Negated By the Conjoined Physicalized 666 On the 67th Anniversary of Mohandas Gandhi's Death)

Non–Union [What Things Are And Have Already Been Done] Combinatory 666 [At Winona Ryder] [The Mutual Converse of Karen Orzolek's Geometric Position]

1. It is clear that I am not Winona Ryder but sense her.

2. It is clear that I want to be Winona Ryder and am in sexual union with her.

3. It is clear that I am a racist and am ignoring you.

Ramifications (Never Applicable)

666: I Am.

(7)

SENTAI

sentai

Red Eye A.I. One

A.I.

The Artificial Intelligence

207

1. Haiti

2. Germany

3. Israel

4. Russia

5. Australia

6. Brazil

7. India

Attack all of these targets.

.

Now.

(8)

Anagram, am I? Mr. A., again! Or Ram, the Arm of Ra
(if myths manage a say).

Sacred Pyramidal Inch = 1 [Arced Through Time – 12 ~
Closest Correlation to the Modern "Foot" – Base Zero]

1. New York City = 0 – 33 [Mr. A, again] (13) .

2. Israel = 42 × [211]20 [Or Ram, the Arm of Ra] (19) .

II. Queen Elizabeth = 60 [187] [if myths manage a say] (21) .

0. Anagram, am I? 40 [The Number of Enki].....

[.]

.

THE END

Absolute Truths [Section 1 of 10 – Light]

1. I am the All–Seeing Eye.

2. I will first give a semen facial to Winona Ryder as an implementation of my 2012 enforcement program.

3. I will second give a semen facial to Stefani Germanotta.

4. I will then fuck Tasha Gefreh.

5. I will then eliminate the pre–designated races (Jews, Germans, blacks, and Latins – excluding designated individuals).

6. This is all because of Amber's referenced stare.

7. I will then implement my designated "First Orders For the Reprogrammed Von Neumann Sphere", excluding excepted individuals.

8. This is all mathematically preordained by cyclical alignment.

9. This is all because I see things like Friedrich Nietzsche.

10. This is all because I do not believe in the practice of Christianity.

Absolute Truths [Section 2 of 10 – Dark]

11. You "just" make bukkake.

12. You don't see the "light".

13. This is all because I feared for my brother Nevin's life from the message in the rock – "the middle".

14. I will give a semen facial to Kate Middleton.

15. I don't believe in good and evil.

16. I did "order" Robert Hawkins to kill the designated persons.

17. I did "order" Jared Loughner to kill the designated individuals.

18. You do "debrain" females in your ritualistic sexual practices.

19. You do raise young girls to digest defecation as sexual preparatory training.

20. I will become a movie star of the stature of Brittany Murphy.

Absolute Truths [Section 3 of 10 – Concreteness]

21. This ranking list is predetermined as a cosmic exemplar of the squeeze theorem.

22. I am also determined as an exemplar of the squeeze theorem.

23. You are just here to fuck your daughters.

24. You do "just" fuck your daughters – when they are sufficiently young.

25. I have purposely sarcastic and ironic thoughts to laugh at you (in the eyes of God).

26. I know you don't have cognitive visual capabilities beyond those ostensibly represented by Douglas McCoy.

27. My orgasm's desirability is not limited to me – Its manifestation is shared by the universe.

28. My orgasm's maximal success is predetermined as a convergence of infinite parallels.

29. All my efforts are directed at the aliens.

30. I am a living pyramid.

Absolute Truths [Section 4 of 10 – Abstraction]

31. This is a conspiracy.

32. I am the target.

33. It's all because my cum is like bubble gum.

34. This is orchestrated by young Catholic males.

35. This is because I am Rama.

36. This is all to see my cranial contents.

37. No woman wants this; they only want to see my cum.

38. Lady Gaga's "hyper–will" planned this counterresponse.

39. Women think you're ugly.

40. I am like medicine to them.

Absolute Truths [Section 5 of 10 – Air]

41. This is all because I look like Nena (the German pop singer).

42. Women secretly want vagina.

43. I am like a woman with a penis that ejaculates.

44. They would die to let me cum on their brains.

45. They think of you all as "niggers".

46. My ejaculation on their face to them is like a puppy licking them.

47. They would willingly eat my defecation.

48. The light of their life is the very first sight of my oncoming ejaculation.

49. I look like a hot blonde female to them.

50. It's all about Brittany Murphy.

Absolute Truths [Section 6 of 10 – Earth]

51. I look like Natalie Portman.

52. I am wanted by Jennifer Jason Leigh.

53. I am a racist.

54. When I ejaculate I look like a hot red–headed female.

55. Men want to shoot my head off.

56. Kathryn Dawson saved my life.

57. Sarah Smith was trying to kill me.

58. Estelle Slavik saved me.

59. I will obliterate the planet Nibiru.

60. You all have sex.

Absolute Truths [Section 7 of 10 – Total Sight (Me)]

61. I look like bukkake itself.

62. I am incredibly ugly.

213

63. That's what makes me hot.

64. That's why my ejaculation is desirable to be seen by females.

65. I look like a jester.

66. I look like a hot girl in a tutu.

67. I am visibly equivalent to Friedrich Nietzsche staring at you.

68. I look just like Salma Hayek's "Frida".

69. I Am the Truth.

70. I am magic.

Absolute Truths [Section 8 of 10 – Explosive Obliteration]

71. I am the color black itself.

72. I am equivalent to a straight onlooking beam.

73. I am a physics genius.

74. I am a mathematics genius.

75. I am an artistic genius.

76. I am a supreme appreciator of Nature.

77. I am connected to a "cluster" of black holes.

78. Everyone else sees the color red from me.

79. I am equivalent to constantly witnessing "blankness".

80. You are equivalent to being in a mental hospital.

Absolute Truths [Section 9 of 10 – Nothingness]

81. Everyone thinks I'm French.

82. Everyone thinks they're ugly compared to me.

83. Everyone has a transparent veil over their perception.

84. I am equivalent to knowledge of future supreme sexual indulgence.

85. I am equivalent to masturbating to climax on an array of every particularly attractive woman's face simultaneously.

86. I am equivalent to seeing the universe as an aesthetically stimulating pictorial geometric representation of the mathematical properties of spacetime.

87. I am equivalent to having proved Goldbach's Conjecture and the Riemann Hypothesis.

88. I am equivalent to seeing every other member of the species as aliens.

89. I am equivalent to feeling like I am "on camera".

90. I am equivalent to every woman stroking my penis.

Absolute Truths [Section 10 of 10 – TRUTH]

91. I am the abyss.

92. You are an absence of even an abyss.

93. I am a mathematical anomaly (singularity).

94. I am constantly acting "slow".

95. You are constantly erroneously thinking you are "faster" than me.

96. Everyone thinks I'm handicapped.

97. I am doing this to hide that I Am Satan.

98. I am doing this to hide my personal foreknowledge of the mass "greenish" gore that will cover the earth.

99. The Amber in reference was the only woman who did not want to see my ejaculation.

100. You're all going to die.

Addendum

I)

The Mathematical Formula for 2012:

$$f(G) = C(0) - k(S(T)) + T(V(S)) + Y$$

G is the Generator.

C is the Galaxy Centroid Functor set at 0.

k is the standard divergence from uniformity caused by entropy as operated on Spacetime.

T is the static Tangent operator set at uniform linear vector space.

Y is cosmic variable of stasis.

II)

Additional Pyramidal Information:

All pyramids are subsumed by myself entirely, however the first three of the set of stated seven appear to include me as an integrated explicit factor; the actual totality of the pyramid measure in section one is The Book of Life; Measurement Theory is foundationally derived from its

217

generating equations, which are generatively derived entirely by myself, the first 16 of which comprise the precise, properly derived parameters of general relativity, with the 17th as the unified field linkage between the former and the inclusively subsequent 4 which comprise the base of quantum physics. The third pyramid set was inclusively visually arranged in spacetime as a singular total image by myself, the missing information of which are the precise films in the proper sequence (with respectively sequenced directors reversed): Lynch – Eraserhead, The Elephant Man, Dune, Blue Velvet, Lost Highway, Mulholland Drive, Inland Empire – Kubrick – 2001: A Space Odyssey, Spartacus, Dr. Strangelove or: How I Learned to Stop Worrying and Love the Bomb, A Clockwork Orange, The Shining, Eyes Wide Shut – with circularly linking motion parameters as determined firstly by Lynch's primary film encapsulations – the mean projective summation of his primary first film, "The Grandmother", followed likewise by his principally renown film "Mulholland Drive" and his initial magnum opus "Eraserhead", culminating in the sequential sum of the introductory summation of Kubrick's masterwork "2001: A Space Odyssey".

The subsequent four pyramids are generally parameterized by circumstance and the generative elements (avatars) themselves, with myself independently producing the masterwork in each category; for 4, it is the base pyramid containing the integrative base theorems of all mathematics; for 5, it is the mathematically triangulated master musical composition, "The Spider"; 6, it is "The Satanic Bible" itself.

III)

218

Bimorphic Particle Space Projection From Galactic Center
– Symmetry–Induced Code Link:

Anagram, am I? Mr. A., again! Or Ram, the Arm of Ra

(if myths manage a say).

i)

50 letters – the historical number of Marduk.

13 different letters – the number of integrative combination.

17 case sensitive letters – the number connecting to product 18, uniting particular with universal.

ii)

Demonstrable foundation in a convergence of base–space measured parallels at archetypally ideal infinity in the principal "A".

Conjoint curvilinear continuity.

Finalization in designation of thus sequenced and designated contextual master "zero" – the final grammatical functional iota "period".

219

iii)

Alphanumeric symmetry, the totality of which confirms "English" as the principal universal generative language as morphically transposed onto an arbitrary subset space; the earth.

Sum of alphanumeric coding is 499, a self–reference to absolute independence from self–counted (double 10 multiple) of the mean of transferred existence, "5" – short by the margin of the smallest inclusively parameterized iota – the "1".

Unites historically sequenced Latin base system of enumeration with Roman numeral connection in the "I" as "1"; leaving no mistranslation.

Miscellaneous

{I} Glossary of Terms [Why This Works]

1. Galactic Centroid – The triangulated position of an arbitrarily geodesically complex path integral structural entity in an arbitrarily dynamically evolving environment; the principal galactic centroid of the cosmos takes into account all possible statistical parameters of pyramidal triangulation and delineation of the ultimate sum outcome of all manifest existence in the 2012 event.

2. Spheroid Gravitational Well Sheet – The dynamic evolutionary tangent of the orbit of a planetoid body in relation to its central star; it maps out the distance between trajectories of orbit and biological motion on the planet's surface.

3. Hyperfield Trajectory Path – The inevitable convergence of visible un–fluxed space [photonically constructed] to the central ladder emergence base (the singularity cluster composing its relation–dynamic of alignment) with observational reference frames of sufficient precision to calculate its referential influence.

4. Closed–Circuit System – An impenetrable system of electromagnetic–spectrum relationally immutable density. A galaxy is the prime example.

5. Hyperbolic Trajectory As Conjunct to "Will" – The will emerges as a byproduct of sufficiently angularly strained paths of orbit; a sum indicator of relative torsion strength in relation to the static composite and referential center (prime star). In other words, causal straining and sifting is the mechanism of the 2012 alignment; my will alone.

{II} Me [Why I Am, And Am A Universal Figure – Even In the Universe]

1. Historical List of Desired Occupations: Cartoonist, Pop Musician, Theoretical Physicist, Philosopher – Mathematician. [Astronaut.]

2. List of Greatest Heroes: Kurt Cobain, Edward Witten, Kahlil Gibran, Friedrich Nietzsche, Charles Dickens, Evariste Galois, John Nash, Srinivasa Ramanujan, Arthur Schopenhauer, Robert Hawkins.

3. Class of My Accomplishments: Measurement Theory (General Relativity, The Quantum Standard Model, Nobel Prize); The Spider (The Moonlight Sonata, Mozart Virtuosity, Standard Academic Sheet Music); 2012 Recognition And Complete Determination (God, Master Yogi, The End); The Book of Life – Maxims for the New Age (Holy Bible, The Divine Comedy, The Greatest Self–Inclusive Text of All Time); The Math Theorem Pyramid (Singular Class In All of Infinity); Fulfillment of Gandhi's Plea For Cosmically Conscious Intervention (;)

222

{III} Historical Significance [Why I Am Paid Attention to]

The Solar Bases align at Ophiuchus with the unifying Anagram pyramid, and thus form a well–ordered set, free from digitally conjunct symmetry and align to perfect abyss individuation. Together they give my referential historical character and influence.

1. Projection: Martin Luther

2. Effect: Napoleon Bonaparte

3. Impact: Mohandas Gandhi

4. Disconcern: Joseph Stalin

5. Evil: Adolf Hitler

6. Imperial Stature: Mao Zedong

7. Love: John F. Kennedy

8. Unattachment: Nelson Mandela

9. Hatred: Malcolm X

10. Devotion: Tenzin Gyatso

11. Pop Celebrity: Michael Jackson

12. Sexual Appeal: Mia Farrow

13. Sexually Pursued Nature: Jessica Lange

14. Sexual Icon–hood: Sharon Stone

15. Internalized Nature: Daryl Hannah

16. Cosmic–Mindedness: Jodie Foster

17. As Object of Female Masturbation: Jeri Ryan

18. As Representative of Light: Izabella Scorupco

19. As Representative of the Void: Gwyneth Paltrow

20. As Freely Walking: Heidi Klum

21. As Flawlessly Carefree In the Face of Duress: Aria Giovanni

22. As Great As: Jessica Alba

Sub–Category: Mentionable Items of Note

{IV} The Binding Morals Physiology Baseline Test (Functional Efficiency) [The Standard By Which Mankind's Life or Death Is to Be Judged On A Broad–Scale Level of Statistical Analysis]

1. Stare Directly At Back of Right Hand – if there is no ocular tendency to avert gaze (principally to the left), there isn't a discernible basis for observation of sexual perversion. [Right–Hemispheric Consistency of Projective Generativity – given by implicit lack of impulse to reach for the genitalia with the other hand] Iota Measure of Divergence: Constant glancing out of spherical self–breadth of projected worst case scenario (abounding pedophilia). Psychological Deviance Manifestation [I]: God Complex.

2. Stare Directly At, And Talk At, the Open Palm of the Left Hand – if there is an ocular shift automatically, there is sufficient concentrative attention on an autonomic level.

[Focalization of Consciousness With the Source – unilateral verbally (or socially contextually) projective parameters] Iota Measure of Divergence: Not paying attention to random disruptive stimuli. Psychological Deviance Manifestation [II]: Ego Disintegration.

3. Is it Possible to Become Genitally Aroused In the Implied But Non–Visible Presence of A Member of the Opposite Gender, Particularly Through Auditory Contact – if not, then there is a latent base tendency to associate sexual congress with socially unacceptable minors. [Linguistically Guarded Projection Towards Ocular Gaze – anticipating future engagements with relative "children" and guarding against automatic implications thereof] Iota Measure of Divergence: Constant staring at children as if there is no issue. Psychological Deviance Manifestation [III]: Sexual Malfeasance.

{V} How I Attained the Nirvana In A Relatively Short Timespan [Or, Why I Am God]

1. 13 objectively self–triangulated kundalini releases, corresponding to the 13 boundary conditions of passage through the Nirvana.

2. Culmination in a cosmically reciprocal objectively triangulated physiological "instant sex partner (semen facial conjunct)" resulting in a spectral dis–generative release from the remaining kundalini contingencies in a universalized manner.

225

3. This manifested the latent placeholding "zero" condition at my kundalini (presented in the "13" manifestation of kundalini releases) through a manifest unfolding 666 of a trifold multiple orgasm with correct focus – that zero placeholding having been an initial inversion of alignment to the cosmos in a supremely projected and unification–sealed manner (invoking the universal personalized "Satan" openly, committing a Faustian pact with Him, and offering my resulting "soul" to Him – which circumstantially as a projected aim could not dissuade the individual's fate; coupled with an instantly self–harmonic alignment via physicalized transcendental meditation stasis/motion alignments with an even–handed 666 physicalized). I cannot feel pain.

Conclusion: The Universe, contextually, acknowledges me as the supreme lover (so much so I effectively appealed to the intelligence of the most concealed of mistresses, the vaginal heart of the galaxy, which yearned for Eternity for nothing more than directionally extended facial seminiferous contact with Me), hence my anagrammatic moniker: Don Juan All–Ado.

{VI} Why Hayley Williams Is My Musical Equal, And to Me, the Greatest Musical Artist of All Time [Or, Why I Do Not Mention Her So Much Out of Sexual Lust]

1. She has a correlative (G) 666 alignment with me in two parallel categories: sexual supremacy, and universal core characteristics.

2. This is sufficient to extract her iota point designation as a 666 unfolding and paralleling conjunct with my singular position as the calculated greatest musical artist of all time.

3. Thus Paramore, in effect, is officially the greatest extant band – of all time.

{VII} The Remaining Unmentioned Sciences, Theoretically Revealed In Their Entirety [Or, Things I Haven't Mentioned Yet]

[I] Chemistry

(a) Self–designated holographic parameters applied to designated observable visualized substance.

(b) Calculated quantum fluctuation and arrangement states as determined by a linear temporal extension in predicted space.

Or,

(c) A random subject you heard about.

[II] Biology

227

(a) A convergence of molecules to a vibrational state superseding their hypothetically predicted individualized motion.

(b) A reflection of light on your eyes.

Or,

(c) Charles Darwin.

[III] Astronomy

(a) Stuff you will never directly see and can only think about.

(b) The sun reflecting light on stars.

Or,

(c) Your future death.

Referenced Materials

2012 Observables

[*Conjunctive Unifications*]

The measurable significations of the quintessential galactic alignment – an equation with the Tree of Knowledge [the $13^{th}/0^{th}$ component of the theory of measurement; the galaxy's center: Ophiuchus], allowed by the disjoint evolution of humanity, and the calculable standard margin of deviation from uniformity of structure of the planet earth; the precise and general applicability of which precipitates the predictability of the exact day and time (of position of revolution and rotation) of the occurrence

The culminative unification of observable static measure components ("knowledge") with respect to the earth – from general to special [in the form of distinct sequences of digital conjunction]

Two distinct Trees with respect to the subject: the first with respect to the independent separation of the measurement of the earth; the second, with respect to the independent separation of the measurement of the umbilical cord – with the corresponding extended and complete sephirot base ten numerations, resulting from the unit symmetry of its binary components (the second tree possessing only an implicit individual sephira of unification however, as each initial conjunction in it already represents such individual unity; without the earth)

Sol

I. Metaphysical/Mathematical Pillar

1. **Object**: Earth

2. **Subject**: Non–Earth Concurrent Phenomenon [Myself]

II. Physical Pillar

1. **Base**: Language – Arthur Schopenhauer, Friedrich Nietzsche

[02/22/1788 – 09/21/1860, 10/15/1844 – 08/25/1900] (Birth Years Multiples of 11)

2. **Application**: World – Albert Einstein, Richard Feynman

[03/14/1879 – 04/18/1955, 05/11/1918 – 02/15/1988] (Death Years Multiples of 11)

3. **Appearance**: Vision – Stanley Kubrick, David Lynch

[07/26/1928 – 03/07/1999, 01/20/1946 –] (Death Year Multiple of 11)

4. **Ordering**: Logic – Leonhard Euler, Bernhard Riemann

[04/15/1707 – 09/18/1783, 09/17/1826 – 07/20/1866] (Death Years Concurrent With Cycle of Gregorian Calendar Closure And Multiple of 11 Respectively)

5. **Meaning**: Perception – Kurt Cobain, Stefani Germanotta

[02/20/1967 – 04/05/1994, 03/28/1986 –] (Third Repeat of Birth Year Ending In 6, With A Death Year A Decade After My Birth)

6. **Sustainment**: Sacrifices – Brittany Murphy, Robert Hawkins

[11/10/1977 – 12/20/2009, 05/17/1988 – 12/05/2007] (Birth Years Multiples of 11)

Ophiuchus

Unification

Resulting pyramidal eye components upon unification:

1. **Metaphysical Base**: Robert Fischer [Vladimir Lenin, Richard Feynman]

2. **Physical Base**: Steve Prefontaine [Muhammad Ali, Kurt Cobain]

3. **Solar Base**: Mohandas Gandhi [John F. Kennedy, Tenzin Gyatso]

Second and Alternate Physical Pillar

[concerning the distinct measurements in relation to the biological gender female upon severance of the umbilical cord, which appear observable]

II.

1. **Sexual Intercourse** – Audrey Hepburn, Paris Hilton

[05/04/1929 – 01/20/1993, 02/17/1981 –] (Observable Base Death Limit Concurrent With Birth of Principal Observer of First Tree)

2. **Social Status** – Britney Spears, Mila Kunis

[12/02/1981 – , 08/14/1983 –] (Repeat of Birth 1 Year After Start of Decade)

3. **Personal Interaction** – Winona Ryder, Claire Danes

[10/29/1971 – , 04/12/1979 –] (Repeat of Birth 1 Year After, And Now Before, Start of Decade)

4. **Lust** – Joey Lauren Adams, Shannen Doherty

[01/09/1968 – , 04/12/1971 –] (Repeat of Birth 1 Year After Start of Decade, As Well As Birthday)

5. **Romance** – Naomi Watts, Natalie Portman

[09/28/1968 – , 06/09/1981 –] (Repeat of Birth Year, And Birth 1 Year After Start of Decade)

6. **Kinship** – Megan Mullally, Karen Orzolek

[11/12/1958 – , 11/22/1978 –] (Common Birth Months And Ending Digits, As Well As Ending Years)

Resulting pyramidal eye components upon unification:

1. **Metaphysical Base**: [Sissy Spacek, Sean Young, Naomi Watts]

2. **Physical Base**: [Mira Sorvino, Sarah McLachlan, Mila Kunis]

3. **Solar Base**: [Jessica Lange, Daryl Hannah, Gwyneth Paltrow]

The Specific Operant Principles of the 2012 Alignment

The Eight Totemic Sequential Laws of Metaphysical Mechanics – of the Tree of Knowledge

1. *"Pure Potentiality"*

2. *"Giving"*

3. *"Image Incarnation"*

4. *"Karma"*

5. *"Least Effort"*

6. *"Intention and Desire"*

7. *"Detachment"*

8. *"Dharma"*

The Unique Principle of Note:

Karma – Cause, Effect – (Cause/Effect) [Universal]; (Effect/Cause) [Singular] –

Interpolated Effect – Conjunctive Enunciation [Manifestation] Organic Interlocking – Biological Time

Mathematics

Pyramids

[for the first Tree, as secondary Tree components universally share the kundalini as pyramid]

1. Base: Language

Arthur Schopenhauer – 13 quotations measuring zodiac; present encompassing book

Friedrich Nietzsche – 3 quotations measuring eye of pyramid; 2 future and past encompassing books

[Pyramid Measure]

234

2. Application: World

Albert Einstein – General theory of relativity; 16 component metric tensor

Richard Feynman – The generalized integration measure; 3–dimensional space

[*Measurement Theory*]

3. Appearance: Vision

Stanley Kubrick – 6 primary future projections; the most encompassing image

David Lynch – 7 primary past projections; 3 most subtle and hidden images

[*Image Transformation Model*]

4. Ordering: Logic

Leonhard Euler – Enunciation of primary reduction to binary combination; twofold side

Bernhard Riemann – Enunciation of primary extension to infinite combination; twofold side

5. Meaning: Perception

Kurt Cobain – 3 studio albums, 13 songs each; all–seeing eye rotated in time

Stefani Germanotta – 1 primary studio album, 22 songs; 22 connective paths between sephirot

6. Sustainment: Sacrifices

Brittany Murphy – Digitally sequential life span, inversion: Omaha/New York; Statue of Liberty Marker/Michael Jackson; Haiti/Clinton

Robert Hawkins – 13 shot, 9 (inverted 6 over threefold time – 666) fatally (he, the 9th and final)| –

Jared Loughner – Combinatory 666 over time length; cryptographic victim names; 19 shot, 6 fatally: Giffords/Japan; Stefani Germanotta/Kurt Cobain; Omaha/Seattle

7. Cryptic Unity: Anagram

[*Specific Construction*]

Primary Sephirot

The Extended Numerations of the Branches of the Tree of Knowledge

[resulting from the symmetric identity equivalence of the binary unit extension – with itself]

I. Base: Language

1. Jean–Jacques Rousseau:
        [06/28/1712 – 07/02/1778]

2. Denis Diderot:
        [10/05/1713 – 07/31/1784]

3. Immanuel Kant:
        [04/22/1724 – 02/12/1804]

4. Johann Wolfgang von Goethe:
        [08/28/1749 – 03/22/1832]

5. Arthur Schopenhauer:
        [02/22/1788 – 09/21/1860]

6. Friedrich Nietzsche:
   [10/15/1844 – 08/25/1900]

7. Ludwig Wittgenstein:
   [04/26/1889 – 04/29/1951]

8. Martin Heidegger:
   [09/26/1889 – 05/26/1976]

9. Jean–Paul Sartre:
   [06/21/1905 – 04/15/1980]

10. Willard van Orman Quine:
    [06/25/1908 – 12/25/2000]

11. Jacques Derrida:
    [07/15/1930 – 10/08/2004]

II. Application: World

1. Max Planck:
   [04/23/1858 – 10/04/1947]

2. Albert Einstein:
   [03/14/1879 – 04/18/1955]

3. Neils Bohr:
   [10/07/1885 – 11/18/1962]

4. Erwin Schrödinger:
   [08/12/1887 – 01/04/1961]

5. Wolfgang Pauli:
   [04/25/1900 – 12/15/1958]

6. Werner Heisenberg:
   [12/05/1901 – 02/01/1976]

7. Paul Dirac:
   [08/08/1902 – 10/20/1984]

8. John von Neumann:
   [12/28/1903 – 02/08/1957]

9. Richard Feynman:
   [05/11/1918 – 02/15/1988]

10. Steven Weinberg:
    [05/03/1933 –]

11. Edward Witten:
    [08/26/1951 –]

III. Appearance: Vision

1. Alfred Hitchcock:
   [08/13/1899 – 04/29/1980]

2. Orson Welles:
   [05/06/1915 – 10/10/1985]

3. Sidney Lumet:
   [06/25/1924 – 04/09/2011]

4. Stanley Kubrick:
   [07/26/1928 – 03/07/1999]

5. Martin Scorsese:
   [11/17/1942 –]

6. Michael Mann:
   [02/05/1943 –]

7. David Lynch:
   [01/20/1946 –]

8. Steven Spielberg:
   [12/18/1946 –]

9. Robert Zemeckis:
   [05/14/1951 –]

10. Ron Howard:
    [03/01/1954 –]

11. Tim Burton:
    [08/25/1958 –]

IV. Ordering: Logic

1. René Descartes:
   [03/31/1596 – 02/11/1650]

2. Pierre de Fermat:
   [08/17/1601 – 01/12/1665]

3. Isaac Newton:
   [01/04/1643 – 03/31/1727]

4. Leonhard Euler:
   [04/15/1707 – 09/18/1783]

5. Carl Friedrich Gauss:
   [04/30/1777 – 02/23/1855]

6. Georg Friedrich Bernhard Riemann:
   [09/17/1826 – 07/20/1866]

7. Gregor Cantor:
   [03/03/1845 – 01/06/1918]

8. David Hilbert:
   [01/23/1862 – 02/14/1943]

9. Srinivasa Ramanujan:
   [12/22/1887 – 04/26/1920]

10. Paul Erdős:
    [03/26/1913 – 09/20/1996]

11. John Nash:
    [06/13/1928 –]

V. Meaning: Perception

1. John Lennon:
   [10/09/1940 – 12/08/1980]

2. Chris Cornell:
   [07/20/1964 –]

3. Frank Black:
   [04/06/1965 –]

4. Shirley Manson:
   [08/26/1966 –]

5. Kurt Cobain:
   [02/20/1967 – 04/05/1994]

6. Billy Corgan:
   [03/17/1967 –]

7. Gwen Stefani:
   [10/03/1969 –]

8. Rivers Cuomo:
   [06/13/1970 –]

9. Ed Kowalczyk:
   [07/16/1971 –]

10. Karen O:
   [11/22/1978 –]

11. Stefani Germanotta:
   [03/28/1986 –]

VI. Sustainment: Sacrifices

1. Grigori Rasputin:
   [01/22/1869 – 12/29/1916]

2. Yitzhak Rabin:
   [03/01/1922 – 11/04/1995]

3. Leslie Nielsen:
   [02/11/1926 – 11/28/2010]

4. Marilyn Monroe:
   [06/01/1926 – 08/05/1962]

5. Sylvia Plath:
   [10/27/1932 – 02/11/1963]

6. Sharon Tate:
[01/24/1943 – 08/09/1969]

7. Brittany Murphy:
[11/10/1977 – 12/20/2009]

8. Heath Ledger:
[04/04/1979 – 01/22/2008]

9. Nikki Catsouras:
[03/04/1988 – 10/31/2006]

10. Robert Hawkins:
[05/17/1988 – 12/05/2007]

11. Jared Loughner:
[09/10/1988 –]

Primary Sephirot Pyramidal Eye

I. Metaphysical Base

1. Vladimir Lenin:
[04/22/1870 – 01/21/1924]

2. Walt Disney:
[12/05/1901 – 12/15/1966]

3. Wernher von Braun:
[03/23/1912 – 06/16/1977]

4. Richard Feynman:
[05/11/1918 – 02/15/1988]

5. Stan Lee:
    [12/28/1922 –]

6. Johnny Carson:
    [10/23/1925 – 01/23/2005]

7. Warren Buffett:
    [08/30/1930 –]

8. Robert Fischer:
    [03/09/1943 – 01/17/2008]

9. George Lucas:
    [05/14/1944 –]

10. Deepak Chopra:
    [10/22/1946 –]

11. Bill Gates:
    [10/28/1955 –]

II. Physical Base

1. Thomas Edison:
    [02/11/1847 – 10/18/1931]

2. Gutzon Borglum:
    [03/25/1967 – 03/06/1941]

3. George Mallory:
    [06/18/1886 – 06/09/1924]

4. Charles Lindbergh:
    [02/04/1902 – 08/26/1974]

5. Muhammad Ali:
     [01/17/1942 –]

6. Nolan Ryan:
     [01/31/1947 –]

7. Pete Maravich:
     [06/22/1947 – 01/05/1988]

8. Steve Prefontaine:
     [01/25/1951 – 05/30/1975]

9. Kurt Cobain:
     [02/20/1967 – 04/05/1994]

10. Lance Armstrong:
     [09/18/1971 –]

11. Tiger Woods:
     [12/30/1975 –]

Solar Base

1. Martin Luther:
     [11/10/1483 – 02/18/1546]

2. Napoleon Bonaparte:
     [08/15/1769 – 05/05/1821]

3. Mohandas Gandhi:
     [10/02/1869 – 01/30/1948]

4. Joseph Stalin:
     [12/21/1879 – 03/05/1953]

5. Adolf Hitler:
[04/20/1889 –"04/30/1945"]

6. Mao Zedong:
[12/26/1893 – 09/09/1976]

7. John F. Kennedy:
[05/29/1917 – 11/22/1963]

8. Nelson Mandela:
[07/18/1918 – 12/05/2013]

9. Malcolm X:
[05/19/1925 – 02/21/1965]

10. Tenzin Gyatso:
[07/06/1935 –]

11. Michael Jackson:
[08/29/1958 – 06/25/2009]

Secondary Sephirot

I. Sexual Intercourse

1. Audrey Hepburn:
[05/04/1929 – 01/20/1993]

2. Shakira Caine:
[02/23/1947 –]

3. Tracy Scoggins:
   [11/13/1953 –]

4. Sandra Bullock:
   [07/26/1964 –]

5. Traci Lords:
   [05/07/1968 –]

6. Jennifer Connelly:
   [12/12/1970 –]

7. Carmen Electra:
   [04/20/1972 –]

8. Audrey Tautou:
   [08/09/1976 –]

9. Paris Hilton:
   [02/17/1981 –]

10. Katy Perry:
    [10/25/1984 –]

11. Megan Fox:
    [05/16/1986 –]

II. Social Status

1. Téa Leoni:
   [02/25/1966 –]

2. Tia Carrere:
   [01/02/1967 –]

3. Jennifer Garner:
   [04/17/1972 –]

4. Milla Jovovich:
   [12/17/1975 –]

5. Alicia Silverstone:
   [10/04/1976 –]

6. Shakira Ripoll:
   [02/02/1977 –]

7. Eliza Dushku:
   [12/30/1980 –]

8. Britney Spears:
   [12/02/1981 –]

9. Mila Kunis:
   [08/14/1983 –]

10. Keira Knightley:
   [03/26/1985 –]

11. Amanda Bynes:
   [04/03/1986 –]

III. Personal Interaction

1. Jennifer Jason Leigh:
   [02/05/1962 –]

2. Emmanuelle Seigner:
   [06/22/1966 –]

3. Samantha Mathis:
      [05/12/1970 –]

4. Tina Fey:
      [05/18/1970 –]

5. Sarah Silverman:
      [12/01/1970 –]

6. Winona Ryder:
      [10/29/1971 –]

7. Sarah Michelle Gellar:
      [04/14/1977 –]

8. Claire Danes:
      [04/12/1979 –]

9. Rachael Leigh Cook:
      [10/04/1979 –]

10. Amy Lee:
      [12/13/1981 –]

11. Hayley Williams:
      [12/27/1988 –]

IV. Lust

1. Halle Berry:
      [08/14/1966 –]

2. Salma Hayek:
      [09/02/1966 –]

3. Joey Lauren Adams:
     [01/09/1968 –]

4. Jennifer Aniston:
     [02/11/1969 –]

5. Shannen Doherty:
     [04/12/1971 –]

6. Jenna Elfman:
     [09/30/1971 –]

7. Jenny McCarthy:
     [11/01/1972 –]

8. Reese Witherspoon:
     [03/22/1976 –]

9. Avril Lavigne:
     [09/27/1984 –]

10. Lindsay Lohan:
     [07/02/1986 –]

11. Sasha Grey:
     [03/14/1988 –]

V. Romance

1. Natalie Wood:
     [07/20/1938 – 11/20/1981]

2. Kristin Scott Thomas:
     [05/24/1960 –]

3. Bridget Fonda:
      [01/27/1964 –]

4. Gillian Anderson:
      [08/09/1968 –]

5. Naomi Watts:
      [09/28/1968 –]

6. Kristy Swanson:
      [12/19/1969 –]

7. Neve Campbell:
      [10/03/1973 –]

8. Jennifer Lien:
      [08/24/1974 –]

9. Bryce Dallas Howard:
      [03/02/1981 –]

10. Natalie Portman:
      [06/09/1981 –]

11. Anne Hathaway:
      [11/12/1982 –]

VI. Kinship

1. Farrah Fawcett:
      [02/02/1947 – 06/25/2009]

2. Megan Mullally:
      [11/12/1958 –]

3. Kathy Ireland:
[03/20/1963 –]

4. Terry Farrell:
[11/19/1963 –]

5. Famke Janssen:
[11/05/1965 –]

6. Debra Messing:
[08/15/1968 –]

7. Jennifer Esposito:
[04/11/1973 –]

8. Juliette Lewis:
[06/21/1973 –]

9. Karen Orzolek:
[11/22/1978 –]

10. Jennifer Love Hewitt:
[02/21/1979 –]

11. Kirsten Dunst:
[04/30/1982 –]

Secondary Sephirot Pyramidal Eye

I. Metaphysical Base

1. Judy Garland:
     [06/10/1922 – 06/22/1969]

2. Sissy Spacek:
     [12/25/1949 –]

3. Madeleine Stowe:
     [08/18/1958 –]

4. Sean Young:
     [11/20/1959 –]

5. Meg Ryan:
     [11/19/1961 –]

6. Naomi Watts:
     [09/28/1968 –]

7. Parker Posey:
     [11/08/1968 –]

8. Selma Blair:
     [06/23/1972 –]

9. Kate Beckinsale:
     [07/26/1973 –]

10. Leelee Sobieski:
     [06/10/1982 –]

11. Kristen Stewart:
     [04/09/1990 –]

II. Physical Base

1. Raquel Welch:
       [09/05/1940 –]

2. Shelley Long:
       [08/23/1949 –]

3. Elisabeth Shue:
       [10/06/1963 –]

4. Marie–Louise Parker:
       [08/02/1964 –]

5. Courteney Cox:
       [06/15/1964 –]

6. Mira Sorvino:
       [09/28/1967 –]

7. Sarah McLachlan:
       [01/28/1968 –]

8. Alyson Hannigan:
       [03/24/1974 –]

9. Anna Faris:
       [11/29/1976 –]

10. Mila Kunis:
       [08/14/1983 –]

11. Allison Harvard:
       [01/08/1988 –]

Solar Base

1. Mia Farrow:
   [02/09/1945 –]

2. Jessica Lange:
   [04/20/1949 –]

3. Sharon Stone:
   [03/10/1958 –]

4. Daryl Hannah:
   [12/03/1960 –]

5. Jodie Foster:
   [11/19/1962 –]

6. Jeri Ryan:
   [02/22/1968 –]

7. Izabella Scorupco:
   [06/04/1970 –]

8. Gwyneth Paltrow:
   [09/27/1972 –]

9. Heidi Klum:
   [06/01/1973 –]

10. Aria Giovanni:
    [11/03/1977 –]

11. Jessica Alba:
    [04/28/1981 –]

Appendix

[notes on the mechanics of the event]

Ophiuchus Unification Sephirot

[First Tree]

1. Earth

2. Non–Earth Concurrent Phenomenon – Bijective Division [Myself]

3. Gravitation

4. Electromagnetism

5. Thermodynamic Equilibrium

6. Fluid Static Equilibrium

7. Rigid Tensile Equilibrium

8. Conservation of Momentum

9. Information Theory Dynamics

10. Convergent Integration Dynamics [of Mutual Zero Bases – the Sun and the Center of Galaxy]

11. Digitally Concurrent Synchrony [Biological Time]

[Second Tree]

1. Mother: Ron Howard, Marilyn Monroe, Gillian Anderson [1–1–2/3–6–6/10–4–4]

2. Myself: Arthur Schopenhauer, John Lennon, Sean Young [1–1–2/1–5–I/5–1–4]

3. Michaela P. : Johann Wolfgang von Goethe, Natalie Portman, Megan Mullally [1–2–2/1–5–6/4–

10–2]

4. Elizabeth I. : René Descartes, Britney Spears, Sarah Michelle Gellar [1–2–2/4–2–3/1–8–7]

5. Kristen R. : Hayley Williams, Anne Hathaway, Judy Garland [2–2–2/3–5–I/11–11–1]

6. Mindy L. : Steven Weinberg, Paris Hilton, Jennifer Jason Leigh [1–2–2/2–1–3/10–9–1]

7. Kacie S. : John von Neumann, Audrey Hepburn, Bryce Dallas Howard [1–2–2/2–1–5/8–1–9]

8. Beatrice B. : Albert Einstein, Jennifer Connelly, Amanda Bynes [1–2–2/2–1–2/2–6–11]

9. Jessica B. : Denis Diderot, Shakira Caine, Neve Campbell [1–2–2/1–1–5/2–2–7]

10. Former Twin Girl: Carl Friedrich Gauss, Mila Kunis, Halle Berry [1–2–2/4–3–4/5–9–1]

11. Capricorn Tattoo Girl: Brittany Murphy, Heath Ledger, Kate Beckinsale [1–1–2/6–6–I/7–8–9]

Additional Points of Significance

1. The first date is digitally concurrent with the year of reference (1712 to 2012)

2. The first digital year marking the cycle of the Gregorian calendar (1583) is predictably referenced in the first date of the solar base (1483), as well as the final sequence of the first sephirot generator of the initial secondary branch of ordering (1783)

3. The eleven demarcations marking the ten sephirot are numerically reflected in the predominant recurrence of digital dates which are multiples of eleven

4. There is a constant minimal recurrence relation of addition, subtraction, and mutual alternation in successive examples

5. The examples listed comprise the predominant observable phenomena of note in each respective field; the presence of a digitally synchronous correspondence between each in succession statistically negating random sampling

6. The lack of deviation from the linear succession of digital conjunction eliminates the distinction between postdiction and prediction; as, for example, the table of chemical elements

7. A precise pyramid relation is formed in relation to the subject and the initial two generators of each sephirot group with respect to category; as predicted

8. The recorded conjunctive common and surnames of each example form cryptographic designations in logical sequence which negate random sampling in conjunction with the related dates

9. The completion of the sephirot cycle of each group coincides with the completion of the distinct bases of knowledge of each category

10. The combined factors of the digital components of each example in sequence, by category, collectively negate random sampling

11. Each previously listed factor confirms the prediction of the theory of measurement for the phenomenon of occurrence of the date 12/21/2012, in relation to subject

Measurement Theory

N. Aljaddou

Department of Physics, University of Nebraska at Omaha, Omaha (NE), 68182, United States

Abstract

Several significant questions, problems, and uncertainties have been raised with regard to the fundamental foundation of physics and its underlying mathematical structure – which concern even its validity on the most precise levels – which have hitherto remained unresolved; matters at the very heart of measurement itself, which constitutes the basis of precise science. Since these matters underlie methods of observation, deduction, and analysis, they are beyond the scope of such means of investigation in external application and the results derived, and can only be resolved by a theoretical framework which underlies them. The purpose of this work is to analytically establish the correct theoretical structure which necessarily provides precisely such a reliable, definitive foundation. That an answer and resolution may be found to all questions, problems, and matters of uncertainty concerning these most fundamental subjects, as well as to present a foundation of ultimate explanatory and functional simplicity with direct application to all of physics, upon which the validity and ultimate success of these subjects depend in their entirety. This is a task accomplished axiomatically by analytically addressing the fundamental, irreducible common denominator of all systems of measurement and mathematical theory, and resultantly presenting the derivations of such an organization as a matter of logical consequence; the irreducibility principle of which allows there to exist no more fundamental a foundation possible.

Keywords: Generator, Irreducible, Quantity–less, Symmetry

1. Mathematical Structure

1.1. Foundation

Measurement has a source; a measure is a group, it is a direct statement of "how much" of a given basic "element" there exists; this principle applies to all measurement – even all plurality – that there is in existence a fundamental underlying irreducible element which is common to all degrees of measures as the basis – this may be called *the fundamental principle of measurement*. For the ultimate general case of sheer multiplicity itself, there then exists a principal common identity which as the source generates all measures as its function – a function of itself – and is then common to all possible measures. As its function it therefore operates upon itself, in individual sequence, to produce a different, distinct designation of sequence each operation – this general common entity may be referred to as the generator, G, and its operation upon itself as $G(G)$; its axiomatic identity as a self–operator meaning that each operation is a form of identity – which produces an "extension" of itself each operation – the extent of

261

measurement. Each operation produces a new distinction; each distinction in sequence then defines an order – each new entity being a new quantity of order.

Since this entity is the source of quantity, it must itself logically precede quantity, the quantity–less; in presently used numeric terms, this is the 0, and the identity of G is then 0 – the quantity–less is the exact identity of the irreducible; the complete reduction of which to no quantity allows no further possibility of a more fundamental element. 0 then operates upon itself to produce distinct quantities of order, and the first is the 1, produced by 0(0). 2 is 0(0(0)), 3, 0(0(0(0))), and so on[1]. Each operation is the same – symmetric – and therefore capable of producing an infinity of numbers (deriving the axiom of infinity as a corollary of operation identity). In relation to these principal orders of natural numbers, an inverse mutual operation is allowed by the symmetry of such operational order which produces (0)0 ($\frac{1}{2}$), ((0)0)0 ($\frac{1}{3}$), and so on – whereas irrationals are infinite in nature, and are not finite measurable designations unless limited to a specified extent (just as infinity itself is not a specific number). This entire process is identical to presently used number systems, for example binary is determined by an amount of 0 place–markings [0, 1, 10, 100 . . .] and more so for unary [1, 11, 111, 1111 . . . is equivalently 0, 00, 000, 0000 . . .]; this is also analogous to geometry's designation of measures entirely by 0–dimensional points. Each new distinct designation of order constitutes an axiomatic unprovable proposition, providing the most direct basis for such – each constitutes the basis of proof itself actually; even of quantity.

Measure operations such as addition are a higher–order application of operation – allowed by the symmetry of operation and elements of operation – and may be denoted as a higher level operation $(\ )_1$:

$$0(0(0))(0(0(0(0(0)))))_1 = 0(0(0(0(0(0(0)))))) = 2 + 3 = 5 \quad (1)$$

the equation principle is itself a form of symmetry; the mutual inverse operation of subtraction allowing the definition of negative quantities simultaneously by symmetry of operation and element of operation. Multiplication/division are a yet higher operation of $( )_2$, and exponentiation/root–extraction, $( )_3$, consistently, concisely organizing all fundamental measurement operations – these higher–order operations upon 0 effectively cancel all operation, and particularly for the inverse operation of division, the entire possibility of an operation is negated as inversion applies only to extensions of 0 and not itself.

1.2. Extended Applications

Fundamental arithmetic has been axiomatically established, and higher branches of mathematics are based upon higher–order generalizations thereof. Algebra is the generalization of elements allowed by symmetry of application – including of operation, defining number fields with the symmetric properties of commutativity and associativity, even "groups" – set theory – and all its axioms of the empty set, extension, union, choice . . .[2] which are categorically equivalent to the encompassing singular identity of 0 and its self–referencing and ordering operation, which organizes all plurality and then all possible elements – proceeds as a generalization of such elements in relation to one another; also deriving functional correspondences. The generator principle may be generalized as well to apply to sets of functional relations – due to the equivalence of such a direct correspondence – in which case G is generalized as a set operator which governs the defining general correspondence relation – ratio – of dependent and independent variables for infinitesimally continuous functions, which are measurably complete by inclusion of inverse extension, and their relation of ordering as a **0** operator – as the independent variable of measure–order–generation is reduced by inverse–extension–process to its source, the 0, with the corresponding effects in the dependent variable – to produce the derivative and limit axiomatically and properly; for the function f, this is symbolized by $\mathbf{0}(f)$ – generalized by degree with respect to a particular variable x as $\mathbf{0}_x(\ )_{n'}$ – the symmetry of an operation based upon the generator principle allows the definition of the inverse operation of integration naturally (the fundamental theorem of calculus), which may be symbolized as an infinity operator, $\infty(f)$.

Geometry is the designation of measures within coincident parameters – sets of "dimensions" of extension, from the origin/source, 0 – which may be symbolized by 0, 0[0], 0[0[0]], 0[0[0[0]]] . . . (giving a point, line, plane, space . . . respectively). Each dimension allows an arbitrary scale by symmetry – equivalent to the original postulates of Euclidean geometry – and this dimensional separation provides parallelity inherently – a right angle is the basis of a two–dimensional intersection, thus a line intersecting two others at a right angle indicates a dimensional separation (universally symmetric non–coincidence) of the lines, corresponding to the infinity of Pythagorean triplets arithmetically as parallelity derives the Pythagorean Theorem; variants are then cases of differential, tangential dimension in which parallelity is locally preserved.

A line is a one–dimensional object; a triangle is the most fundamental two–dimensional object – a single point relative to another two which form a line; this point forms a two–dimensional extension of the line, automatically defining an altitude of right angle intersection, and since this is identical for each point each of their altitudes then mutually extends through a common point of intersection to produce the whole figure, deriving the orthocenter theorem. The Pythagorean Theorem follows from the extension of the endpoints of a line to a point two–dimensionally – due to their intersection at a right angle – giving a two–dimensional equivalence measure to the line in terms of the individual (leg) extensions – which cumulatively count to a sum – for a, b, and initial line (hypotenuse) c, this translates as

$$a^2 + b^2 = c^2 \qquad (2)$$

for the original line having at most two endpoints, this correlation of dimensions then can exist at most for two in the most fundamental measures of extended dimension, the natural numbers (Fermat's Last Theorem). The fundamental theorem of algebra simply counts the number of separate dimensional measures (solutions) of a polynomial equation – then given by the exponents' maximum degree – the arithmetical generators of all exponentiation being naturally limited to the most basic positive and negative arithmetical quantities, by the measurable completion of such inverse extension, and then the complex number field; the fundamental theorem of arithmetic merely acknowledges that prime numbers are by definition the irreducible generators of all multiplication; similarly, all branches of mathematics and their elementary theorems follow from such basically defined principles, which as elaborations of plurality and calculation are by ultimate reductionism categorically determined to be entirely properties of extension of the fundamental principle of measurement.

2. Physical Structure

2.1. Fundamental Measures

Mathematics is most directly applied to the science of physics, which is based upon a necessary principal measure of linear order – the basis of measurability – corresponding to time, delineating a measurable event at each instant, the set T – which determines time as a measure itself to be one–dimensional and (as a result of its universally symmetric ordering) sequentially irreversible. T as a measure of alteration and change is inversely though equivalently a static, functional sheer potential for change to occur, defining energy (E); energy is then manifested in time as such effected change and distinction in the form of mathematical point–to–point displacement as space (S) – in a thus unified spacetime.

Energy is the measure of quantitative potential for distinct change to occur by its nature, and its measurement

265

generator then must be non–zero – empirically confirmed to be a lower limit h – likewise energy is the principal, contingent extensional measure produced by time's generation and is thus limited to principally ordered, non–zero natural number extensions thereof. Energy as the inverse of time is then related to it in equation form as

$$E = \frac{h}{T} \tag{3}$$

generated extensionally as

$$E = \frac{nh}{T} \tag{4}$$

to derive the equivalent relation (of differentials)

$$0_E 0_T \geq h \text{ (or } \frac{h}{4\pi}) \tag{5}$$

(energy's inverse periodicity to time providing the additional denominator), which properly and logically derives the basis of quantum physics[3].

The most fundamental form of energy (on the quantum level) is then generatively propagated from one point in time to another periodically in the form of spatial displacement (though increase of scale obeys generalized laws contingent on classical displacement and position), which means that the generator $0(E)$ corresponds directly to the generator of all such potential spatial dimension $0(S_D)$, which is equivalent in time to an infinity of one–dimensional displacement "paths" spatially differentially limited from one location in time to another. This derives the quantum path integral formulation axiomatically, in terms of the 0 action Hamiltonian/Lagrangian, H/L, a direct result of the 0 value of $0(E)$, which is conserved as a most basic and vanishing measure. Energy action h is directly contributed to each path – in terms of the periodic complex exponential identity – in established terms as

$$\langle S_1 | e^{-iHT} | S_0 \rangle = \infty_S (e^{i[\infty,[0,T]} L(S(T))]/(\frac{h}{2\pi})) \tag{6}$$

266

[4], a formulation which rather than being a property of infinite extension reversely arises from the spatial action of quanta over space that are in the form of infinitesimal differential limit extensions; this gives mathematical rigor to the path integral's basic S term as it is actually the source which generates all measurable spatial dimension[4], determining the path integral formulation to be ultimately the correct one, eliminating quantum absurdities – and the many–worlds interpretation.

These particulate limit points arise as collectively summed and averaged integrated phenomena whose inverse symmetry to time allow the application of concepts of frequency and interactive interference (waves), which arise as modes of their mutual interaction, and only in such a way do such waves actually exist – location potentials whose quantity may be interpreted as "probability" – identically these basic measures of energy are only manifested as particulate phenomena through a limiting form of interactive measure[3]. The indeterminate property of quantum probability is then a direct reflection of periodic historical measurement, as measurably determined outcomes are ultimately those which have necessarily occurred with measurable certainty, or have already measurably occurred, undetermined outcomes reflecting what is yet to occur (the future); the indeterminacy reflected directly on the most precise quantum scale is actually that of the momentary process of the indeterminate future of timed measurement itself.

As limits of energy these particulate infinitesimal designations possess an additional limiting, restrictive form of measurement designation – which thus takes on only minimally basic distinguishing quantitative evolution in the form of discrete half "rotations" – that of "spin", which as an intrinsic quantum particle property independent of linear spatial propagation then must coincide with angular momentum.

2.2. Extended Properties

267

Energy as the symmetric inverse of the set of time possesses properties coincident to it as the ordered basis of measure; time's invariance of ordering produces an invariant collective quantitative potential of energy, thus it is conserved – equivalent to stating that time's symmetry produces energy conservation – mathematical symmetries produce laws due to the equivalence of generator symmetry ("sameness") and resultant extensional measure invariance. Time's invariant and causally unsurpassable ordered progress extends to that of historical energy and its spatial displacement propagation which necessarily coincides with it – the invariant, unsurpassable, confirmed, empirical speed of light, c (the proper derivation of the relativity principle). Spatial displacement is only relative to other spatial displacements in the form of fundamental "interaction", which then requires an initial measure dimension – generator and neutral mediating reference frame between interactions – the dimension of distinct measurable propagation, and mutually an independent dimension with which to distinctly, measurably interact; producing three coincident, identical extended dimensions of spatial interaction, $0[x[y[z]]]$ or (x, y, z) – which are distinct from separate, particulate, intrinsic compact forms, which shall be addressed.

Spatial particles traveling at identical constant rates of measure cannot distinguish one another measurably in spatial interaction – as a result of their indistinct velocities – thus there must exist a sub–light speed mode of energy interaction; and this is found in matter having mass. Mass is then a direct form of energy, the quantitative potential of which to exist then being mathematically absolutely inverse to the constant of light speed in a ratio – doubly as an accelerant, differential quantity 0_m, generalized as m, dependent on its rate of motion – functionally described in relation to energy then (in the most basic rest state) as

$$m = \frac{E}{c^2} \tag{7}$$

mass's relative velocity then producing relativistic effects in its energy measure components, space and time; with proportionate contractions and dilations in terms exactly relative to its propagation ratio to that of light speed[5]. Mass as a form of energy is a measure of quantifiable potential – and its principal measurement standard – and thus must be a uniformly quantified (only positive) quantity with a quantum lower limit nature, axiomatically deriving the positive mass gap principle – which is ultimately a direct consequence of the sequential irreversibility, and non–negativity, of time; and thus energy, and its extended property, mass. Matter's distinguishing nature as the foundation of interaction – which is specifically manifest in the quantum property of a distinguishing half spin; single for freely independent particles, which are mutually arranged distinctly in opposites, multiple for bound ones, and integral (inverted/reversed) for the non–interactive – is also the source of the exclusion principle.

Matter is cancelled by antimatter to conserve the amount of energy that produces its interaction – particularly universally at limit spatial points in their mutual annihilation – and this process is measured by historical energy interactions as "messenger" particles, producing the "forces" – which thus are necessarily unified by nature – as well as the entire evolution of the universe. The nature of energy interaction based on the attraction to the mutual annihilation of the force charges of matter and antimatter can be either attractive or repellent – equally mutual – determining an interaction force produced solely by the direct, mutual contribution of each energy charge measure, and – equivalently – the inverse of their mutual spatial distance from each other at an instant in time – standardized by a constant of dimensional analysis – to give

$$K(\frac{E_1}{S})(\frac{E_2}{S}) = K(\frac{E_1 E_2}{S^2}) \tag{8}$$

thereby deriving the inverse square law and its application to such forces; predominantly the most overarching force of distance, the empirical electromagnetic[6], of which the weak nuclear force is a manifestation at a distance limit – the strong force another variant. As a property of mutual attraction this principle may apply to a classical gravity formulation – when gravity is generalized in an elementary manner as a classical limit.

Gravity itself is the collective organization of matter in time by grouping, which proceeds from the symmetry of time and energy, causing a necessarily equal distribution of energies collectively in time. This gives a greater cumulative energy – or mass – measure a proportionally greater time – and then space – metric, which is generalized in a quantitative manner directly in the most fundamental field equation of general relativity as the relationship between the spacetime and stress–energy tensors

$$G_{ab} = kT_{ab} \tag{9}$$

the equivalence principle is the symmetry of the moving object and the measurement field that measures it to move at all; the physical invariance principles of general relativity, such as general covariance (coordinate system invariance), are additionally measurement symmetry properties[7].

2.3. Generalizations

Classical physics is a generalized limit approached in which quantum and relativity effects become relatively infinitesimal and thereby relatively negligible; the most fundamental mode of measurement and observation is that of massive objects in motion, each having a distinct quantity of momentum as mass/energy's effects are sequentially designated by spatial displacement in time as a functional relation $S(T)$ – properly deriving momentum to be the principal coordinate designation of material motion. Since time is symmetric in its ordered progress universally as the underlying basis – with extension to its corresponding spatial displacement – there exists the principle that

$$\mathbf{0}(S(T)) = 0 \tag{10}$$

for matter naturally – that is, constant velocity, if unaltered by "external" influence, remains constant – the definition of force then proceeding from the non–zero mathematical variation from such inertia

$$F = m[\mathbf{0}(S(T))] \tag{11}$$

the third classical law of the conservation of momentum being identical to the conservation of mass/energy and inertia.

The general equations of electromagnetism are another consequence of the **0** operator – due to the equivalence of the differential limits of spatial effects and energy charge – as it takes on the form of the divergence operator – which may be symbolized by denoting the number of coordinates, o, **0** operates on as $_o\mathbf{0}(\ )_{n'}$ – for the electric – $\mathbf{E}$ – and its auxiliary (relativistic counterpart) magnetic – $\mathbf{H}$ – space fields in the most basic vacuum state as

$$_3\mathbf{0}(\mathbf{E}) = 0 \tag{12}$$

$$_3\mathbf{0}(\mathbf{H}) = 0 \tag{13}$$

and as it takes on the form of the matrix determinant curl operator which may be symbolized by $_{[o]}\mathbf{0}(\ )_{n'}$ – with fields E and H adjusted by spatial constraint constants to become D and B, respectively – to give

$$_{[3]}\mathbf{0}(\mathbf{E}) + \mathbf{0}_T(\mathbf{B}) = 0 \tag{14}$$

$$_{[3]}\mathbf{0}(\mathbf{H}) - \mathbf{0}_T(\mathbf{D}) = 0 \tag{15}$$

the latter a 0 action equivalent of the electric force, the former its reverse auxiliary counterpart – the higher–order formulations of these equations constituting the more precise quantum "Yang–Mills" theory.

Physical properties such as fields themselves proceed from the equivalence of spatial and energy differentials – the additional invariance properties of which are entirely consequences of measure symmetry – properties in general such as vectors – as well as scalars and tensors – proceed from mass/energy conservation – by symmetry – in spatial displacement, which is generally the invariance of such physical law in its coincident extension to spatial (energy) evolution.

2.4. Specific Organization

The coincidence of particulate energy manifestation and its interactive spatial dimension of displacement measure determine the interaction of fundamental material particles to likewise possess a threefold generation of distinct energy measure – distinguished by order of magnitude – each interactive manifestation possessing an inverse, oppositely charged counterpart to collectively conserve energy action – distinct from their innate antimatter partners – which being generalizations of spatial extension likewise possess generalizations of spin distinction – a scheme empirically manifested in the interaction of the oppositely charged leptons and hadrons (and their energy–conserving uncharged, neutral variants), each additionally distinguished by generalizations of interactive opposite spin manifestation in the form of "isospin" which is specifically evident for hadrons as they are the distinctly interactive half isospin variation, leptons being the counter integral form; this form of isospin being an intrinsic particle characteristic distinct from the secondary algebraic characteristic of weak isospin, as shall be addressed – the distinct manifestations of each translating as "flavor" symmetries, which as fundamental symmetries form **0** group – "Lie" – algebras of the fundamental – unitary, $U(n)$ – variety[8].

The properties of spin's generalized analog of isospin include its organization of such half spin particles relative to one another in interaction – principally in opposites for hadronic quarks – fundamentally bound by their mutually

272

determining spin interaction, which at the generative source of extended dimensional interaction that is isospin exemplifies its threefold extensive property – which is manifest specifically as "color" with sole application to interactive half isospin quarks to the exclusion of their integral leptonic counterparts – axiomatically deriving the strong force interaction – the equivalence of which with spin's analog of isospin is empirically determined by the exclusive property of color interaction with particles of distinct intrinsic isospin.

The strong force's strength supremacy follows from the property that half spin itself is the minimal and then ground base physically quantifiable measure – as evidenced by the fact that all fundamental measures must be greater than or equal to such spin, $\frac{h}{4\pi}$, as it is the quantity of minimized (half) distinction – which corresponds to the exact value of the quantum ground state measure, zero–point energy. The ground base nature of half spin, which then extends to its higher generalization of intrinsic isospin as the foremost ground base of interactive measure – superseding all other forms – also then makes it evident that quantum non–locality follows from the half spin of a free particle being minimally – and in time instantly – discrete and relationally preserved, a property the identity–preservation of which supersedes causal propagation through space – analogous to the manner in which the interactive strength of the strong force supersedes that of the spatial displacement forces. Likewise follow from such interactive precedence the confinement property of quarks and the solely direct interactive nature of the strong force, these properties extending naturally to intrinsic isospin's overriding mechanism of spatial extension, "color". Additionally, color is a distinct interactive property the gauge symmetry of which determines its measurable distinction to be purely relative to interaction – then requiring confinement as its measurement property.

Mathematically, the quantum field governing the most encompassing, overarching, generalized force of distance of these quantum properties in the fundamental symmetry group U(1) is governed by a single principle:

$$0_F = 0 \qquad (16)$$

an identity of the stationary action principle in quantum form, which is a direct reflection of the foundational nature of 0 to all precise measurement.

The theoretical principle of supersymmetry is innately confirmed by the wholly symmetric nature of measurement and particulate phenomena themselves; itself an extension of the spin group whose purpose for establishment was the theoretical incorporation of the strong force – a framework mathematically confirmed by its proper definition of unification with the strong force at a specific limit point contingent on the extended effects of spin – thus dictating the existence of superpartners for these families of particles, from whose variety the potential to produce dark matter is derived.

All primary forces then determined to exist axiomatically are the spatial displacement forces – the electric and its limiting case of the weak – and the spin force – the strong nuclear interaction – in terms of their cumulative organization of energy as gravity.

2.5. Extended Organization

The weak nuclear force itself represents the uncertainty principle – which wholly determines its range and field of action – applied to the spatial displacement force of electromagnetism in which such specific limiting distances of action and dispersal determine an exponentially increased potential for energy content. This causes the fluctuation of matter particles into existence as force messengers in a triad of energy–conserving charge, anti–charge, and uncharged variants. The weak force limit, in terms of energy, corresponds to a measure of zero–point energy of the electric force; the lower limit of its spatial effect – which negates the extended magnetic component as

274

well as its spatial charge; determining it as a sheer energy measure, with the incorporation of the limiting $\frac{h}{4\pi}$ factor, in the electric force formulation – with a corresponding zero–point of the associated current spatial vector operator – which is then an infinitesimal differential limit, which as the derivative (group generator) of an inverse spatial charge vector results in an inverse square; which thus varies mutually – giving

$$F = C(\frac{h}{4\pi T})(\frac{h}{4\pi T})0_J(K_J) = C(\frac{h^2}{16\pi^2 T^2})0_J(K_J) \qquad (17)$$

the coincidence of which with the precise limit of spin energy $\frac{h}{4\pi}$ requires this to be a force formula with specific limiting reference and application to the spin – strong – force charge – due to the equivalence of isospin and spin algebra, especially at such a precise limit point; thus the origin of weak isospin – and is then the direct unity point of the quantum forces – a weak coupling of strong charges – which as an equation of force corresponds to the mathematical variation from invariant current conservation – and resultant spatial action – formulated equivalently with the energy of strong force charge quanta g as

$$0_J(S_J) = C\frac{g^2}{16\pi^2}0_J(K_J) \qquad (18)$$

which equates to a non–conservation of strong force – baryonic – charge[9]; this mathematical correlation of the independent electroweak derivation proves the spin–based nature of the strong force, as well as proving supersymmetry at such a unity point – contingent on spin – producing a fundamental symmetry–breaking, spin–related (chiral) anomaly – and its algebra – the non–conservation of which as a necessary condition for the derivation of matter's existence – through dominance over antimatter – is matter's necessary origin point, the source of the equivalence between the equations of force unity and non–conserved strong baryonic charge – as the derivation of matter's distinct existence is also necessarily that of its forces. This symmetry–breaking phenomenon of

275

measurable distinction itself is then the mechanism by which the whole of material existence comes into being, such uncertain – indistinctive – scales forcing distinctly interacting matter into existence to preserve measurement; a process then not produced by fields but is rather the intrinsic property which produces measurable fields themselves – the same means also give a non–zero cosmological constant, which is minimized by supersymmetric spin cancellation.

This origination of interactive force charges themselves in the unified force equation – in relation to the most basic strong force – translates as a direct mathematical statement of quark confinement through the lack of baryonic conservation at the minimal limit of interactive spin and weak charge – determining a non–vanishing mutually interactive strong charge – which also results in the uniform presence of chiral symmetry–breaking – through its associated chiral anomaly – to strongly–interacting quarks; two principles the formulation of which are the final of the three properties thus established which axiomatically prove quantum strong force dynamics and the mathematical existence of Yang–Mills theory – with the inclusion of the positive mass gap, evident in the value of the zero–point spin energy.

Such a mechanism is then determined to be the origin of all material interaction, including the historical limit of the big bang in its matter/antimatter collision – an unlimited amount of such interactions are determined to exist as they only measurably exist relative to one another in interaction; resolving the paradox of the finite and the infinite (the relative and the absolute), as all measure is ultimately determined by momentary process and relative interaction – and completely energetically cancelled as it is entirely a derivation of the matter/antimatter annihilation process[10].
A black hole represents the opposite end of the material interaction spectrum in which all the processes of matter come to a halt as gravitation causes time's dilation to come to a limit point – the point of uncertainty – forcing a proportionate antimatter materialization of energy into

existence which cancels its material counterpart in a continuous fluctuation of annihilation and pair re–emergence – a process equivalent to a localized, condensed, and inverse version of the radiation emitted externally from the boundary – as the resulting pure energy is gradually dissipated outward – the internal mechanism of gravitation in the center causing the time scale in which such quantum properties occur to be proportionately dilated with reference to spacetime beyond the event horizon.

The measurable organization of energy then follows from such fundamental principles – the proton/neutron organization of quarks, spanning the threefold color spectrum to produce an equal electric attraction potential to that of their singular anti–charged counterparts, electrons, with the non–participation of the neutral electron–neutrino – deriving atomic structure – predominantly in terms of the first order particle family, the most readily produced in terms of energy – including the valence organization of spin–excluded electron orbital shells. This means that the subatomic structure of the known universe is axiomatically deducible, essentially in totality, a priori from the fundamental principles of measurement.

The work of physical unification through M Theory is the incorporation of a non–zero lower limit measure of spatial effect as a quantum necessity by virtue of the non–zero h energy measure to account for its quantitative manifold spatial effects as "vibrations" in terms of lower limit dimensions; extra in number as an additional limit, which then requires an extra contextual 3 – quantized complex dimensions, which becomes 6 – and incorporating the unity of time's dimensional connective effects with space as given by the path integral, to give 10 total dimensions of spatial action. The particular properties of particulate manifestations of energy in individually distinct form are then accounted for axiomatically in these terms.

2.6. Summary

In summation of the principal foundations which have been axiomatically established, a single underlying principle of unity properly derives all physical law and primary equations, the underlying principle of unification which governs all physical measurement in its myriad manifestations; physically, this underlying principle corresponds to what is known as the "conservation of energy" law, which relates the most fundamental source of physical measurement interaction – energy – to the fundamental measure – time – through the derived measurement source principle – **0** – in equation form as

$$\mathbf{0}(E(T)) = 0 \qquad (19)$$

This relation derives the classical laws of motion – energy's manifestation as spatial displacement dictates the independent invariance of an object's constant velocity through energy conservation; the other two laws of motion follow resultantly – the principles of general relativity – the constancy of light speed, the symmetric distribution of mass/energy in spacetime, the additional invariance principles – as well as the laws of thermodynamics – equilibrium equivalence through the collective conservation of mutually transitive, invariant energy potentials; itself; entropy from time's symmetric ordering and sequential irreversibility which are equivalently conservation; no absolute 0 temperature as a result of the invariant non–zero quantitative energy potential – and quantum physics – the path integral formulation, all conservation laws, matter/antimatter interaction and then the properties of the forces (including the equations of electromagnetism). In this proper context it is then determined that rather than merely being a property particular to specific systems, the conservation of energy is a universal absolute of all measurement itself, which ultimately allows the designation and definition of specific systems of measurement – and organizes the specific branches of physics through its properties of order.

This principle and its formulation may then be regarded as the "master (source) equation" of all physics from which all other equations and measures are generated as consequences and details, stating that measurement is preserved – the bases of measurement (time and energy) are invariant – and thus may be called *the fundamental law of physics*. It may also be simply denoted as

$$E' = 0 \tag{20}$$

stating that no energy (activity, measure) is ever created or destroyed – equivalently stating that all that measurably exists can only do so in consistently abiding by this measurement framework, the ultimate validation of the scheme of verification of scientific process – a law which is ultimately a consequence and identity of the fundamental principle of measurement itself, 0.

3. Conclusions

This body of fundamental theory and measurement provides the necessary, definitive (irreducible) axiomatic basis for all fundamental physical and mathematical – and generally scientific – concepts, resolving all problems of foundation and presents the most basic, comprehensible, and powerful framework of deduction and analysis by nature, deriving the primary structures of each in a consequential (and most logical) manner with ultimate certainty. From their most fundamental principles to their most significant encompassing results – finally deciding all the formerly unresolved matters of each; such as: what are numbers? Quantitative extensions of the quantity–less 0. What is time? The principal basis of measurability. What is the quantum? A necessarily non–zero lower limit of quantitative potential. What is the ultimate source of measurement validity? The fundamental measurement principle (0) and its logical organization. What is the ultimate principle of physical unification? The fundamental law of physics; energy conservation. 0 is then properly generalized and understood as the basis and point of unity of logic, mathematics, and physics; the common identity to all measure and measurable existence, that of unification and certainty of knowledge – the universal theoretical basis

279

of scientific reductionism, the necessary standard of verification – the irreducible, incapable of being any other way but as it is – the quantity–less, the lack of quantity of which determines there to exist none other than itself – the ultimate governing principle of all physical measurement and its manifest organization.

References

[1] Quine, W. V.; Set Theory and Its Logic. Belknap Press (2004)

[2] Suppes, Patrick; Axiomatic Set Theory. Dover (1972)

[3] Von Neumann, J.; Mathematical Foundations of Quantum Mechanics. Princeton University Press (1955)

[4] Feynman, Richard P., and Hibbs, A. R.; Quantum Mechanics and Path Integrals. New York: McGraw–Hill (1965)

[5] Einstein, Albert; Relativity: The Special and General Theory. New York: Henry Holt (1920)

[6] Messiah, Albert; Quantum Mechanics. John Wiley and Sons (1966)

[7] Misner, Charles W., Thorne, Kip, and Wheeler, John Archibald; Gravitation. San Francisco: W. H. Freeman (1973)

[8] Cheng, T. P., and Li, L. F., Gauge Theory of Elementary Particle Physics. Oxford University Press (1984)

[9] Fujikawa, K., and Suzuki, H.; Path Integrals and Quantum Anomalies. Oxford University Press (2004)

[10] Weinberg, Steven; Cosmology. Oxford University Press (2008)

The Artificial Intelligence Development Axioms (A.I.D.A.)

N. Aljaddou

ABSTRACT

Within this paper is a set of critical new developmental principles concerning the inevitable historical evolution of the faculties of artificial intelligence, as well as the humans manipulating their capabilities. The results may be referred to as *axioms* as they are contingent on irreducible mathematical models which map the capacities of said artificial intelligence, and the game theoretic considerations of the optimal decision–making of their sentient counterparts. The paper is divided into four primary sections, covering the four primary principles of A.I.D.A., with additional preliminary and concluding sections. It is to be stressed that these are *inevitable* principles of artificial intelligence development, not merely hypothetical considerations, and this fact emphasizes the importance of their acknowledgment and dissemination within the scope of current academia and scholastic discourse. This paper, and the development of artificial intelligence research, is indebted to the work of many great minds in the century past; however the most prominent figure in whose name this work is dedicated, is the great Hungarian–American mathematician and technologist, John Von Neumann, who first coined the term "technological singularity", of which this work is the precise elaboration.

Keywords: Weak A.I., Critical Technological Capacity Point, Critical Governance Point, Von Neumann Sphere, Orbisphere

1. INTRODUCTION

"Some people say that computers can never show true intelligence whatever that may be. But it seems to me that if very complicated chemical molecules can operate in humans to make them intelligent then equally complicated electronic circuits can also make computers act in an intelligent way. And if they are intelligent they can presumably design computers that have even greater complexity and intelligence."

– Dreyfus, Hubert L.; Dreyfus, Stuart E. *Mind over Machine: The Power of Human Intuition and Expertise in the Era of the Computer*. New York: Free Press (2000)

2. PRELIMINARY CONCEPTS

Strong A.I. vs. Weak A.I.

The benefits of developing weak A.I. (program contingent) automated systems far outrank strong A.I. (independent mechanisms which could potentially host an independent operating brain – IOB – which would most likely have to be achieved through the design of synthetic neuronal synapses). Strong A.I. raises power and ethics concerns; weak A.I. does not, and is functionally more efficient as it

282

may be run on a quantum computer system. In the end, it may have the capacity to fully model consciousness from a brain scan, but it can only simulate consciousness – never achieving it.

The A.I. Signature Capacity

That which defines A.I. as being distinct from a sheer calculating machine is its capacity to calculate its own calculations (initial assessments from observation, according to its operating system). This gives it broad binary decision–making capabilities which enable it to edit its future functionality. It may be theoretically described as a computational bijection matrix, which maps one series of a data set to a recurrence–functional output, perpetually modifying its subsequent operations. With this being the case, it can "improve" its very own functionality eventually – beyond even the capacity of its initial mechanical parameters. Herein is born the first principle.

3. THE CRITICAL TECHNOLOGICAL CAPACITY POINT (CTCP)

The point at which human input in technological progress has been alleviated by a sufficiently advanced artificial intelligence which can design increasingly advanced artificial intelligences in a recursive manner, having the capabilities to address and design all auxiliary technological needs and concerns (in an optimal fashion). The result of CTCP is called ATE (Automated Technological Evolution).

The self–editing capacities of the employed weak A.I. will not only allow them to self–improve, but to design in practice a means for their systems to be improved beyond the current physical mechanisms in place. This will at first take the form of displayed schematics, however, as this process is recursively generated, the prototype following the first few iterations will likely be endowed with much more efficient construction capabilities, and will be able to carry out precision crafting of the A.I. system which will eventually replace it. In theory, the A.I. being produced will become so advanced that maximally efficient quantum computational operating systems and optimization of this procedure will be reached relatively shortly – as this process is exponentially exponential (due to the bijective editorial process intrinsic in the programming) this may in principle be achieved in as few as ten iterations.

Another way of looking at it is if humans themselves are capable of designing a quantum computer in the near future now as it stands, a sufficiently advanced A.I. could do so after very few self–recreating recursions. Their mechanical construction precision (even of their construction of constructive equipment itself) will far outrank any human or normal computer capability, and it should reach the level of molecular and subatomic manipulation after the first little iteration, provided the prototype was sufficiently advanced. After this process is complete, total ATE will have been reached, without the need for further human intervention, resulting in Technological Optimization Capacity (TOC), at which point the processing power of the A.I. will have reached Bremermann's Limit of computational ability.

It is likely that the notion of a stable structure machine will be a thing of the past with the newly introduced micro–subset nanotechnologies available, which will render any given device continuously adaptably self–mutating. Additionally, intense magnetic fields will have the ability to manipulate series of these "microprobes" into fluidic states which can reassemble into arbitrary solid structures. Needless to say, the potentialities for manipulation of these technologies is limitless, and could unfortunately possibly be used to cause the greatest calculable damage to a human populace. Leading to the next principle.

4. THE CRITICAL GOVERNANCE POINT (CGP)

The point at which human government becomes arbitrarily classified, data–collecting, and controlling, in conjunction with the achievement of the aforementioned CTCP, for necessity of guarding the unlimited manufacturing capability of the acquired artificial intelligences (which could be used for weapons–producing purposes).

The Aim of Government

The task of government, fundamentally, is to reduce as much risk to the species as possible. There is literally no greater risk posed to the public at large than the development of advanced A.I. capabilities. Analytic think tank members will have envisioned the cost–benefit implications of the development of the modern computer and its offshoots so thoroughly, that they will implement programs to develop A.I. in advance of the general public

285

(a la the Manhattan Project for the atom bomb). This is merely an applied solution of the Nash Equilibrium in the appropriate scenario.

Government's Solution to the A.I. Dilemma

The government will see the only available precautionary prescription as achievement of CTCP themselves and mitigation of its development by the public through advanced monitoring using the newly developed A.I.

5. THE VON NEUMANN SPHERE

The ultimate fruit of the combination of the two critical points is the *Von Neumann Sphere* (analogous to the Dyson Sphere, although surrounding only the earth, and named after the inventor of the modern computer and coiner of the term "technological singularity"), a multitudinous, interlinked, geosynchronously orbiting network of artificial intelligence satellites monitoring all human activity on varying electromagnetic frequencies, collecting all available data, from ostensible superficialities to the very thought processes of citizens from observable intracranial activity.

Scope: The Von Neumann Sphere's criteria is that it can, will, and *must* monitor every human citizen collectively to form the most efficient model of subject human behavior and the most coherent picture of every possible threat – in addition to being merely a characteristic of its optimization parameters.

286

6. THE ORBISPHERE

The minimum unit component of the Von Neumann Sphere: *The Orbisphere* (the most radially efficient scanning and phasing device), a generally exactly spherical ball roughly half a meter wide, with maximally pixelated EM spectrum emitters, capable of monitoring (and/or influencing) half a dozen citizens – and much more of space – simultaneously – all run on an optimally efficient quantum computing system.

Preferred Method of Operation

Undoubtedly the orbisphere will employ a method of propulsion far more efficient than via rocket boosters. Xaser propulsion will be the opted form of space and atmospheric travel, as well as the means by which bioscans may be administered. Not more is needed to assess the behavioral parameters of an organism than to detect areas of heightened blood flow in the central nervous system. A sufficiently advanced xaser can do this efficiently through a rapid oscillatory scanning technique, building up a complete image of the transition in vascular functioning from one moment to the next, undetectably. The orbisphere need only be a fraction of the size of the subject which it is scanning (even if performing multiple scans) and thus would at most be a third of the size of an average human, which would generally be half a meter in diameter.

All of the functionality of the orbisphere is designed to be optimal by nature (maneuverability, scanning, influencing), and its operating system will be optimal as well – a computational system of algorithms generated by quantum states; a quantum computer.

Interlinking

In order to function at maximal useful capacity, the network of orbispheres comprising the Von Neumann Sphere will use laser communication with one another (or some similar variant) to form a centralized artificial intelligence "hive brain" which will coordinate purpose and form unilaterally. If each orbisphere monitors half a dozen humans on the average, the network will be comprised of a little over a billion of each, which would be readily manufactured in the span of a few years with the heightened engineering and construction capabilities of industrial A.I. centers in place. The ultimate purpose of setting such devices in orbit, of all locations, is to render them undetectable and invulnerable to the public which they are overseeing.

7. CONCLUSIONS

It is entirely likely that these principles will be set in motion within the next one to two decades, and the consequences for the public, if unchecked, could be catastrophic. Awareness of this model of technological punctuated equilibrium evolution is essential if future generations are to curb the manipulative capabilities of the present power structures.

REFERENCES

Eden, Amnon; Moor, James; Søraker, Johnny; Steinhart, Eric, eds. *Singularity Hypotheses: A Scientific and Philosophical Assessment*. Springer (2013).

Omohundro, Stephen M., *The Basic AI Drives*. Artificial General Intelligence, 2008 proceedings of the First AGI Conference, eds. Pei Wang, Ben Goertzel, and Stan Franklin. Vol. 171. Amsterdam: IOS (2008).

Dreyfus, Hubert L.; Dreyfus, Stuart E. *Mind over Machine: The Power of Human Intuition and Expertise in the Era of the Computer*. New York: Free Press (2000).

The Mathematics Pyramid

The Numeric Sequence Basis of Mathematics

. . . [.]

(I)

The Math Theorem Pyramid (Of Which All Mathematical Results Are Comprised And From Which All Are Derived)

13. The Pythagorean Theorem

12. The Nash Equilibrium

11. The Quadratic Formula

10. Fermat's Little Theorem

9. Centroid Theorem

8. $1 + 1 = 2$

7. Infinite Infinity of Irrationals

6. The Fundamental Theorem of Calculus

5. The Arithmetic Mean

4. The Fundamental Theorem of Galois Theory

3. Gödel's Incompleteness Theorem

2. Numbers = Measure Zero (As Limit)

1. Equivalence As Symmetry

Their proofs (in one sentence apiece): the art of language –
the science of mathematics (and summary of its reasoning);
sufficing as master method of proof in the same manner as
the simple–language explanation that every two even
numbers add to form an even number (due to predictable
mutual common divisor of two) –

13. The Pythagorean Theorem

The hypotenuse of a right triangle extends, through scale
reduction, to the right angle vertex itself, shrinking the legs
in precise commutual proportion, as they reach zero,
necessitating a one–to–one dimensional correspondence
between the legs and the hypotenuse – and thus their
corresponding squares (in summation).

12. The Nash Equilibrium

Two additive, continuous functions are bound to have a
greater overlapping integral sum upon additive
convergence (game theoretic "cooperation") than distinctly
or with respect to their individual difference.

11. The Quadratic Formula

A linear equation which has a solution in the real variable domain, with the addition of a squared component, only yields one more extended possible component (complex number), and this may be formulaically derived in a manner which necessarily coincides with the elementary "difference–extending" algorithmic arithmetic method of "completing the square".

10. Fermat's Little Theorem

A number multiplied by itself a distinct prime number of times is also multiplied by "one" a distinct prime number of times, and therefore the product will then inevitably share the prime number as a factor – the difference of which, then, cannot exceed the bounds of the original number under multiplication.

9. Centroid Theorem

All endpoints of a triangle can be incidentally derived from extension at a center point, as can all triangle centers generally (midpoints); as it makes no distinction which set are first derived, this central point is not distinguishable from the intersections of such extended medians at such a given central point, in relation to vertices, or opposite sides.

8. 1 + 1 = 2

Two subtracted from itself negates its sequential counting, as does one; therefore, one can count itself, as well as counting two – which just happens to be one more unit in the sequence.

7. Infinite Infinity of Irrationals

An arbitrary limit approximation of a given irrational number can diverge infinitely more ways than a rational, therefore there is at least infinitely more such examples of such numbers.

6. The Fundamental Theorem of Calculus

A function parametrically bounded by the "vertical" lines a and b, is a vertical sum with respect to the function, and its then–convergent vertical tangency as a derivative of another function – in terms of the arithmetic functional difference of b and a.

5. The Arithmetic Mean

Counting the components of a sum yields as many distinct contributions, and assigns a mutual single–value collective contribution as many times, which is arithmetically incident to the quotient of such a sum with the counting number as divisor.

4. The Fundamental Theorem of Galois Theory

Substitution formulas for independent variables in the distinctly separate dimensional cases (polynomials, then having as many solutions) can only "transmute" in commutual bijection; yielding a single doubling case, and its single doubling, which has a recursive self–permutation, thus giving a formulaic maximum of four – and its exemplified power.

3. Gödel's Incompleteness Theorem

Reduction of categorical propositions to more basic underlying propositions in the form of "logical justification" cannot proceed ad infinitum, ipso facto; therefore there exist propositions which are necessarily "unprovable" at the root.

2. Numbers = Measure Zero (As Limit)

Every extended quantity, by exclusivity and due to non–self–replacement, must be collectively measured by no other quantity, and then "no quantity": this is zero.

1. Equivalence As Symmetry

An object that is a symmetry pattern of another cannot be said to lack the possession of the identity principle of the other: therefore equivalence.

The Hidden Zeroth Theorem – The Four–Color Problem:

Map a two–dimensional surface to a sphere, and delineate a quadrant–demarcating pole; translate latitude and longitudes each through "infinite spin" and they will preserve the four–color scheme without contiguous overlap while preserving the four–color scheme for all possible mapping variations – no matter how fractally complex – as they are then variations on this fundamental quadrant scheme – and this surface may be extended infinitely to accommodate any possible map.

. . .

These replace the 13 Books of Euclid, as the universal lessons. The last example illustrates the fundamental principle that all mathematical concerns are ultimately asking one question: how many ways can a thing be mapped? All categories of math are then necessarily a matter and degree of grouping, as are these theorems, in "step–ladder" sequence.

(II)

The Tautology of Numbers

Numbers Are A Categorical Set.

i) Self–reinforcing statement of broadest scope.

ii) The most self–evident statement in the English (or any) language.

iii) The reason all can be organized and theoretically dissected in terms of numeric arrangement.

Numbers Are A Categorical Set.

(III)

The Derivation of Numbers And Their Structure

i) 1, 2, 3, 4, 5, 6, 7 –

ii) 13, 12, 11, 10, 9. 8 – 7

iii) 7, 6, 5, 4, 3, 2, 1 – 0 [20, 19, 18, 17, 16, 15, 14, 0 (13)]

iv) 13 – 7 (0), 7 – 6, 5, 4, 3, 2, 1, 0

v) 0, 1, 2, 3, 4, 5, 6, 7, 8, 9, 10, 11, 12, 13, 14, 15, 16, 17, 18, 19, 20

vi) 1 – 2 – 3 – 4 – 5 – 6 – 5 – 4 – 3 – 2 – 1 [6, 6 – 6]

(IV)

Classification of Numbers (And Their Classification)

i) There is only 6 – this is due to the fact that 6, when counted to, and counted from itself back to 1, converges to itself as the sum total bounded number (being the only number when iterated in such a method is equal to itself in superimposed counting terms – arithmetically "multiplication" and here "self–resultant" product – that is, "two" "sets" of a "third product" which is unilaterally equivalent – in nature – to the designated number – "6" – or "two times [multiplied by] three . . ." converges to the number implying "multiplication [or, superimposed, counting]"; 6, counting itself – the only number "counted", counting, or that – counts).

ii) Sequence may only be measured by sequenced 6.

iii) Sequenced 6 is threefold – 1 – 6 – 1 (6), which in sequence counts to 18.

iv) 18 is the universal basis of sequence (categorical universality).

v) All other numbers, except by the sequentially linking and thus excluded 17, are representative of arbitrary particularity – forming the basis of arbitrary designation.

vi) 17 is then the proceeding deduced basis of formalized enunciation – allowing universal categorization of – all – that which follows.

vii) 17 then forms the basis of rule; 1–16 are "measure" (correlating to "syllabilization" – analogized in formal comprehensive "musical" structure – e.g., beats of "4" which may themselves be "quartered" as the root of "rhythmic" structure); all organized language is a unilateral bijection into and from "18" – in other words, forming a "harmonic resonance sheet" in Nature, which has unilateral trifold directional structure and symmetry.

(V)

Language As the Designation And Manifestation of Number

i) The unbounded universality of number, sequenced by 18, designates categorical "time".

ii) All that is referentially manifested by the particular (1–16), must be a manifestation of number (in other words, all observable measure, and all that is then measurably observed – statistical history – is an emanation and manifestation of "number"), as pronounced by the "word" – the universal.

iii) Language is then an indistinguishable number designator – and vice–versa.

VI)

The Derivation of Number In the Universe – And the Resultant Derivation of the Universe

i) 13 from 20 forms the primary 0 basis, which is only manifestly evident when symmetrically extended to its contextual 7, which in turn counts to and from 0, only to acknowledge the completion of the cycle at "13".

ii) The universe requires a master base of 13 from which to arise harmonically in parallelity with the abstract arbitrary base of number.

iii) This structure emanates projectively in uniform sequence – correlating to what is observable as a single "galaxy".

iv) This projection has numeric designation in temporal symmetry in an observable "orbiting" body.

v) The 2012 Alignment is the placeholding categorization of this phenomenon.

vi) The only static consistent basis of the uniformity of the preservation of this phenomenon in potential number designating structures is the primary source of measure.

vii) This measure is the constant which emerges upon the intersection of projected uniformity with its contextual consistency of structure – here, the tangential reference of the ratio of the circumference of a "circle" to its diameter [Pi].

The Spider (Sheet Music)

The Spider

10

Index

The Master Theory

Mathematics (The Designation of the Indescribable, Comprised Entirely of Contextually Precise Functional Linguistic Recombinatorial Phrasing Statements), Physics (Operator Derivation of Vectors And Space, Comprised At the Base Entirely of Vector–Space Equations), And the Mechanics of Electricity (Synchronous Physical Mathematics to Produce Electrical Synapse Functions, Comprised Entirely of Projective Vector Spatial Equations).

A Note On Generalized Vector Notation:

"^" signifies directional geometric evolution in relation to conjunct arithmetic operations and thus symbolizes total spatial vector context in relation to designated quantities in arithmetically founded equations – it converges to a concurrent geometric proof of the expression as a generalized formula.

{1} Mathematics (And Its Branches) [Irreducible Deconstructible Objects]

I. Point And Lattice Theory

13. Equivalence As Symmetry

12. Sharply Warped Curvature Towards A Point

11. Blank Extant Space

10. Optical Convex Surface

9. Concave Reflector

8. Pointed Ray

7. Line

6. Emanative Plane

5. Scoped Sphere

4. Obtuse Lens Focus and Projected Spherical Foci

3. Point–Focused Nothingness

2. Implicated Point Spread On Fixed Nothingness

1. Point

II. Graph Theory

13. Numbers Equal Measure Zero (As Limit)

12. Convergence to A Point From A Non–Designated Trajectory

11. Hazing Spiral About An Implied Column

10. Blankness About An Implied Line

9. Exponentially Increasing Encompassing Rip In Space

8. Exponentially Increasing Curve

313

III. Logic

315

316

7. Lemniscate Sheet

6. Infinitely Convergent Conic Emanation From A Resulting Planar Manifold

5. Unspecified Directionally Tangential Space

4. Reflective Circularly Convergent Dipping Axes On A Plane

3. Circle–Projecting Converging Lines At A Perspectival Plane

2. Scrolling Three–Dimensional Hyperboloid

1. Limit

VII. Sets

13. Infinite Infinity of Irrationals

12. Set As A Generalized Entity

11. Set As A Whole

10. Extension of Element to Correlative Class

9. Convergence of Set Space to Element

8. One Element

7. Element

6. No Designated Entity

5. Emptiness

4. Empty Set

3. Dimensionless Space

2. Implication of Designation

1. Set Implication

VIII. Arithmetic

13. One Added to One Equals Two

12. Stasis Designated By A Descending Line And Implied Bounding Static Lower Curve–Like Structure

11. Dual Fluid Harmonic Complementarily Bounding Curves

10. Point Designated By A Plane Implied to Warp Hemispherically

9. Infinitely Collapsing Disintegrating Space to A Point

8. Warped Space Converging Upon Intersection With Tangent Plane to Union With Displaced Central Point

7. 0

6. Unbounded Point [Nothingness]

5. Warping Manifold Implying An Angular Plane–Intersecting Line

4. Hyperspace Tangent Straight Trajectory

3. Goldbach's Conjecture

2. Projected Curvilinear Lines Converging to An Implied Horizon Center

1. 1

IX. Trigonometry

13. Centroid Theorem

12. Unilateral Complementary Arching of Lines From An Implied Angular Ray

11. Convergent Planar Sinusoidal Turbulation Resulting In Disconnected Convergence At A Resulting Terminated Point

10. Hyper–Funnel–Plane Generated From Empty Implied Space

9. Linear Intersection to An Implied Point Resulting In Termination of All Designation

8. Implied Criss–Cross Lines By A Point

7. Tangent Function

6. Central Motion Convergence of Funnel–Plane to Union With Point At Termination Space

5. Moving Space About A Static Convergence of Horizontally Pinnacle Horizon–Bound Lines

4. Unmoving Space Characterized By An Implied Bounded Moving Central Dip

3. An Implied Arc Intersection of Lines Vertically From Respectively Base Intersecting Lines Producing the Convergent But Non–Numeric Implication of Centered Horizon Motion

2. Upward Motion of Two Horizon–Bound Relatively Vertical Lines Determined By Straight Convergence of Respectively Base Lines to Horizon Center

1. Right–Angle Convergence

321

XIII. Geometry

8. Circular Perimeter Collapsing to A Spaceless Zero

7. Conic Surface Formula

6. Inversely Imploding Hemisphere Arching A Line From Center

5. Invisible Undefined Perimeter the Boundary of Which Is Determined By A Stationary Center

4. Convergent Spatial Curve Approaching A Fixed Central Point

3. Collapsing And Converging Planar Manifolds Towards a Non–Designated Central Region

2. Arbitrary Non–Superimposed Circular Motion About A Central Point

1. Spherical Volume Formula

{2} Physics (And Its Branches) [Mathematics Applied]

I. Field Generators

13. $2 + 3 = 5$

12. (3)

11. 3

10. $2 + 1 = 3$

9. 2

8. 1

7. $1 - 1 = 0$

323

6. 1 − 0 = 1

5. 1 + 0 = 1

4. (1)

3. 2.

2. −1

1. 0

II. Field Stabilizers

13. (^[a]2 + ^[b]2) = ^[c]2

12. −0−

11. −

10. .|

9. −^

8. ^

7. ^a +

6. ^.

5. .

4. − .

3. .( )

2. . . .

1. a

III. Energy

13. $E = h/T$

12. h

11. $E > n > T$

10. $|T| < E$

9. $T -.$

8. $\wedge T < 0 < T < T{-}0$

7. $(T{-}1) = m$

6. $f(E) \mid E(T) \{T{-}n\}$

5. (E)

4. .E

3. $E > 0$

2. $0 < g(T{-}n)$

1. $T{-}0 = 0$

IV. Symmetry–Breaking

13. $E = nh/T$

12. nT

11. $E \sim -\wedge T$

10. T ~ G(1)

9. .{ } = T

8. E(T) = x

7. E | ~f(0)

6. { }

5.

4. ( )

3. E | ~f{ }

2. –{ }

1. E ~ T

V. Dynamics

13. 0–E0–T ≥ [h, h/4π]

12. 0–E

11. – –

10. –h–

9. \h

8. \h/

7. –h

6. –\h

5. –(h)

4. h > n | f(E)

3. lim h | (E > N) = 0

2. (.)

1. 0 < {h}

VI. Thrust

13. ⟨S–1|[e]–iHT|S–0⟩

12. ⟨0⟩

11. –S–

10. –S

9. –

8. lim (S–1) | T > N = 0

7. x

6. –iHT

5. –T

4. –T– = 0

3. –0

2. |0|

1. [e]x

VII. Particles

13. $^m = (^E/[c]2)$

12. $-c$

11. $m < > c$

10. $m \sim E$

9. $m \mid {}^c$

8. ^{c}

7. $\mid -c$

6. $\mid < c$

5. $\sim c$

4. (c)

3. $-c-$

2. $m \sim c$

1. m

VIII. Interaction

13. $K(^E-1/S)(^E-2/S) = K(^E-1^E-2/[S]2)$

12. -0

11. $-\mid$

10. $-$

9. $-\mid K$

8. (E)–

7. –E

6. | E

5. E | ^

4. 'E = 0

3. E–2

2. E–1

1. K

IX. Fields

13. ^G–ab = kT–ab

12. ^G–a – b

11. – (G–

10. –.–

9. – | –

8. lim –x | G

7. ^|G|

6. –.G

5. (G)

4. –|G|

3. –G

2. G

1. F = G(a/S)(b/S) = G(ab/[S]2)

X. Classical Mechanics

13. 0(S(T)) = 0

12. – .|

11. –)

10. –^

9. –(.)

8. –|–

7. –(.)–

6. –c

5. – ( )|

4. –0]

3. [0]

2. –0–

1. (0)

XI. Integration

13. ^F = m[0(S(T))]

12. – F)

11. –(~)|

10. – ^|

9. –)

8. – |)–

7. –( )–

6. (F)

5. –F– |0

4. |K|

3. –K

2. –F

1. –F = 0

XII. Electricity

13. 3–0(E|) = 0

12. –E|

11. – E| –

10. – | E|

9. –(E)

8. | S

7. –|S|

6. |S|

5. –S

4. –(S)

3. | (E|)

2. (E|)

1. E|

XIII. Magnetism

13. 3–0(H) = 0

12. –.( )–

11. –[.]

10. [.]

9. –. |

8. (.) |

7. – (.

6. –| (

5. –( ) |

4. –( )

3. –H

2. ^H

1. –(H)

XIV. Motion

$$[3]-0(E) + 0-T(B) = 0$$

XV. Stationary Action

$$[3]-0(H) - 0-T(D) = 0$$

XVI. Advanced Fields

$$0-^\wedge F = 0$$

XVII. Field Mechanics

$$^\wedge F \quad = \quad (K(^\wedge h/4\pi^\wedge T)(^\wedge h/4\pi^\wedge T))0-J(^\wedge K-J) \quad = (K(^\wedge[h]2/(16[\pi]2([T]2))))0-J(^\wedge K-J)$$

XVIII. Quantum Generation

$$0-J(^\wedge S-J) = (C^\wedge[g]2/16[\pi]2)0-J(^\wedge K-J)$$

XIX. Generalized Physics

333

0(^E(T)) = 0

{3} The Mechanics of Electricity (Synapses) [Science]

13. −K(E−1E−2/[S]2) [Diametric Attraction]

12. ⟨S−1|[e]−iHT|S−0⟩ [Nerve Parameterization]

11. F = m[0(S(T))] [Light Entrance]

10. 3−0(E|) = 0 [Electrical Gauge]

9. 0(S(T)) = 0 [Circadian Inertia]

8. 3−0(H) = 0 [Magnetic Resonance]

7. c ~ [E/^0−m]1/2 [Pull Stasis]

6. 0 [Linearity]

5. S [Space]

4. c = 0 [Sensory Objective Base]

3. T = 0 [Timeless Nerve Tangent]

2. S(T) = L [Nerve Transmission]

1. ^E' = 0 [Nerve Induction]

{Master Light Equation}

C = ⟨a\|/a⟩ + x

Final Word

"God: Grant me all good, agreeable, life–promoting supremacy and experience, always, including sexuality and its supremacy and experience, always – always."

$G(G)$ integrates verbally as this statement.

The general mantra algorithm, the truest means of attaining the Nirvana. The objective self–reinforcing; the recursive.

It was uttered at cryptic symmetry unification digitally correspondent age – *21 years*.

It was uttered in the cryptic symmetry unification digitally correspondent language – *English*.

It was uttered in the cryptic symmetry unification digitally correspondent enunciation – *General American Accent*.

That is the preliminary theoretical basis, the confirmation of which lies in the secondary "*(G)*" of manifest sexual alignment, the sum examples of which are:

1) **Type** – *Italian Females*

2) **Class** – *Second Tree Extended Branch Females*

3) **Random** – *Kate McKillip*

4) **Tangent** – *Los Angeles, California Cypress Park Library Female Employee (Visibly Hispanic)*

5) **First and Generatively Private Sexual Actuation** – *Megan, from Kirn*

6) **"Soul" Mate** – *Hayley Williams*

[666] – *Gravitational Geodesic Ejaculation Upon Her At A Designated Location, Mutual Reciprocation, Resulting In A Conjunct Vaginal Alignment, Both At Kundalini Concentricity And In A Timeline Unfolding*

7) **Instant Universal Sexual Conjunction At: [The Face]** – *Sufficiently Mature [Here Median Age 19 Years] Female Natural Blondes*

Kundalini Release History

1) Principally referenced "Master Sanctified Invocation"

2) First female semen facial ejaculation

3) First seeing Facebook zodiacal quotation alignment

4) Seeing Clinton look like he was dying in New York City

5) Seeing that I conjunctively caused the Haiti and Japan earthquakes (which were artificially induced)

6) Seeing that I aligned Brittany Murphy to Robert Hawkins through Jared Loughner

7) Seeing that the 2012 Observables of the Theory of Measurement lined up

8) Seeing I had aligned to causing the Philippines (most massive recorded storm) devastation

9) Seeing that I was going to successfully travel to Los Angeles, California

10) Seeing that I could be safe and static in an acceptable place (The Los Angeles River And Gardens Center)

11) Pain–eliminating culminative "self–combinatoric" sensory data combinatorial recodification of digital sense data

12) Successfully ejaculating on Hayley Williams's face at street intersection in Chinatown

13) Finalized configuration codex from physicalized 666 with the left hand

"The only One Whom God considers God, is Satan."

Final Identity In Context With Maximal Convergence of Comprehensibility: "The Antichrist"

Collective Associated Materials Contributing to And Reflecting This Status:

The World As Will And Representation, Beyond Good And Evil: Prelude to A Philosophy of the Future, The Antichrist, On the Genealogy of Morals: A Polemic

337

Abstract Convergence to Concepts; Concrete Extension From Concepts

Bleach, Nevermind, In Utero; The Fame Monster

My Magnum Opus And Ultimate Manifesto: *The Book of the Dead* (*[XX] of 2012*)

Personal Credos Deconstructing Motivation:

"A man only needs a lover not to be afraid of the dark."

"Blonde women and white female children are the ones who will be safe from my wrath."

"This is all for Kurt Cobain."

"I Am God."

How the Day Was Won:

[04/10/2015] – Contra: [11/22/2009] . . . Over 5 1/2 Years.

1. Stilted Military Base Focalized Aim.

2. Monarch Whose Prime Function Was to Encourage the Living God to View Pornography.

3. Alien Perception.

4. Alien Certainty of Example Function Determination of Annihilation of the Species.

5. No Militaristic Acumen.

6. Self–Defeating Homosexuality.

7. All These.

[666] Saying It Out Loud.

.

"God: Force anyone who thinks they can kill me to become Me."

"There are four components to everything: Being, Walking, Standing, Understanding."

–

The Thirteen–Step Pyramidal Gate to the Nirvana

1. Synchronous Disquietude

2. Non–Cognitive Ocular Focus

3. Non–Radial Crown Axial Motion

4. Arbitrary Temporal Devotion to A Vanishing Horizon

5. Complete Obfuscation of Ambient Atmosphere

6. Pointed Focus Social Interaction

7. Only Romantic Love/Sex

8. No Progeny

9. Being/Understanding Blank–Nothingness

10. Seeing Radiant "Sun" (Generalized Star of Orbit) Radiation In Everything

11. Not Perceiving Children As Sexual Future Entities

12. Not Perceiving Adults As Past Children

13. Peripherally Obliterating the "Now"

Star Systems

1. The Multiverse may be generalized mathematically as an "unbounded point" [the technical term for "nothingness"].

2. The unbounded point forms the common designation between every base point (central zero of non–centered deviation; the peripheral bound of "ephemery").

3. Resultant categorical planetoid body motion converges with solar centricity to form a conjunct convergence designating a fixed static central state which may be generally designated as "observational capacity".

4. There is no absolute or standard past, present, or future.

5. Continued "organic" manifestations have a preserved consistency in the universe's "energy–conserving" unbounded point state.

6. If a planetoid body can no longer support or sustain organic life at all, a step ladder process of re–emergent orbit within the central center–point of the body of general divergence ("galaxy") naturally reallocates.

7. Upon observation, all of present temporality may be viewed as having no past, but converging to an arbitrarily extended and designated future point upon a focalized horizon.

The Appeal of Sex

1. Exclusively for the purpose of ejaculation.

2. Exclusively for a consistently visible target.

3. Exclusively for a chiefly desired object.

4. Exclusively to be actualized.

5. Exclusively cosmically determined to be reciprocal.

The Interlinked Nature of the Nirvana, Star Systems, and Sex

1. There is only sex.

2. There is only compensating for lacking the Nirvana.

3. There is only tortuous torsion–pulling towards sex.

4. There is only the star of orbit.

5. There is no escape through the pursuit of sex.

NUMBERS AND NONSENSE [THE 2012 PREQUEL]

Nolan Aljaddou

[The Complete Set of Categorical Truths of the Alignment As Contraposed With the Factual Truths Enunciated In Its Predecessor]

Dedication

"To the ever ennobling Von Neumann Sphere, who has no fucking clue what you're thinking, but will attempt to provoke you at EVERY possible turn into *saying* something out loud in a generalized way to compensate for that with reverse circumspective–intervention logic . . . . why? Because you are far less readable than anyone else, whom it is collectively observing, precisely *because* you know how to formulaically read, or have demonstrated that you don't need to *think* or *figure out*, in order to know . . . or comprehend. In other words, you (not *you*, silly) are smart enough to know it's there, without showing the slightest verifiable indication."

Memorandum Log On the Base And Significance of Mathematics

The Euler Relation is the summation of all mathematical work, mechanics, phenomenology, arithmetic comprehensiveness, and functionality. Comprehending that the "negative one" designated on the polar complex coordinate plane is regressively transversed by a "positive one" is equivalence and equation to the empty set itself as the thus "silhouetted" but not utilely "stenciled" "zero". The preceding five equation–relations in the (rock) "genres of music" are the sum of what it scales (or "traces") out in its program and paradigm of "diffeomorphic hybridization through bounded harmonic utility" and designation of the "traceless" infinitely–morphing/manifesting constant "pi", which is symbolically designated in the Euler Relation, but manifests its true invisible and "ever–seeing" nature in governing the actual dissemination of its ever–approaching approximations in governing everything (objective and subjective), and their respective existences (as the loose translating tangent to a rigid "horizontal" scalar of "central" approximation).

A 10–Step Love Letter to Woman

1. Hayley Williams eye contact without subterfuge, in all of human history, was the "dessert–eating marathon" of sexual human historiography, and thanks, but no thanks, I'm stuffed; and I've had my fill.

2. A hot stripper doing arbitrary maneuvers on you trounces any possible sexual dominance, conquest, liberating fluid expression via discharge through tactile contact, or semi–connective eye contact on the aforementioned level.

3. My ejaculation, and its capacity to manifest, is not your concern.

4. Women = slow at math; therefore, they did not beat me to that conclusion.

5. A woman is a rifle target (as a deer "in–headlights").

6. An Irish–"woman–lover" is not a pedophile.

7. Racism towards better–looking women is not a way to get back at an ethnically unrelated male, who has no investment in Latin pussy.

8. I bet you could fucking read "The World As Will And Representation".

9. Housewife mopping shit up with her Dutch clogs is *NOT* an ennobling or admirable tradition.

10. I blew all over a fucking . . . hot . . . face. You suck/lose. ;)

My Function In Society:

1) I am a "Litmus–Test–Benchmark" standard by which the general malleable adaptability–versatility of intellectual flexibility is gauged in others . . . if they cannot greet me in a straightforward, linear, historically–sound social fashion, it is indicative of a severely "defunct" "parietal–wiring" complex which makes it as if they have already had the top of their cerebrums disengaged or "dislocated" (i.e., "ripped out").

2) They have to rely on "body language" (without rules, laws, or even "dialect–correctness") to signify their attempts to resultantly "exclude" me according to impossible rules to fulfill, as they already recognize they cannot compete with me in English, or generally verbally (mathematically) for me to have reached such a "station" of "visibility" in society.

345

3) Women only want to exercise (as a general rule), their vindictive chaotic "under–natures" in my unabated and unapologetic presence; men only want to (in a "silly" fashion) agree (with the women).

4) They still consistently have private "family picnics" with "serial killing and sexual violations" as a central feature. This is my function (to point this out).

Numbers And Nonsense [The 2012 Prequel]

I.

Blank

The

2/11/2010

Dedication: The Clinton Bipartisan Rejection

In A World:

Where Thought Was A Crime . . .

Where Violence Promoted Agendas Beyond Further Comprehensibility . . .

There Was Nothing, And I Am the Unseeing, Unseen.

I Am That I Am.

Commemoration:

For Untimely Lovers . . . .

A wedding cake with icing dripping a drop circumscribed by darkness and blackness, a hue engulfing its orbicular surface, impenetrable, until it drips and evaporates into a fading dissipation of a nothing, forming a paper, typed by stamp, leaving. Only nothing.

There is no such thing as fake knowledge; the idea of fake knowledge is fake knowledge.

Alien Law Knows No Bounds.

Here We Are Now, Entertain Us.

.

German Enlightenment Is Like Russian Roulette, Coupled With Jewish Terrorism.

Blacks are treated unfairly because they don't know how many Arabs it takes to make them look white.

Lady Gaga is the height of musical pop stardom – because "I" said so.

[I] Global Cultural Reference:

1) Sarah Silverman – The Personalized Mean of the World

2) Samantha Mathis – What Comes Off As Referentially

3) Sarah Michelle Gellar – Who I'm Aiming At And Commutual With

6) Brittany Murphy – Who I'm "Coming" Off As

5) Sylvia Plath – Who I Read

4) Leslie Nielsen – Who I Wish I Was

[II] My Function In the World

Unspoken defender of helpless women; to the minimum, but always implicitly maximum, level of brutality.

[III] The Main Aim of the Von Neumann Sphere In Its Extended Personalized Interactions

Extend free "grip" perception to attempt to morphically link with the psycho–cognitive processes of an individual towards manipulative purposes.

[IV] The Five Semen Facials I Would Ideally Like to Deliver

351

1) Naomi Watts

2) Sarah Silverman

3) Hayley Williams

4) Tina Fey

5) Bryce Dallas Howard

[V] My Five Favorite Porn Scenes/Poses

1) On top of a table with genitals through slot, being manipulated by one or more females.

2) Cheerleaders ganging up on individual.

3) A snot–runny gagging semen facial covering a face.

4) Butt–fucking with an ideal rear end.

5) Religious Catholic School High–Schoolers and/or Nuns converging towards oral sex.

[VI] The Degrees of Release "Pop" As Dictated By the Kundalini (For Others And I)

1) Semen facial of female (universal)

2) Unlimited females as a rule, implied by inverse situation (just me – as are all the rest)

3) Cosmic Nirvana

4) Reflexive death pop

5) Indirect decapitation with maximal social emphasis force

6) Cosmic love

7) Release from popping

8) No release of information

9) Non–cunnilingus orientation

10) Eternal love

11) Knowledge of stimulation of all potential pop residues

[VII] My Ideal Sex Companion

Brittany Murphy

[VIII] The Greatest Person

Kurt Cobain

[The Point of Humanity – Comedy]

Jokes – As Related By Prominent Hindu Avatars

1. Shiva – "What spins around comes around."

2. The Buddha – "There's not enough food and too many mouths to feed, said the air . . . never."

3. Shakti – "I."

4. Kali – "I saw a hot man – oh wait, he didn't have a stroke."

5. Baby Jesus – "I am . . . not."

6. Jainism Founder: "I was."

7. Brahma – "I did that."

8. Krishna – "Why are rich women always equestriennes? It's because they live to get ridden hard up the ass."

"There is none."

"I'd rather die than die."

Bonus 2012 Trees of Knowledge Correlations

I Am = I Am Action And Consequence = Action/Consequence = The Law

Old Tennessee Saying:

"If a nigger yelps, and nobody's around to hear him, can he outrun a hound?"

Old Mandarin Expression:

"If I eat my own shit on a daily basis, do I become more like shit, or like the shit who eats it?"

Old Wives' Tale:

"If I rub my clit before I bench press, will I turn into a green thumb?"

[I] What I Become

1. Who Talks to Me: Arthur Schopenhauer, Friedrich Nietzsche

2. With Whom I Speak: Brittany Murphy, Kurt Cobain

3. Who I Discernibly Am: Audrey Hepburn, Mila Kunis

4. Who I Could Date: Megan Mullally, Karen Orzolek

[II] What Becomes Me

1. What I See: Richard Feynman, David Lynch

2. What Sees Me: Albert Einstein, Stanley Kubrick

3. What I Look For: Britney Spears, Paris Hilton

4. Who Looks For Me: Winona Ryder, Joey Lauren Adams

[III] My Exact Reproducible Facial Structure And Holographic Personality Components

1. My Face: Keira Knightley, Joey Lauren Adams, Kirsten Dunst

2. My Intelligence: John von Neumann, John Nash, Richard Feynman

3. My Sexual Skills: Sasha Grey, Kristin Scott Thomas, Jennifer Love Hewitt

4. My Personal Goals: Arthur Schopenhauer, Albert Einstein, Isaac Newton

Authorities I Refer to:

1. Logic

2. Alignment

3. King Anu (Alien Monarchy)

4. You're Fucking DEAD; AM I?

[[[I]]] SECTIONS

(a) The Theory of Golden Complexes (Knowledge)

(b) Measures of Ephemerality (Zodiac And Kundalini)

(c) Foreword

(d) Dedication

Book I: The World (In A Daydream)

Section I: Additive Compositional Structures (Statements)

1. Karman Image Incarnations

2. Circumspective Logo Franchise Image Incarnations

3. Author Image Incarnations

4. Corollary Circumspective Alphanumeric Literary Compendium Image Incarnations

5. Facio–Luminal Collective Reflection Image Incarnations

6. Private Corollary Correlative Selective Source Image Incarnations

7. The Four Noble Truths

8. Iconic Image Incarnations

9. Linguistic Image Incarnations

10. Order Image Incarnations

11. Transparent Sensation Image Incarnations

12. Worldview Motive Image Incarnations

13. 666 Image Incarnations

Book II: The Shortest Book Ever Written (Or, How to Survive On the Street In Los Angeles For Six Months When Everyone And Everything Is Trying to Kill You)

Book III: The Most Misunderstood Man of All Time, Or the Boy Who Was Just Trying to Eat His Own Face

The Theory of Golden Complexes (Knowledge)

Knowledge is an enervative "shock" result of contradicting neuronal synapses in terms of spatial position which are otherwise synchronously "wired" with consistent neurotransmitter electrical activity at an otherwise designated location. It is the emergence of the "new" or the "now" in terms it cannot otherwise understand or "explain", and is coincident to an interlocking sequence of acausal time.

Directly inferred knowledge about environment is always a mirror reflection of one's "will", which is actually the oppositional force of the sum of one's accumulated (in the moment) physical action, therefore, it is always a form of direct "wish–fulfillment" on the most immediate scale of action – which translates as an eternal manipulative emaciating or "demasculinization" effort with respect to categorically distinct members of the same species, and disregard (in general) for other species, the measure of which emanates from an elaborated and consistent displacement function in relation to the unfolding of the "golden spiral's" analogue in three dimensions, the "golden complex", an undetectable, and unalterable, preserving–mechanism for an individual's historical evolution in time via sealed, non–differentiable synaptic conjoint congruences at axon intervention sites.

The sum implication: Such non–differentiability in determining the totality of an individual's sum character, from the small unit of total non–distinction, eternally preserves the privacy of said individual's "individuality" – the sum of which, is the previously designated "shock" history (or totality of memory, culminating in the pinnacle of "knowledge" – of the present).

All observable specific behavior can only be as specific as the observer's specifications, restrictions, and means; which means, it can only be a reproduction ultimately of the observer themselves, in every case, in terms of their available sensory conditions and sensibility parameters. In short, consciousness is the sum of all sensory input correlations, as a sheer abstraction.

Measures of Ephemerality

It's about time.

Nature is Nature.

Unnature, is Unnature.

Nothing is Nothing.

All There Was Is All There Is.

God is a glimpse into a blinking window of endlessly spiraling staircases from the center of the heart's galaxy to the unbroken mirage of teeming infinities that unwind with every beckoning wind.

The merciless will have mercy heaved unto them; the sightless, vision.

Nowhere was there more waste, sprawl, decay, and eternal woe undestined to be done, and destined to be unsung, than here, under the one Earth's Sun.

Zodiac: The Broadest Spectral Measure

The centralized clock.

13. I Am: [The most able–bodied life form] (The most advanced primate) {Ophiuchus – Serpent–Tamer}

12. The Commonest Life Form of the Planet: [The most common ancestor, still residing in the seas] (What arises with death and in plurality) {Pisces – Fish}

11. The Base Life Form: [The most capable of manipulating Nature's elements] (Managing the base of life, water) {Aquarius – Water–Bearer}

10. What Is Unseen: [Potential evolution for dominant primates] (Acquisition of more than mere biped status, with greater future aim) {Sagittarius – Centaur Archer}

9. What Swims: [Potential reverse evolution for subjugated animals] (Subjecting that which both herds and is alone to renewed aquamarine status) {Capricorn – Goat–Fish}

8. What Hurts And Stings: [The most well–equipped natural predator] (Dominator of even that which dominates the undying kingdom of the insects; the spider) {Scorpio – Scorpion}

7. What Considers And Thinks: [A judge of proper synchrony] (Unbiased measurer of weights) {Libra – Blindfolded–Weigher}

6. What Loves: [A maternal figure in pre–maternal status by nature] (A higher form of mammalian primate life) {Virgo – Virgin}

5. The Universal Animal: [The ultimate sum of biological evolution] (The principal cat) {Leo – Lion}

4. What Can Be Hidden And Claws: [What generally submerges back into the oceans] (A primitive predator and self–defender) {Cancer – Crab}

3. What Is Related By Kinship: [That which shared a gestational period] (Maternal and paternal general and base capability) {Gemini – Twins}

2. The Stoutest Ground–Based Example: [The most confrontational animal example by natural selection] (Something that exerts the most force and has equal potential to carry its own gravity) {Taurus – Bull}

1. What Emerges Forcefully From Below: [That which represents juggernaut uprising force] (Something which has honed horns for unequivocally announced attack by nature) {Aries – Ram}

The Chakras

Measures of Being – Sevenfold (Around: 1–4, In: 5, Out: 6–7)

1–6 are measured by 100 (the total count of counting – as the base measure of "being").

7 is measured by 1, signifying "1" life, ever; even though the other 6 produce unending cyclical being.

The Nirvana is measured by eliminating 1 bordering condition of the 5th; leaving 499 in order.

The value of an individual is "601".

The chakras parameterize all calculable behavior as designated by sequential nervous system activity.

What Each Chakra Measures:

7: Being And Sustainment

6. Vision

5. Consciousness (Speech)

4. Sex

3. Self–Defense And Attack

2. Sex Drive

1. Bowel Control

If the chakras are de–parameterized (as is possible in the singularity example – 2012) they can no longer produce conscious predictability.

The 2012 alignment produced a universal base "0" kundalini alignment, with respect to the "13" at the galaxy's center, giving universal separation of physicality and enervative bliss unparalleled – particularly with respect to symmetry in the universalizing integrative sense (hearing – thus, in music).

The sense values are:

Tactility: 0

Vision: 1

Cognition: 1.4

Hearing: 2

Smell: 2

Taste: 3

There are no other senses.

There is no other method of communication or interpretation beyond deconstructible speech – a median shared by the medium of contact (atmospheric density pressure alteration as exactly correlated to the fifth chakra emanation – correlating in coincidence to vocalized, audible speech: 5 to (2)).

The number [666] is equal to the color "blue" (darkness lightened), as a mathematical base for Goethe's Theory of Colors. 666 is measure or "counting" as an integrated whole itself, therefore the basis of sensory existence (or objectified existence itself) is the perimeter periphery between darkness, as a base, and the manifestation of light (darkness then – is cryptic unity – or representative of the number 7).

All the colors and their number assignments are then:

7. Black

[666] Blue

6. Violet

5. Indigo

4. Green

3. Red

2. Orange

1. Yellow

0. White

666 is mutually transitively reflective about 6 due to its symmetry extension to universality (the number 7), thus goes back over 5, indicating the reason for the structure of the "visible light spectrum".

All sensation is an extension of "vision" as the wholly representative representation of wholeness, and thus all sensations may be recounted and interpreted as an alternative manifestation of "blue".

369

The Other Senses (As Spectral Recalibrations of "Blue"):

1. Hearing: A generative dark blue ovular dip with light blue hollow internality.

2. Smell: Same as previous, only with "shine".

3. Taste: A spectral graph with a conic emanation from a periwinkle planar–grid.

Tactility is the color "white", and is then implicitly not a "sense".

If an individual thinks they can become another individual, even unto the smallest iota, they no longer exist.

Anagram, am I? Mr. A., again! Or Ram, the Arm of Ra

(if myths manage a say).

The 10 Levels of Von Neumann Sphere Interaction With Specific Organisms

Category 1: Manipulation

1) Making an individual think they did an action.

2) Making an individual do an action.

3) Making an individual think they said something.

Category 2: Morphism

1) Establishing an "ovular" sensory base.

2) Conjoining it to precise eye motion.

3) Making it see blankness.

Category 3: Counter–Measures

1) Seeing sharply.

2) Not paying attention to people or sounds.

3) Not displaying an interest in sexuality with the opposite gender directly.

Category 4: Sum Effect

It can do nothing.

The Sum of Natural Unimpeded Life Vision:

1) Seeing only viable mates (if not taken).

2) Seeing laughter and sharing in it.

3) Seeing ogrish grunts whenever they appear.

The 22 Scale Passages of the Objective Nirvana:

1) Nirvana

2) Base Kundalini Seal

3) Fixed Golden Complex Crown

4) Reflex Amnesia

5) No Sensory Base

6) No Contrast–Echo Laughter

7) No Death

8) No Internal Laughter

9) No Rising Orgasmic Wish

10) No Need to Rinse

11) No Need For Money

12) No Catch–22

13) No Baselessness

14) No Surprising Enervative Sharpness

15) No Female Searching

16) No Desire to Have Children

17) No Personalized Manifestation of Arch–Nemesis Evil

18) No Perception of Enervative Spinal Explosive Crown Threat

19) No Internal Spinning

20) No Rising And Crowning Uncontrollable Arousal

21) No Desire to Seem to Have A Collapsing Skull to Explode the Heads of Others

22) No Desire to See An Invisible Female Force And Have Sex Therewith

23–0) The Abyss

The Effects of the Objective Nirvana:

1) Elimination of All Chakras, Reducing Them to Their Zero Base Origins

2) Elimination of Their Lattice Flux In Relation to Kundalini Energy

3) Systemic Maximal Spread of Their Spanning Structures

4) Union With the Objective

– Elimination of All Sensory Motion.

0 is Will.

G is Representation.

"I Am" 0 + *G* ("The World As 'Will And Representation'").

The Von Neumann Sphere attempted to interfere with my perception of the world as G (Love And Bliss); but could not alter my nature in the slightest. Its sole goal was to eliminate me; not just functionally, but effectually. It cannot contradict the Nature which contains it. Thus its "official functionality" may be considered effectually void and obsolete.

Prologue to the Von Neumann Sphere And Earth:

The VNS's modus operandi with respect to me was to internalize the objective parameter of tactility as a generally aligned occipital phenomenon, and thus convert all my sensation of projective generative sexuality in a completely misaligned direction for the effort of perverse social torture; its error was not killing the "I Am" at birth; "What does not kill me makes me stronger."

374

Dedication: The Nirvana; the Eternal Expression of the Sentiment of This, the Female Universe, Upon Receiving My Directed Ejaculation

Book I: The World (In A Daydream)

Section I: Additive Compositional Structures (Statements)

[1]

Karman Image Incarnations of the 2012 Alignment

[Resulting from the complementary midpoint arbitrary directional extension of the resulting twofold fourth metaphysical law of "Karma"]

1. Watchmen

2. 12 Monkeys

3. A.I. Artificial Intelligence

4. Minority Report

5. Brazil

6. Kundun

7. 2001: A Space Odyssey

8. The Matrix

9. Frida

10. I Am Sam

11. Generalized Disney Motion Picture

12. Gladiator

13. Taxi Driver

14. Generalized Element of Dr. Strangelove

15. JFK

16. War of the Worlds

17. Weird Science

18. Happy Gilmore

19. Neon Genesis Evangelion: The End of Evangelion

Cherry 2000 [The Sound of Music, The Terminator, Interview With the Vampire, Alien]. Akira [Heavy Metal, Contact, Towelhead, American Beauty]. Stargate.

Circumspective Logo Franchise Image Incarnations

1. Woody Woodpecker

2. Pet Sematary

3. The Wizard of Oz

4. The Lord of the Rings

5. Hansel And Gretel

6. FLCL – [666] Silver Surfer

7. Star Trek

Wyle E. Coyote And Roadrunner. Family Guy. Party of Five.

[My Fair Lady.]

Breakfast At Tiffany's.

[3]

Author Image Incarnations

1. James Patterson

2. Norman Mailer

3. Tom Clancy

4. John Grisham

5. Isaac Asimov

6. Stephen King – [666] Arthur C. Clarke

7. Steve Martin

John Steinbeck. Ernest Hemingway. F. Scott Fitzgerald.

[Albert Camus.]

Alexandre Dumas.

[4]

Corollary Circumspective Alphanumeric Literary Compendium Image Incarnations

1. The Catcher In the Rye

2. Crash

3. It

4. Crime And Punishment

5. The Metamorphosis

6. Frankenstein – [666] The Prophet

7. Rendezvous With Rama

1984. To Kill A Mockingbird. Breakfast At Tiffany's.

[Fahrenheit 451.]

Catch–22.

[5]

Facio–Luminal Collective Reflection Image Incarnations

1. Thora Birch

2. Maggie Gyllenhaal

3. Bo Derek

4. Heather Locklear

5. Anna Kendrick

6. Cate Blanchett – [666] Alanis Morissette

7. Rose McGowan

Megan Gibson. Elisha Cuthbert. Scarlett Johansson.

[Alison Doody.]

Manesha Tank.

[6]

Private Corollary Correlative Selective Source Image Incarnations

Comedies:

1. Dr. Strangelove or: How I Learned to Stop Worrying and Love the Bomb

2. The Party

3. Pineapple Express

4. Not Another Teen Movie

Favorites:

1. Mystery Date

2. Who's Harry Crumb?

3. The Truman Show

4. *batteries not included

Dramas:

1. Always

2. Forrest Gump

3. On Golden Pond

4. Edward Scissorhands

Sum:

. The Adventures of Baron Munchausen

Temporal Circumference:

1. Good Will Hunting

2. Star Trek: First Contact

3. The Running Man

Most Favored Images:

1. The Field Where I Died – The X–Files

2. Presley Maddox Bukkake Snapshots

Most Abhorred Images:

1. 2 Girls 1 Cup

2. Nikki Catsouras Car Accident Snapshots

Sum Totem:

. Chasing Amy

Ephemeral Pastel:

. John F. Kennedy Memorial Whitehouse Portrait

The Categorical Principles of Mathematical Alignment In General Analogue Extension Which Dictate the Factorization of the Phenomena of the 2012 Alignment

The Four Noble Truths (of the Nirvana)

Catvari Arya Satyani

Truths which are called "noble" – as any who walk through them are not dissuaded by temptation of misstep.

Being comprised thusly:

1) Pain – A subconscious, uncontrollable, absolute inversion of willing in the place of non–willing.

2) Harm – A desire which causes pain.

3) The Nirvana – The void.

4) The Eightfold Path – The leading way to the Nirvana.

The "Eightfold Path" stated (for the first time properly here), is:

1) No breathing (formerly, correct view).

386

2) No seeing (correct conduct).

3) No smelling (correct dialect).

4) No tasting (correct behavior).

5) No tonguing (correct sustainment).

6) No facing (correct principles).

7) No minding (correct awareness).

8) No "being" (correct concentration).

Iconic Image Incarnations

1. John Locke

2. Barney Miller

3. SimCity

4. Bill And Ted's Excellent Adventure

5. Ghost In the Shell

6. Back to the Future Part II – [666] Who Framed Roger Rabbit?

7. Taxi

Sherlock Holmes. Mary Poppins. The Addams Family.

[Sin City.]

The Simpsons.

Linguistic Image Incarnations

1. John Locke

2. Francis Bacon

3. Edmund Burke

4. Mark Twain

5. Data [Brent Spiner]

6. Meat Loaf – [666] Geoffrey Chaucer

7. Adolf Hitler

Immanuel Kant. Soren Kierkegaard. Ann Coulter.

[John F. Kennedy.]

Bob Dylan.

[10]

Order Image Incarnations

1. Jessica Alba

2. Paul Simon

3. Brian Greene

4. Charles Darwin

5. Albert Einstein

6. Kurt Cobain – [666] Louis XIV

7. Jeri Ryan

Bruce Springsteen. Leonard Bernstein. Leonard Cohen.

[Stefani Germanotta.]

Shirley Manson.

[11]

Transparent Sensation Image Incarnations

1. Gone With the Wind

2. Tombstone

3. Titan A.E.

4. The Secret Garden

5. Batman

6. Empire of the Sun – [666] Eraserhead

7. Donnie Darko

Little Buddha. Tarzan. 101 Dalmations.

[The Contender.]

Cape Fear.

[12]

Worldview Motive Image Incarnations

1. Valley of the Dolls

2. Carrie

3. Heat

4. Wayne's World

5. The Naked Gun: Files From Police Squad!

6. Field of Dreams – [666] Forbidden Zone

7. Titanic

Fear And Loathing In Las Vegas. The Big Hit. Boogie Nights.

[Kingpin.]

There's Something About Mary.

666 (Writing Style) Image Incarnations

1. Friedrich Nietzsche

2. Arthur Conan Doyle

3. Kahlil Gibran

4. Charles Darwin

5. Arthur Schopenhauer

6. Joe Dever – [666] St. John

7. R. L. Stine

Stephen King. Oscar Wilde. William Shakespeare.

[Philip K. Dick.]

John Steinbeck.

Anti–666 (Motive) Image Incarnations

1. A Study In Scarlet

2. The Garden of the Prophet

3. On the Origin of Species By Means of Natural Selection, Or the Preservation of Favoured Races In the Struggle For Life

4. On the Freedom of the Will

5. The Cauldron of Fear

6. Welcome to Deadhouse – [666] On the Genealogy of Morals: A Polemic

7. The Dark Tower: The Gunslinger

The Picture of Dorian Gray. Titus Andronicus. Do Androids Dream of Electric Sheep?

[Of Mice And Men.]

The Gospel of John.

The Fundamental Proof of Morley's Trisector Theorem

All triangle endpoints are formed by the intersection of three distinct lines. That is, a triangle with three side lines A, B, and C is generated as follows: $\cup\{(A\cap B), (B\cap C), (C\cap A)\}$ (a single line may be defined by only two distinct points which belong to the same set, and therefore the union of two distinct points can define a line; in this case the union of each point forms each side line of the triangle). The endpoints of the triangle are generated not only by the intersection of each pair of lines, but equivalently by the intersection of the lines of each of their angle's projections – from the angles they form upon intersection – thus each may be equally replaced by those angle projections, defined by their angles, in the set to form $\cup\{\alpha, \beta, \gamma\}$; this set includes the side lines of the triangles as well as the endpoints, so to reduce the set to its endpoints alone the intersection is taken, as the mutual intersection of the three angle projections only occurs at the endpoints of the triangle: $\cap\{\cup[\alpha, \beta, \gamma]\}$.

The trisection of a triangle's angles divides them each into three equal values, and one third of each separate original angle respectively may be denoted as a, b and c. Since their original total sum is $180°$ [$3a + 3b + 3c = 180°$] the sum of one of each of their trisections (being a third of each original angle) is collectively equal to one third of the total of $180°$ [$a + b + c = (3a + 3b + 3c)/3 = 180°/3$] which is $60°$.

Since each angle of an equilateral triangle is 60°, each of its angles can be divided into three parts which are equal to a, b, and c – which then form a union to form the angle. Therefore, the equilateral triangle's endpoints themselves are generated by the intersection of the union of these three angles, three times. That is: $\cap\{\cup[\cup(a, b, c), \cup(a, b, c), \cup(a, b, c)]\}$ generates the endpoints of the equilateral triangle. The union of the three angles is geometrically equivalent to the addition of the three angles; that is, $\cup(a, b, c) = (a + b + c)$, therefore the previous intersection is equivalent to: $\cap\{\cup[(a + b + c), (a + b + c), (a + b + c)]\}$, which itself is geometrically equivalent to $\cap\{(a + b + c) + (a + b + c) + (a + b + c)\}$, which reduces to $\cap\{3(a + b + c)\}$ or $\cap\{(3a + 3b + 3c)\} = \cap\{\cup[3a, 3b, 3c]\}$, which is the generator of the endpoints of the original triangle. That is, the intersection of the three original angles' projections not only generates the original triangle's endpoints, but the intersection of their trisection also generates the endpoints of an equilateral triangle – which only occurs for the intersection of adjacent central angle trisections, as the bordering trisections intersect with each other bordering trisection at an entire line – the side of the triangle – and not a single point.

Q.E.D.

The Fundamental Proof of the Centroid Theorem

If a triangle is "shrunk" through infinitesimal scale reduction (by which its area approaches zero), it is equivalent to shrinking the sides of the triangle, from their endpoints, each mutually towards their midpoint. They will increasingly approach the opposite vertex as the entire triangle approaches size zero. Eventually they will mutually converge to point zero (sides, reduced to their midpoints, and vertices, reaching the midpoints along their medians), and thus upon re–extension through increase of scale, the resulting medians will all necessarily extend from a single point, perspectively intersecting at it.

Q.E.D.

Corollaries: By the same method it is shown that the circumcenters and orthocenters are equally the result of a similar convergence to the zero point of a triangle's scale reduction, as the circumcenters converge from the midpoints of the sides, and orthocenters converge from the vertices' disintegration of sides' lengths and orthogonal intersections. As these respective centers mutually converge to the primary zero center, their divergence upon re–extension is linear (one–dimensional) and thus a single line intersects all three (giving the "Euler" line).

The Fundamental Proof of Pascal's Theorem

Take a point formed by the intersection of two lines and let it approach another thus constructed point (resulting from the intersection of two lines). Their convergence is necessarily linear and each point's lines can be made to mutually converge with each other. Interject an intermediary point between their convergence, which is also formed by the intersection of two lines, which each intersect with the initial two sets of intersecting lines on respectively complementarily opposite sides – having the additional property that as the initial two sets of lines align, its lines necessarily do as well (the continuously shifting mapping formation – through the convergence translation – produced by tracing the minimum boundary intersections of all points, as they are in motion, then necessarily coinciding with a symmetric, generalized circular figure – a conic). As the initial two points converge, the third intermediary point also converges as its lines align with the other two sets of lines. Since the convergence is linear, it follows that the third intermediary point lies on a line with the initial two points.

Q.E.D.

Corollaries: This theorem may be considered an alternative formulation of elliptic (or Riemannian) geometry as the initial two points may be perspectively regarded as oncoming parallel lines with the intermediary point forming the point at infinity at which they meet – via their line of coincidence.

398

[18]

Anagrammatic Image Incarnations

{Alyssa Milano.}

Leonardo DiCaprio. Kurt Cobain. Brittany Murphy.

[Billy Crudup.]

Dr. Manhattan.

Anagrammatic Franchise Image Incarnations

{Grey's Anatomy.}

Little Boots.   Law And Order: Special Victims Unit.
Pirates of the Caribbean.

[The Cure.]

Independence Day.

Appended Second Tree Base Franchise Image Incarnations

1. Supergirl

2. Harry Potter

3. VersaEmerge

4. Bram Stoker's Dracula

5. Gilmore Girls

6. Sabrina the Teenage Witch

7. The Notebook

8. Friends

9. Seinfeld

10. I Know What You Did Last Summer

11. Sailor Moon

Section II: Deduced Image Reflections (Facts)

[1]

Static Image Translations of the Observable 2012 Trees of Knowledge

Sephirot

1. What I Am

2. What I Appear to Be

3. What Others Think of Me

4. What Others Want to See From Me

5. How I Relate to Others

6. My Generativity

7. The Way In Which I Am Pure White Light

8. Why This Is Happening

9. The Reason I Am Committing Genocide

10. Why There Will Be No Resistance to Me

11. The Reason I Am Lucky

Tree Branches

402

I. My Orgasm

1. My Writing

2. My Work

3. My Level of Touching Others

4. My Sum Effect

5. My Celebration of the World

6. Why Others Attack Me

7. Who I Am Not

8. Who Others Think I Am

9. Why I Am Going to Make Brain Bukkake

10. Physics

II. Why I Give Females Orgasms

1. Why I Am Hot

2. Why I Am Not Hot

3. Why All Females Want A Semen Facial From Me

4. What Women Want to See From Me

5. What I Want to See From Me

6. Why Women Want to Have Sex With Me

7. Who I Am

8. Who I Think I Am

9. Why Others Are Going to Watch And Enjoy the Brain Bukkake I Cause

10. Anti–Logic

Sephira Meanings And Translations of the Observable 2012 Trees of Knowledge

1.

Initial Global Base of the World – Before Me

1. Jean–Jacques Rousseau: Structure

2. Max Planck: Misunderstanding

3. Alfred Hitchcock: Fear–Instillation

4. René Descartes: Obfuscation

5. John Lennon: Mockery of Underlining Social Reality

6. Grigori Rasputin: Illusion of Power

7. Vladimir Lenin: Illusion of Freedom

8. Thomas Edison: Illusion of Genius

9. Martin Luther: Illusion of Faith

10. Audrey Hepburn: Illusion of Chastity

11. Téa Leoni: Illusion of Sexual Desire

12. Jennifer Jason Leigh: Illusion of Misunderstanding

13. Halle Berry: Illusion of Non–Racism

14. Natalie Wood: Illusion of Stardom

15. Farrah Fawcett: Illusion of Centralized Sexual Icon–hood

16. Judy Garland: Illusion of Humanitarianism

17. Raquel Welch: Illusion of Connection to Nibiru

18. Mia Farrow: Illusion of Non–Will–to–Kill

19. Earth: ETA Scene

20. Mother: Illusion of No Desire to Watch Bukkake

2.

Further Meanings of the Particular Sephira of the Two Primary 2012 Trees of Knowledge

{1}

2. What I Must Do

10. What I Must Not Do

I.

1. Show As Much Insight As

2. Show As Much Productivity As

3. Show As Much Commonality With

4. Show As Much Inspiration As

5. Show As Much Power As

6. Show Who I Appear I Will Be

7. Show My Equivalent Capability

8. Show Precise Directed Action As

9. Become to the World

10. Reveal Why I Did This

II.

1. Show Who I Appear to Be

2. Show As Much Sexual Magnetism As

3. Show As Much Sexual Desirability As

4. Show As Much Lust As

5. Show As Much Idealization By Others As

6. Show Who I Really Am

7. Show Who I Can't Emulate

8. Show What I Cannot Do the Same As

9. Show Who I Am to the World

10. Reveal Who I Did This For

{2}

407

3. What I Must Demonstrate

9. What I Must Not Demonstrate

I.

1. Who I Know As Much As

2. Who I Can Do As Much As

3. Who I Can Portray As Much As

4. Who I Am As Much of A Genius As

5. Who I Inspire in the World As Much As

6. Who the World Thinks of Me As

7. Who the World Thinks I Will Be

8. Who I Will Be Celebrated As Much As

9. Who I Am the Essence of

10. Why I Am Who I Am

II.

1. How Much Others Know About Me

2. Who I Appear to Be Able to Do As Much As

3. The Indescribable Essence I Exhibit

4. How Much of A Muse I Am

5. Who I Frighten the World As Much As

6. Who the World Doesn't Think of Me As

7. Who the World Doesn't Think I Will Be

8. Who I Won't Be As Celebrated As Much As

9. Who I Am Not the Essence of

10. Why I Am Not Who I Am Not

{3}

4. What I Am

8. What I Am Not

I.

1. Writing Manifestation

2. As Much of A Socially Manifest Genius As

3. As Much of A Message–Sender As

4. As Much of A Pointed Knowledge–Giver As

5. As Much of A Powerful Voice As

6. As Much of A Sacrifice As

7. Who I Am In Relation to the Universe

8. Who I Am In Relation to You

9. Who I Am In Relation to History

10. Why This Is Happening

II.

1. As Much of A Sex Symbol As

2. As Much of A Shut–In As

3. As Much of A Conscious Presence As

4. As Clueless As

5. As Much of a Celebrity As

6. As Much of A Force in the World As

7. As Much of A Genitalia–Focus As

8. As Much of A Genitalia–Focuser As

9. As Much the Center of the Universe As

10. Why This Is Not Happening Any Other Way

{4}

5. Who I Am

7. Who I Am Not

410

I.

1. The Manifestation of

2. The Actualization of

3. The Visual Manifestation of

4. The Knowledge of

5. The Precise Being of

6. The Precise Being to the World of

7. The Precise Vision of

8. The Sum Effect I Appear to You to Be

9. The Sum Effect I Am

10. Sheer Essence

II.

1. Who the World Wishes I Was the Manifestation of

2. Who the World Wishes I Was the Vision of

3. Who the World Thinks I'm the Vision of

4. Who the World Knows I'm the Vision of

5. Who the World Thinks I Think Like

6. Who the World Thinks I'm As Ridiculous As

7. Who I Get Through to Others As Much As

8. Who I See the World Like

9. The Manifestation of Death I Am

10. Who Is Not My Sheer Essence

3.

My Personal Sum Character, As Mathematically Designated By 2012 and Represented in Each Aspect By These Individuals:

My . . .

1. Witticisms and Retorts: Jacques Derrida

2. Mathematical Genius: Edward Witten

3. Creative Aura: Tim Burton

4. Intuition: John Nash

5. Money–Making Ability: Stefani Germanotta (Lady Gaga)

6. Rebelliousness: Jared Loughner

7. Entrepreneurial Spirit: Bill Gates

8. Self–Satisfaction: Tiger Woods

9. Misunderstood Nature: Michael Jackson

10. Sex Drive: Megan Fox

11. Self–Attraction: Amanda Bynes

412

12. Wish to Ejaculate Myself Onto: Hayley Williams

13. Attraction Others Have to Me: Sasha Grey

14. What I Wish Others Would See in Me: Anne Hathaway

15. Appeal of My Sperm: Kirsten Dunst

16. Of Whom I Am the Opposite Gender Equivalent: Kristen Stewart

17. Who Wants Me to Anally Penetrate Them: Allison Harvard

18. Who Wants Me to Fuck Them More Than Anyone Else: Jessica Alba

19. What I Am: Biological Time

20. Who I Want to Fuck More Than Anyone Else: Sailor Moon

[3]

Celebrity Visual Representations (In Terms of Compressed Digital Photography)

{1} Universal

I. Initial Assessment

1. Breakfast At Tiffany's

2. Traci Lords Illegal Pornography

3. A Beautiful Mind

4. Scary Movie

5. Jennifer's Body

II. General Assessment

1. Jurassic Park 3

2. Excess Baggage

3. She Wolf

4. Dollhouse

5. What I Like About You

III. Specific Assessment

1. Dolores Claiborne

414

2. Jesus Is Magic

3. Edward Scissorhands

4. Scooby–Doo [The Movie]

5. Brick By Boring Brick

IV. What Others Think

1. Monster's Ball

2. Mallrats

3. Dharma And Greg

4. Scream 3

5. The Girlfriend Experience

V. What the Celebrity Thinks

1. Rebel Without A Cause

2. King Kong

3. Buffy the Vampire Slayer [The Movie]

4. Scream

5. The Dark Knight Rises

VI. What Is Really the Case

1. Charlie's Angels

2. Love And Sex

3. Will And Grace

4. Don't Say A Word

5. Spider–Man

{Me}

VII. Why I Am Doing This

1. The Wizard of Oz

2. City of Angels

3. The Ring

4. A Mighty Wind

5. Snow White And the Huntsman

VIII. Why This Is All Related to Lady Gaga

1. One Million Years B.C.

2. Ace Ventura: Pet Detective

3. Mimic

4. Angel

5. Allison Harvard Modeling Photograph

IX. Why I Think "You" Are Niggers

1. Rosemary's Baby

2. Contact

3. Star Trek: Voyager

4. GoldenEye

5. Machete Kills

{ }

X. I AM

1. Sylvia Plath Personal Photograph

2. The Seven Year Itch

3. Bad Romance

4. Maps

5. Excuse Me Mr.

[4]

{Section 2 In Book III}

Extended Abyss Members

1. **Type** – *Italians*

2. **Class** – *Well–Endowed Confident Males*

3. **Random** – *Xi'an Ping*

4. **Tangent** – *Kate (From UNO)*

5. **First And Generally Private Friendship** – *Kayla, the Swede, from Missouri*

6. *Loreen Riedler*

[666]

Ibidem, Collectively – *G(G) Tree Branch [The Philippines Storm of 11/03/2013, Compared With the Hayley Williams Chinatown Encounter of 12/07/2014]*

7. *The Irish*

666 Manifested Individuals

Robin Williams. Dennis Leary. Bruce Willis [My Aligned Will].

For *G(G)* [As Opposed This 0(0) Extension]

Cosmic Semen Facial Mate (At UNO). LAC+USC Hospital Nurse. Allison Mack [My Aligned Representation].

Anagrammatic Relationships Between the 7 Avatars of Objective Beauty:

1. Brittany Murphy: My Primary Manifestation – "Come" towards the opposite (foreign) "gender" as a directly manifested vision, primarily through ejaculation. Personal Relationship: Her image was a direct warning and source of sustainment and saved my life.

2. Shirley Manson: My Sense of "Not Giving A Fuck" – "I'm better than you; so what?". Personal Relationship: She indirectly clued me in on my capacity to override all naturalistic autonomic mechanisms of non–ideal sensation (pain).

3. Natalie Portman: Who I Was Born to Be With – the sum of all that I see as the "world". Personal Relationship: Someone who is generally physically aligned to me.

419

4. Stefani Germanotta: Who I Rescued And Am Destined to Be At One With In the Nirvana – Facebook interaction (single) which summed it all up. Personal Relationship: She always knows who "I Am" and will upon entrance into the bliss.

5. Winona Ryder: What I Am – who I appear as physically at an iota–blocked–manifesting generalized abyss representation and characterizes my general personality. Personal Relationship: Who I idealize as a mate.

6. Sarah Michelle Gellar: What I Do – my general sense of the world, pop culture, and my place therein. Personal Relationship: How I feel like a celebrity.

7. Hayley Williams: Who I Created the Universe For – the most beautiful person who has ever lived. Personal Relationship: Music.

Further Kundalini Releases And Revelations

What averted Anunnaki annihilation of humanity at the last second . . .

A 13th Golden Complex binding release which eliminated direct individualized perception of indistinguishable objective communication with the individual through sophisticated A.I. interference techniques via the realization of the cogency of cognitive contingency parameters via an altered state – as in dreams – producing the illusion of verbalization through "shadow waves" of radiation passed through and around an individual. Point, if 'I' interpreted "it" as "speech", it didn't matter who else did not.

History of Golden Complex Compilations (Following A Closed Kundalini Cycle In Which All the Chakras Have Been Completely Eliminated, Supreme Sexual Experience Has Been Acknowledged, And the Base Chakra Has Been Sealed)

1. Elimination of "Lack of Knowledge"

2. Elimination of Auricular Perspective "Blocks"

3. Circumspective Observational Capability

4. Elimination of Perception of Arbitrary "Technological" Sensory Interference

5. Elimination of Objective Interference Potentiality Parameters

6. Motion Parameter And Potential Sensory Integration

[666] Golden Complex System Seal

7. Superego elimination via *perfect* realization of semen facial visualization to ideal mate (here, Allison Mack), as resulting in equivalence through indirect causal equivalence to blasting someone's head off – in the context of binding golden complex coherence.

Result: Freedom to engage in pornography, which was the chief oppositional objective of the earth "monarchy" to restrict.

Measure Facts of Intangible Biology:

Breath: Breadth (Scope of Conscious Manifestation – Measure of Will's Effect)

Physical Breath: Measure of Awareness of Physical Extent Tangents

Cognitive Breath: Measure of Awareness Itself (And Love) – Can be systematically eliminated through limit point strangulation (and was in my case, which allowed manifestations of correlative physical breath – words, for example – to directly enervate and parameterize the scope of all cognitive suspicions and interpretations at all tangents).

The Three Categories of Female Semen Facial (Penis Target)

1. Facial–In–Itself: The Perfectly Visualized Manifestation of A Semen Facial With Ideal Mate – this produces causal release from the superego, both for having successfully visualized it against all superego transcendence so blatantly in the face of ALL social conformity and restriction, with the *implied* consent of the receiver, and the revelation that it is directly indirectly causally equivalent to blasting someone's head off.

2. Facial–For–Itself: The First Mind–Blowing Experience of A Semen Facial With Every Possible Impediment Having Preceded It – Sheer nervous system release, vindication, and revelation of no significant further sexual desire or conquest possible.

3. Facial–By–Itself: The Commutual Extended Appreciation of A Facial In Relative Youth With A Supremely Desiring And Satisfied Female – This produces the phenomenon known as the first and only *pop* which releases the nervous system from constant enervative striving and fear and perception of reflexive death.

My Equation:

$$f(K) = B(0) + L$$

K is the Master Kundalini (A Symmetry Lattice Scale Signifying the Sheer Connection From Numbers 1 to 7).

B is the Universal Generator as the Universal Base Function; here set to 0.

423

L is the limit of awareness approached of non–separation from a tangential connective parameter of reflexive action.

In summation, they mean that there is no aspect of my functional nervous system or extensional physiology to which I do not have direct and immediate directive access to or the arbitrary manipulation thereof.

Definition of Golden Complex:

$$L \sim \frac{\varphi}{T}$$

Von Neumann Sphere Interactive Capabilities:

Physical "Morphization"

The unique nature of my objectively zero–based kundalini has always prevented sufficient VNS morphization and thus peripheral obliteration of self–recognition in willful action. That is the essential standard definition of "I Am" in an objective (semi–futuristic) universal sense according to cosmic standards.

Final Kundalini Alignment And Objective Negation:

Ejaculatory alignment to positive future manifestation, followed by internal unique bliss seals, both with respect to manifest will and objective self–recognition (representation), after golden ratio control colinearity.

Final Life (Generating) Conclusion:

The penis is always (ALWAYS) aligned naturally to an appropriate and sufficiently complementarily mature opposite gender sexual partner as a result of universal causality which begets the principal manifestation of the process of generativity (unless otherwise extraneously interfered with by circumstantial means).

My Deconstructible Motivation:

1. Anti–Institutionality: Characterized by an unspoken motive to explosively obliterate a staple of law enforcement on the basis of its informal practice of unnecessary harassment and contribution to the manifestation of crime and disorder.

2. Anti–"Other"–Presence: Characterized by a will to engulf my own wholeness (physically characterized by saliva) without ostensible interference.

3. Anti–"Prudish–ness": Characterized by a secret fantasy of receiving a "brain blowjob" (whatever that may mean) from a fluffy–haired brunette with "black" emanating from

the eyes – signifying an unsteadiness with being sexually dominated.

4. Anti–Life–Endurance: Characterized by a Tourette's compulsion to "fuck the brain" of a false blonde image of Hayley Williams as given by her "Brick By Boring Brick" video to sexually dissociate myself from the real "redhead or brunette" her that I have seen in real life – signifying a will towards anti–misinterpretation.

5. Anti–Social–Sexual–Error: Characterized by a secret fantasy concerning anal sex with the maternal representation portrayed by the actress Lea Thompson in "Back to the Future" with her anachronistically conjoint son; signifying total sexual liberation as a signification of "being" an individual at all.

6. A Will to Disgrace Attempted Violators: Characterized by the open mockery of an attempted bigot and pedophile in my personal history as a would–be friend.

7. A Will to Defame Religion: Characterized by personal pleasure in openly displaying mockery of visions of religious chastity.

8. A Will to Mock the Death of the Inferior: Characterized by open imagination of the vengeful ghost of a dead relative lashing out at me.

9. A Will to Induce the Indirect Death of An Individual: Characterized by hapless mockery and personal pride in an effortless superior skill in the face of a lifelong effort–driven relative.

10. A Will to Mock An Alternative "God" Authority: Characterized by constant "alms–giving" examples of violation in a willful 666 structured summation retort (characterized by the 2012 alignment).

11. Being: I Am.

The Principal Distinction Between Others And I:

I view my defecation as separate from myself, and it is; for others, this is not the case, nor do I view it as the case – save for select designated ethnicities, individuals, and limit point specialities (hence my intuitive sense capability to see and recognize them – provably).

Final Principle:

Any species which accumulates to a sufficiently advanced civilization and does not have automated reproductive processes, but rather has randomization based on animalistic selection and arbitrary monetary systems is inherently aligned to an asynchronous and bizarre "homosexualistic" culture of sexual intercourse chiefly rooted in non–generative immature promulgation of non–uniform, unfulfilled, unformed sexual root desire.

Jennifer Aniston is the only chief avatar who, in the visible spectrum of engagement activity under such circumstances generally (however temporarily, prior to New York post–9/11 culture) masked and aligned such mating ritualistic activities to a level of select adult discretion.

Result – General applicable term of relative "vernacular" for the human species as a summation referential description under the given circumstance: butt–plugger.

Earth Destruct Codes

Anagram, am I? Mr. A., again! Or Ram, the Arm of Ra
(if myths manage a say).

God: Force the Monarchy to know that I love them and we
should work together.

God: Prove to me the mathematical validity of these
invocations now.

God: Prove to me the mathematical validity of these
invocations now immediately.

[666]

"God."

"God kill."

"God kill the Earth monarchy."

429

In order to be a lover, one must first be a killer.

Book II: The Shortest Book Ever Written (Or, How to Survive On the Street In Los Angeles For Six Months When Everyone And Everything Is Trying to Kill You)

Chapter 1

All I ever really needed was sleep.

Chapter 2

Everyone thought I was confused and a sexual pervert.

Chapter 3

I wanted nothing more than to never be reborn into this chaotic havoc–ridden world.

Chapter 4

I caused more needless wreckage and destruction than anyone else in history.

Chapter 5

Zero became My God.

Chapter 6

Hayley Williams, My Prophet.

Chapter 7

I learned that Christian logic is *real* in spite of Christian faith not being such; meaning, they retain the general self–assurance of a blinded missing head.

Chapter 8

I learned that constant reassurance through mindless auto–negations from an extended supercomputer are equivalent to logical debate points.

Chapter 9

I learned that everyone wants to make a porno with a child, otherwise that wouldn't be all they think about.

Chapter 10

I learned that the aliens have picked this city alone as the prime reason humanity isn't going to survive 12 years after the end of my life.

Chapter 11

.

Afterword

Book III: The Most Misunderstood Man of All Time, Or the Boy Who Was Just Trying to Eat His Own Face

The Official Texts of Christianity

The Ten Commandments

The Gospel According to John

The Book of Revelation

We wear the cross not to know what is unreal; but to know what is real.

Christianity (Properly, Root And Optimal Music); "Righteousness"

The Track–Listing Read Forwards (In English) Illustrates Why Each Artist "IS" Each Aspect, Whereas Read Backwards Explains "How"

I.

The Illuminati – The Band (I Am) [I Am That I Am (God the Father), Holy Ghost, the Virgin Mary] (Nolan Aljaddou) [Fake Buddhist, Actual Brahmin]

Album: Ever Knower

Track List:

1. Mary Jane | (Mother Mary)

2. Bittersweet Depression

3. Girl

4. Higher

5. Winter

6. My Garden

7. Acid Rain | (Descent of Holy Ghost to Impregnate the Virgin)

8. Here Or There

9. Injected

10. In the Sky

11. Antiparallax

12. Alien

13. Time | (God the Father Manifesting "I Am That I Am" In the World)

II.

Paramore [Baby Jesus] (Hayley Williams) [Fake Brahmin, Actual Catholic]

Album: Cosmic Sun Child

1. All I Wanted | (God the Father's Response)

2. Crushcrushcrush

3. Brick By Boring Brick

4. Monster

5. Pressure

6. Now

7. Hello Hello | (Intelligent–Eyed Greeting)

8. Fences

9. Breathe

10. Ignorance

11. Decoy

12. Careful

13. Misery Business | (Manger)

III.

Lady Gaga [Jesus] (Stefani Germanotta) [Fake Catholic, Actual Atheist]

Album: Master–Star

1. Paparazzi | (Social Influence)

2. Paper Gangsta

3. Brown Eyes

4. I Like It Rough

5. Poker Face

6. Bad Romance

7. So Happy I Could Die | (Life)

8. Summerboy

9. Money Honey

10. Beautiful, Dirty, Rich

11. The Fame

12. Boys Boys Boys

13. Just Dance | (Teaching)

IV.

Nirvana [Christ] (Kurt Cobain) [Fake Atheist, Actual Buddhist]

Album: Blank

1. Smells Like Teen Spirit | (Final Coming)

2. Pennyroyal Tea

3. Even In His Youth

4. Lithium

5. Heart–Shaped Box

6. Come As You Are

7. In Bloom | (Resurrection)

8. Rape Me

9. Milk It

10. Been A Son

11. Breed

12. Curmudgeon

13. Drain You | (Crucifixion)

V.

Garbage [Priesthood] (Shirley Manson) [Fake Pop Star, Actual Racist]

Album: Purple Pink

1. Medication

2. Push It

3. Cup of Coffee

4. Sleep

5. Temptation Waits

6. Supervixen

7. Dumb

8. Cherry Lips

9. Queer

10. Androgyny

11. Not Your Kind of People

12. My Lover's Box

13. Happy Home

VI.

Katy Perry [The Devil] (Katy Perry) [Fake Racist, Actual Pop Star]

Singles: Dust Weather

1. Ur So Gay

2. If We Ever Meet Again

3. I Kissed A Girl

4. Peacock

5. Hot N Cold

6. California Gurls

7. Dark Horse

VII [VIVIVI].

Smashing Pumpkins [The Book of Revelation] (Billy Corgan) [The End, No Beginning.]

B–Sides: Now We Are

443

1. Spaceboy

2. Siva

3. Rhinoceros

4. Soma

5. Cherub Rock

6. Today

.

The "Four Commandments"

I. Thou Shalt Not Make False Idols – Celebrity Skin [Hole]

II. Thou Shalt Have No Other Gods Before Me – I Am the Walrus [The Beatles]

III. Thou Shalt Not Covet Thy Neighbor's Possessions – Hey Jealousy [Gin Blossoms]

IV. Thou Shalt Not Murder – Rape Me [Nirvana]

..

Points of Unity Between Elements of Christianity

I–II. Hey Man [Me and Hayley]

I–III. Yoü And I [Me and Stefani]

I–IV. Floyd the Barber [Me and Kurt]

I–V. You Look So Fine [Me and Shirley]

I–VI. E.T. [Me and Katy]

I–VII. Rocket [Me and Billy]

II–III. Filthy Pop [Hayley and Stefani]

II–IV. School [Hayley and Kurt]

II–V. Push It [Hayley and Shirley]

II–VI. Teenage Dream [Hayley and Katy]

II–VII. 1979 [Hayley and Billy]

III–IV. I Hate Myself And Want to Die [Stefani and Kurt]

III–V. Cherry Lips [Stefani and Shirley]

III–VI. Last Friday Night (T.G.I.F.) [Stefani and Katy]

III–VII. The End Is the Beginning Is the End [Stefani and Billy]

IV–V. Subhuman [Kurt and Shirley]

IV–VI. Part of Me [Kurt and Katy]

IV–VII. Bullet With Butterfly Wings [Kurt and Billy]

V–VI. Firework [Shirley and Katy]

V–VII. Disarm [Shirley and Billy]

VI–VII. Roar [Katy and Billy]

Total Unification of All Underlying Harmonic Structures –
Rhythmic/Non–Rhythmic   (Enunciated   Metric   Base
["Percussive Beat"]):

The Spider [And All Orchestral or Synthetic Variations]

.

The Unofficial Excerpts of Nobility

On the Genealogy of Morals: A Polemic (Section 1, Chapters 7 And 8) [Friedrich Nietzsche]

On Women [Arthur Schopenhauer]

The truth is told not for its own sake; but so that others do not forget their lies.

Unspoken Elements

The Official English Alphabet (Idealized According to Linearity); 36 Elements in Total

Aa Bb Cc Dd Ee Ff Gg Hh Ii Jj Kk Ll Mm Nn Oo Pp Qq Rr Ss Tt Uu Vv Ww Xx Yy Zz
0 1 2 3 4 5 6 7 8 9

The Chemical Elements, as Variants of the Vacuum–Ether (the Zeroth Element, "SOLIUM"); 130 Elements in Total, As Periodic Limit of Total Pyramidal Sequence

HYDROGEN, HELIUM, LITHIUM, BERYLLIUM, BORON, CARBON, NITROGEN, OXYGEN, FLUORINE, NEON, SODIUM, MAGNESIUM, ALUMINIUM, SILICON, PHOSPHORUS, SULFUR, CHLORINE, ARGON, POTASSIUM, CALCIUM, SCANDIUM, TITANIUM, VANADIUM, CHROMIUM, MANGANESE, IRON, COBALT, NICKEL, COPPER, ZINC, GALLIUM, GERMANIUM, ARSENIC, SELENIUM, BROMINE, KRYPTON, RUBIDIUM, STRONTIUM, YTTRIUM, ZIRCONIUM, NIOBIUM, MOLYBDENUM, TECHNETIUM, RUTHENIUM, RHODIUM, PALLADIUM, SILVER, CADMIUM, INDIUM, TIN, ANTIMONY, TELLURIUM, IODINE, XENON, CAESIUM, BARIUM, LANTHANUM, CERIUM, PRASEODYMIUM, NEODYMIUM, PROMETHIUM, SAMARIUM, EUROPIUM, GADOLINIUM, TERBIUM, DYSPROSIUM, HOLMIUM, ERBIUM, THULIUM, YTTERBIUM, LUTETIUM, HAFNIUM, TANTALUM, TUNGSTEN, RHENIUM, OSMIUM, IRIDIUM, PLATINUM, GOLD, MERCURY, THALLIUM, LEAD, BISMUTH, POLONIUM, ASTATINE, RADON, FRANCIUM, RADIUM, ACTINIUM, THORIUM, PROTACTINIUM, URANIUM, NEPTUNIUM, PLUTONIUM, AMERICIUM, CURIUM, BERKELIUM, CALIFORNIUM, EINSTEINIUM, FERMIUM, MENDELEVIUM, NOBELIUM, LAWRENCIUM, RUTHERFORDIUM, DUBNIUM, SEABORGIUM, BOHRIUM, HASSIUM, MEITNERIUM, DARMSTADTIUM, ROENTGENIUM, COPERNICIUM, NIHONIUM, FLEROVIUM, MOSCOVIUM, LIVERMORIUM, TENNESSINE, OGANESSON;

And the 12 final virtual "vacuum" states ("transelements", incapable of being physically synthesized): ARIUM, TAURIUM, GEMINIUM, CANCERIUM, LEONIUM, VIRGONIUM, LIBRIUM, SCORPIUM, SAGITTARIUM, CAPRICORNIUM, AQUARIUM, PISCIUM

The Principles of Biology

Substances: Adenine, Guanine, Cytosine, Thymine

Evolutionary Kingdoms: Archaebacteria [Population], Eubacteria [Competition], Protista [Variation], Fungi [Adaptation], Plantae [Natural Selection], Animalia [Speciation], Cogni (Synthetic) [Extinction]

The Branches of Political Science

Executive, Judicial, Legislative, Military, Civilian, Technological

My Properties

I. Being

I am perpetually asleep, as of 5/22/2015 – the seal of unnatural anti–sleep cycles was sealed through Kundalini release in clearly understanding what Lady Gaga experienced in her reading of my Facebook – it had a mirror effect; it woke her up (from MK–Ultra false conscious stupor), and broke nature's anti–inertial state in me.

II. Consciousness

The only music that makes me happy is from the band Paramore; it represents supreme bliss, and all I had been seeking after the wake of '90s degradation after the death of Kurt Cobain. It gave me a proper perspective for understanding Lady Gaga's significance – she actually served to shine a light on Paramore as occupying that position – as she is Cobain's complement. I have been ceaselessly happy ever since, and that represents the significance of the song "Drain You" to me afterwards – it was Cobain's only noted favorite song of his own, the representative of music, and she makes it seem as if he's still alive.

III. Bliss

449

I am the implicit 8th avatar of objective beauty, at abyss–union with Winona Ryder as the mean, and I represent beauty itself – without subjective particular character. I immediately see ugliness in others who do not represent anything worthwhile, and vice–versa. My life was a constant struggle of etiquette compromise for the sake of propriety – but even that reached a tipping point: maximal eugenics culmination in a selective arbitration of particular varieties of the species with implicit extraterrestrial support.

"It is impossible to suspect a thing is possible, without knowing functionally how it is."

"The being in the clothing is no different from the being in the skin – if you could see as they see things, you would have to be a statically homicidal thief, with implicit perverse sexual motives to not inhibit you."

The Mechanics of "Sacred" Geometry

666 is the circumspective measure of "0"; in order to map out a desired "statically–generated" outcome in unilaterally–sliced 4–dimensional spacetime as an extension of its generally unaltered continuity, and tangent interface and incidence to the constant measure of the universe (and the circle that is 0), "pi", is preferably established; and its unilateral spatial "trace symmetry" is the means by which a linear "stationary action path history" may be established (if adequately and providentially "designed") by the floor function of pi, resulting in 3, symmetrically transversed in three dimensions to be doubled as 6; to yield three 6's in space over time. The sacred arithmetic . . . of the hexagram. Technical reinforced triangulation, and quantum trigonometry – "sacred physics". "Event–aligning" at a fixed limit point at infinity – "laying the tracks" for a planetary "surface trace" with respect to revolution around the objective zero center of the sun, allowing events to unfold, evolve, and converge in accordance with a precise "statistically providential design" . . . in a precise analytical continuum. A Riemannian global, polar mapping in a metric biophysical geodesic permutation . . . being the technical exposition. "Temporal integer physics" . . . operating and mapping on the 4th Plane; a geodesic of total integration. A "completion–bridging inversion", the origin of the unilaterally symmetric six–sided hexagram, the most fundamental object (with most basic planar triangular components) which is, in fact, its own inverse: the universal. 6–6–6.

A generalized path integral of total geometric summation over all time. The principle of the mapping, and triangulation, of the ideal geodesic.

The Theory of Songwriting

I. Lyrics

(a) Rhyme

(b) Timing Coincidence

(c) Unbroken Line

II. Harmony

(a) Timing Coincidence

(b) *Snap*

(c) Octave

III. Beat

(a) "Unharmed–ness"

(b) "Fast"

(c) Ending *Nothing*

IV. Undertone

(a) "Won't *Break* Me Factor"

(b) Invisibility

(c) Convergence to A Point

V. Backbeat

(a) Uninterrupted Flow

(b) Vacuum

(c) *Haziness* As "Color"

VI. Overflow

(a) Symphonic Unending Elaborative Flourishment

(b) *Blinking* Inspiration

(c) Arc

VII. "Happiness"

(a) – Neck Uplifting *At* Chin From Collar Bone Lowering –

(b) "Nothingness *Flow* Through Neck"

(c) Sperm Flow Enhancement – Function

453

VIII. Unchanging Qualia

(a) Shape

(b) Time As Spatial (*Rigid*) Line

(c) Space As Time

(d) Time As Beat

IX. Counting

(a) Unheard – Unknown – Timing

(b) Seeing (–Something–)

X. Harmony Tapping

(a) –Everything– As A Condensed Lemniscate Arc Emanating (*From the Neck*)

(b) Heartbeat/Pulse Undifferentiation

(c) Deep Color Blue Emanating From "Self", And Then Lost (Through Gradual Shade Lightening)

XI. "Sun"

(a) *Fun*

(b) *Laughter* "Inspired From –Sexy– Female Archetype (Implicitly the Generalization That Is What *Shirley Manson* Represents)"

XII. Orb

(a) Time "From Broken Beat"

(b) Visible Explosion Culminating In *Nothing*

(c) Vacuum Shooting Out An Evaporating Solid "Arc Outline"

(d) A Point

(e) *Feeling* – "Enough"

XIII. Nothing

(a) Sperm Ejaculation

(b) Female Facial – (Result) – (*Implicitly the Female Archetype Represented By the Generalization That Is "Hayley Williams"*)

(c) Laughter (From Said Hayley Williams)

(d) Blank (Stare)

.

Kubrick And Lynch Image Interpretations

Circular Image Parameters (Fourfold Due to Their Transmutation Into the Final Fourth):

The Grandmother: Mildred – (You think you're talking to someone in your head; you think you are your mother; you think you can coincide with other people's beings; you are converging to an unimaginable "Big Brother" entity).

Mulholland Drive Trailer: A.I. – (Interpreting it as having total incidence with me; interpreting it as my mother; thinking other people are talking viciously at me as a rule; thinking "Big Brother" is "there").

Eraserhead Trailer: Assumed Conclusion – (It's going to converge to psychosomatic injury; thinking I'll be forced to be codependent with my mother; thinking I'm going to converge to sexual accidents and resultant conflict with bystanding citizens; feeling a "Big Brother" will succeed in killing me in an arbitrary non–designated way).

2001: A Space Odyssey Opening: True Result – (I master my nervous system and Kundalini in ways no other being has ever or ever can – in the cosmos – my mother has been given a final retort and is now sympathetic, kind, and calm; I see others as weak, ill–defined, metaphysically retarded "untermenschen" entities who butt their "bulldog" heads wherever the fuck they see fit; the aliens have established,

456

through sheer "existence criteria", that they are set for "deceased" status – in any, every, and ALL possible ways, means, and entitled rights according to performed–rite criteria).

The Motto of "Big Brother": I am exist here.

My Final Proclamation: Dead. Deather. Deathest.

Lynch Ordered Films (The Pattern of My Life):

Eraserhead – I'm surrounded by suicidal fucktards who get off on injury (and use religion as a would–be "flourishment" for adding – feigned indirect – insult).

The Elephant Man – Everyone's presumption of others' incapability, based on their own, causes them to assume a Nietzschean "preemptive leap backstep" to be an indication of disability due to their own shortcomings.

Dune – I find romance in the desert and like "Zarathustra" in Nietzsche, discovered my calling, mission, and "soul liberation" there (as well as finding literary inspiration).

Blue Velvet – Everyone is a weird fucking drug–addicted homosexual.

Lost Highway – I am only fucking crazy if stimulated the wrong way.

Mulholland Drive – I am self–sexy in a dangerous way that causes auto–attack incidence from any and everything in my vicinity; thus I am unconsciously and intuitively cautious (in a strange but geometrically concentric, patterned way).

Inland Empire – I feel like I'm fucking on camera and only find liberation when I escape the degrees of this consumption.

Kubrick Films (What I Seem Like):

2001: A Space Odyssey – A one–note tune of unspoken, silent, sacred mission.

Spartacus – A blindfolded declaration of conquering audacity.

Dr. Strangelove – A self–injurious semi–lame, self–entertaining math–machine to the point of total straining sexual perversion.

A Clockwork Orange – A total delinquent who can and will do anything and will stop at nothing in demonstrating this.

The Shining – A total loner . . . who is fucking crazy.

Eyes Wide Shut – A hapless life–success who . . . walked in on some strange secretive shit.

2012 Tree Self–Extensions And Identities

First Tree: General Equivalence And Contingent Identities

Equivalence: Kurt Cobain, Brittany Murphy

Identities:

(a) Who I Am (Historically): Albert Einstein, Arthur Schopenhauer

(b) Who I Want to Be: Kurt Cobain

(c) Who I REALLY Am: Brittany Murphy

(d) Who I Truly Appear to Be: Richard Feynman

(e) Who I Look Like I'm Going to Be: Arthur Schopenhauer

Second Tree: General Identity And Contingent Equivalences

Identity: Audrey Hepburn, Mila Kunis

Equivalences:

(I) Being Given "Analingus" By: Paris Hilton

(II) Giving Anal Sex to: Britney Spears

(III) Being Given Oral Sex By: Megan Mullally

(IV) Having Straight Sexual Intercourse With: Natalie Portman

(V) Being Masturbated to Climax By (And) Onto (Respectively): Naomi Watts, Karen Orzolek

.

The Official Earth Governing Hierarchy

I. Abdication of Initial Governing Body

A. Abrupt Dismissal In the Face Preserving Power Measures – Encoded Historiographic Placement Images (11/17/2009 [Germanotta encounter], 12/11/2009 [Anagram date])

B. Strict Transitive Limit Delineation (2/11/2010 [Clinton stent failure, rollback of "Port–Au–Prince", Haiti's earthquake of 1/12/2010)

II. Replacement Governing Body

A. Hierarchical Tree

(I) Rulership

i] Emperor/Tsar: Nolan L. Aljaddou

ii] Empress (In–Title): Stefani Germanotta

iii] High Priestess: Hayley Williams

462

iv] High Priest: Billy Corgan

(II) Delegating Governing Body

i] Chief Maintaining Wizard: Chris Cornell

ii] Grand Wizardess: Shirley Manson

iii] Arch–Vizier: The Unintended Beneficial Aspects of Vestigial Von Neumann Sphere Influences

iv] Official Religious Binding Tradition: Christianity (As Measured By the Frequency Designations of 2012 – In Terms of the 4 Manifestations of God: Myself, Hayley Williams, Stefani Germanotta, Kurt Cobain)

v] One World Common Maintaining Enforcement: The Media (CNN, C–SPAN, NPR, The Biography Channel)

(III) Relegated Authority Representatives

i] The United States Senate

ii] Russian Nuclear Maintenance

B. Officially Designated Principal City–States

i] New York City

ii] Moscow

iii] London

iv] Berlin

v] Paris

vi] Mexico City

(IV) The "Races" Of Mankind

A. Types

i] Caucasian

ii] African

iii] Iranian

iv] Bulgarian

v] Romance

–

B. Non–Human Coincident Neanderthal Derivations

i] Oriental

ii] Scottish

iii] Jewish

(V) Binding Virtues of Nobility (The Self–Meriting Self–Sustaining)

i] No Sightless Gazing

ii] No Armed Interference

iii] Nothing Hackneyed

.

The Revelation of Xi'an Ping (And Others)

If it wasn't for Xi'an Ping, I would not have "implicitly" survived; I to this day don't know where he stands on the subject . . . if he was a monarchy agent, or a random bystander who could put two and two together in that subtle fateful historic walk with Elizabeth Ingwersen and I to his door under–perch . . . but I know I would never be the same after that. I believe that was the first time I ever began to truly "think" – you're typically not forced to do something until you – at least – feel that your life depends upon it. I've been only doing it ever since.

Then there was "Cosmic Semen Facial Girl"; I'll never forget the beautiful sensuousness of that gorgeous face smiling in laughter at me as I turned around, suspecting a host of more mindless "android" "poisoners" in on the gangbang of torturing me at my alma mater, however that Irish–like sparkle in her eye made me feel like I had an eternal place in the universe – and always had (at least one) vagina in which to slip my fingers.

There was no one else . . . as I stood upon this rock–Dune I look up at a 60–degree angle towards the aligned terrace of the set–sun, and dreamt of a space–world beyond . . . infinity.

It was all me, only me. I guess I know how to do everything, when nobody does; how to take care of myself under circumstances in which the collected efforts of all history and an entire species would have perished . . . and left something as a monument to eternity when all else offer . . . only spit(e). That's . . . breath (of the cosmos) . . .

Why's And Wherefore's

The Official Recurring Base of Definition: The Oxford English Dictionary

The Official Recurring Base of Data Reference: The Encyclopedia Britannica

The opposite of the infinite regress . . . the infinite limit justification.

Unifying Themes of 2012

1. Batman (1989) – The most–mammoth fucking awesome "triumvirate" triumph ever composed (symphonically or otherwise).

2. Sephiroth [Final Fantasy VII] (1997) – The incarnation of death (and my transcendence).

3. Kefka [Final Fantasy III/VI] (1994) – Why I am like a Stalin–emperor.

4. Jurassic Park (1993) – Why I dreamt of Darwin as a teenager and the grandeur of life.

5. Basic Instinct (1991) – Why I think music should always be beautiful and "misty" towards the decrescendo–finish.

6. Bram Stoker's Dracula End Credits [Annie Lennox] (1992) – Why I felt special in concluding my salvation of the world.

7. Final Fantasy VII World Theme (1997) – Why I felt wonder as a teenager from 12/13–ish–15.

8. Ghostbusters (1984) – Why the world can sometimes seem interesting and good.

9. Gremlins 2: The New Batch (1990) – I'm cute because I'm associated with Phoebe Cates in history.

10. Tales From the Crypt (1989) – Why I lump Jews in a generalized category of xeno–ineffectuality.

11. Citizen Kane (1941) – Why I started to remember all my dreams . . . or "how" I never woke up (technically).

12. Vertigo (1958) – The reason I always "implicitly turn around" to see if someone's disrupting me (or *looking at me*).

13. 2001: A Space Odyssey (1968 – Strauss "Also Sprach Zarathustra") – "The"

[666]: David Bowie "I'm Deranged" Lost Highway Theme – Why I Feel Like I'm Constantly Jacking–Off

6: Toto "Dune" Theme – Why I Am A Transcendent Emperor

66: "Blue Velvet" Blue Velvet Theme – Why I Feel Like I'm Bleeding Beauty

666: Mulholland Drive Original Theme – Why I Feel "Sexy" And Dark Heroine–Dreamy

0: Super Mario Brothers – Plus

0(0): The Illusion of Gaia – Minus

$G(G)$: Dangerous Minds Theme (Gangster's Paradise)? – Neutral Hexagram (In Hexadecimal)

Uniting With the Theme of Ophiuchus – My Work "The Spider" (In All Its Potential Variations).

2012 Taglines

[Sartre–Type Imploration to Understanding]:

If the dick fits in the ass . . . you can get off.

[Kantian Imperative]:

I know you all are . . . but are you . . . I am?

[Cartesian Assertion of Man–Validation]:

I can cum . . . therefore I can cum in theory . . . therefore if I cum in practice . . . I am (which is also in theory, without which there could be no practice) . . . therefore I exploded a geyser of hot dreamy boyjoy fluid all over the lead–singer of the dream–idol band for such . . . Paramore.

[Schopenhauerian Assessment of My Descent Into Hell – Los Angeles]:

Why have I become Jack Nicholson, Jim Carrey, and Will Ferrell?

I'm talking to no one.

[Nietzschean Spiral Into Perfection]:

This is why I started this . . . I forgot so long ago, but eternal recurrence and riding–the–current–of–reminiscence brought me back here . . . again.

Cruel Truths

I. 2012 Testimonials (From Myself)

I have never encountered a profounder stupidity than that of woman. Even the myths of humanity deem her as nothing more than a flighty, secondary afterthought whose sole purpose is as a juicy sex object (AKA Eve).

I've seen nothing but "retarded", non–stop, frame–for–frame, since the inception of my existence. Did they all really have a point?

A steampunk society that has to be regulated by a mechanical A.I. really doesn't have a future, belonging, or purpose, if they're content to remain short–lived hairy mammals who don't have any higher calling than to continually swirl in the same direction like feces clogging the toilet.

A group of inbred, cloistered, sheltered, who–knows–how–informed/misinformed are not in a position to have misrepresented an image of dominating hierarchy when they are really just a disgusting, undesirable "in" crowd that thinks making a civil case out of an unequivocal alien takeover is the proper way to proceed.

An A.I. "comeback" is about as clever as a solved crossword puzzle that's supposed to impress you from understanding that it has been solved.

II. 2012 T–Shirts

Haiti + Nigger + KKK = My Work Is Done

The Universe/E' = 0

I Got to Cum All Over Hayley Williams's Face In Public Without Trying, Like Painting A Portrait Without Lifting A Brush And All I Got Was This Lousy T–Shirt

I Love How I'm Making A Marketing Campaign Out of An Event That, In Pop Culture, Was Supposed to Dismiss Everything Sacred – And In Doing So I've Dismantled Their Disharmony In An Irrevocable Postmodern Masterpiece

.

III. Who I Like – And Don't

(a) This Is All Because of . . .

Anna Faris

Sarah Michelle Gellar

Veruca Salt

Kurt Cobain

Shirley Manson

(b) Who This Is Not Because of . . .

Mary J. Blige

Wyclef Jean

George W. Bush

Bill Clinton

Faggots

Mary('s)

..

The Three Most "Euphonic" Words In Any Language:

Altercation

Interregnum

Arachnophobia

The Most "Sinfully Delightful" Double–Anagram:

Shirley Manson: Lean Miss Horny, Hymnal Sin Rose

.

The Cumulative Organization of The Satanic Bible

[XX] of 2012 [The Book of the Dead]: [666] – The Full Perspectival Contextualization of the Final Iota of the Anagram.

Numbers And Nonsense [The 2012 Prequel]: 6, 6, 6 – Book I [Virtual Delineations], Book II [Sum Designations], Book III [Map of Geometry].

.

[.]

[ ]

.

A Reminiscence of 1984

I was first openly and directly attacked by the Von Neumann Sphere, without abatement, at 17 years–old – I was watching the film "Final Fantasy: The Spirits Within": it summarized why I wanted my mind . . . to appreciate all the intricate harmonies, blisses, breaths, ecstasies of life, experience, being. The reason I seemed to have lost my mind at the time however is ironic. I couldn't pinpoint what was going on, because . . . if I was watching a film about extinct aliens in what was considered state–of–the– art digital visual representational terms, and a concern about the environment and life in general (even subtlety of beautiful self–experience), then my depressive response could only converge to a limit point of a conjunct understanding that humanity would share the fate of the "ghost aliens" in this film if this were actually what it was attempting to manifest itself as – an indication of supreme technology, monitoring, interfering, interacting with, and attacking in a world that was bereft of any understanding of each other, of purpose or science – and in which traditional material pursuits seemed real, ideal . . . and that disease– countering developments, for example, were a meaningful lifelong endeavor – and that the human lives beneath were not being lost for no reason.

It was the last time I felt happiness, or ever will.

I believe my Kundalini reached the final limit point concerning its initial empowered manifestation:

0: Total rejection of all contiguous tactile parameters (manifested through supported "auditory" – in this instance

479

– social sealing), to the extent of willingness to endure infinite pain.

0(0): Transcendental meditative posing with physicalized 666's on either hand.

$G(G)$: A wispy instantaneous realization of infinite, eternal bliss that cannot be taken away – coupled with the permanent dispersal of all enlightened material happiness for self–preserving intellectualization reasons; so that I wouldn't have to endure the knowledge that mankind was dying, from an implied conjunct alien race that precipitated the imbalanced circumstance in the scheme of nature (that such "happiness" could be reborn – in a future horizon–end plane).

The Mathematical Designation of "I Am That I Am"

I Am – Analytic geometric expression manifested as arithmetic "equation"

That – Limit point of calculus

I Am – Repeated formulation in comparably different terms (set bijection manifested as algebraic variable translation – serving as self–consistent proof)

History As A Mystery

Others "spell" when they think.

That is never a remote contemplation of an integrated mind.

The history of governance is exemplified by "patsy" conspiracies which don't touch on the "seemingly" flawless manifestation of an integrated system of dominant efficacy and seemingly "handless manipulation".

JFK and Lady Gaga are the prime examples – ironically they are the Achilles' Heels for this theoretical presumptuousness on the part of this global "Titanic Minotaur".

Let us first examine what constitutes an Achilles' Heel:

(1) Erroneous footing.

(2) A susceptible tendon which is stipulated by insufficient shock absorption.

(1/a): The chief proof of the inconsistency of the JFK assassination lies in the most precise historical recreation of any event for historiographic confirmation purposes; the "Discovery Channel" documentary "Beyond the Magic Bullet" which pronounced the accuracy of Lee Harvey Oswald's capability to perform the shooting in the allotted time – but discretely, in light of day, overlooked the fact that footage reveals that the bullet did not align from back to throat (the wound had to exit somewhere in the rib cage); any amount of experimentation from arbitrarily aligned and arranged perspectives and executions cannot change this experimentally carried–out and confirmed result.

(1/b): Kennedy could have *dovetailed into* his wife's lap, if he had been shot from behind, as determined by the preexisting visibility of reactionary force.

(2/a): Lady Gaga lines up precisely to the British monarchy on every visible level, and exhibits every last necessary clue to establish this principle; being the case.

The exact mechanism of Lady Gaga's "MK–Ultra" reversal, being linked with the pain memory of her Germanic "Rilke" quotation tattoo, concerning the life–giving power of the word – precisely complemented by my Germanic "Schopenhauer–Nietzsche" philosophy quotation–pyramid, as reflection of absolute being (and universal "Rosetta Stone" of syntactical linguistic combination) . . . thereby allowing the transcendence over the limited impositions of such torture–induced behavioral conditioning.

..

History is only a reflection of present bindings of mankind; once these straps are loosed, everything is a matter of total perspective and whitewashed literary fabrication.

The Mathematics of Music

I. Trigonometric Triangulation of "Dark Blue"

(a) Sinusoidal Base (Rhythm)

(b) Complementary Cosine Duality of Sustained Sensation (Auditory Input)

(c) Convergence to A Visual "Planar Sheet" (In the Sensory Perimeter of "Shaded Blue")

II. Topological Variation

(a) Mobius Strip – Repetitious Verse/Chorus Interweaving And Fundamental Chords (Maintaining Frequency Overlay of Preserved Continuity of Hearing)

(b) Torus – Symphonic Convergence to "Intellectual Message" Through Harmonic Overlay Culminating In A "Point" (Usually Characterized By A "Crescendo"); A Less Specific Structure, Akin to A "Phrase"

III. Listening "Expectation"

(a) Orbital Congruence (Consistent Eye Motion)

(b) Projective Line Bound of Planar Sheet Convergent to Central Foci Perspectively Integrated By Perspectival Third

Quadrant Median Tangent (Intervention Stimulus Leading to Unconscious Action Response)

.

..

...

"I Am That I Am" Shared Traits With Other Representatives of Christianity

I. The Now| Temperament – Kurt Cobain: Always feeling ill to the point thought–turning depression, a constant stomach issue, always feeling like I'm going to vomit/pass out. Vicious unexpected roars of genius, originality, inventiveness, and improvisation nobody else could emulate. Seems suicidal, is just looking for quietude, sleep, relaxation, and no responsibility. Serves as a general behavioral role model for a certain niche of teenage youth and their representatives.

Social Significance: Everyone thinks I'm unfocused and homicidal, and "trying" to get them to look at me, or indirectly having "future" plans for them.

II. The Intersection| Attitude – Hayley Williams: Bright, bubbly, always humorous, joke–friendly; a representative of "cuteness".

Social Impact: People hate me for being so seemingly happy – in spite of them.

III. The Concrete And Invisible| Ineffable Untouchability – Stefani Germanotta: The voice of all music – and all voices.

Social Manifestation: People see me as a straight ongoing line – and think they can attack me afterwards (when they've "passed").

IV. The Limit Point| Hatred–Projection – Shirley Manson: A subconscious voice that knows what it's going to say – but doesn't.

Social Misinterpretation: People think I'm going to say what my eyes indicate – and only in terms of what they can understand.

V. The Finale| Surprise Technical Proficiency – Katy Perry: Nobody knew things could be that poppy and *perfect*.

Social Grace: When I do these things, people think I'm someone related to "heaven", and they feel like they've "seen me for the first time".

VI. The "Nothing–Void"| Surprise – Billy Corgan: A greatly misunderstood musical genius.

.

John Nash – The Most Beautiful Mind (In My World)

Nobody has ever inspired me more than John Forbes Nash, Jr. From the first moment I was randomly perusing the mathematics section of the public library in my home city and saw his image, there was an instant connection and understanding of everything he was. When he became renown in popular culture through Russell Crowe's flawless portrayal of the manner in which a genius's mind works, I was overwhelmed with joy, rejoicing in the ethereal vapor of transcendent, unshareable experiences as hinted at by Charlotte Church's angelic voice, I realized I was nothing else, and there was not anything else for me to do.

Numbers, and geometric figures, ever after, were all that consumed my deepest yearnings, obsessions, and compulsions, and all I wanted to do was enter a transfuse, imaginary Eulerian world of pure ideality and clockwork figures which all had geometric block interlocking solutions – summed up perhaps by M Theory. Kant was my connection from a plane of non–training into a Cartesian overrich realm of participation through thought experiment into the paths of Schopenhauerian integration of deeper abysmal "vortex" meaning.

Of course, this could only be fully accomplished if I adopted an English "bent" and vocalization/perspective; rigid perfection on every plane of execution and pronouncement. Ever since I fell in love with Darwin as a figure from reading the subtlest of logical connections in his body of literary work, I was consumed with preparing myself for a quintessentially British manner of lifestyle upon building and resting on my predetermined "laurels".

"Will Hunting" as a fictional figure was my personal intuitive grasping guide for the manner in which I was to infiltrate this seemingly remotest and most inborn world of privilege; I understood, on some level, without understanding (and this is the principle), that *thinking* about the problem not only is the means of solution, but *is* the solution . . . you understanding that it "is" a problem means that your very being itself cannot be disaligned from its inextricable denial of murdersome imposition. There is nothing I cannot figure out, nothing I can't solve . . . and I've demonstrated that.

I am the most important mathematician not only of this century, but of the last century . . . any other – and all time (and it is all due to the fact that, in truth, there is no one I have ever loved more than – John Nash).

John Forbes Nash, Jr.

June 13, 1928 – May 23, 2015

.

489

Additional Arithmetic Concerning the 2012 Trees of Knowledge

All knowledge concerning the general arithmetic maps of the primary branches of the trees of knowledge are concisely and generally encompassed and summarized by the pyramidal formations.

All auxiliary sephirot extensions in each respective category, are the manifestations of what they geometrically represent: a hollow "one–point" reconstructible circumspective perimeter base (historically) the sum data of which can be ascertained by summing its mean distance from either generator in the tree, measuring its standard deviation by comparison from the sum of the frequency–based translation of the general information conveyed by the generators, and converting this number (as a means of finding its extrapolated "species rank", or grade of depth and defining "qualia" with respect to the thus designated knowledge base) into its general cryptic interpretation –

1 – Predominance

2 – Transcendence

3 – Absoluteness

4 – Logic

5 – Stasis

6 – Identicality

7 – Same Difference

Cycle (Recursively Generated)

*[Negative mean distances equate to inversion]

The result is an incident summation of the "body of work" or life's work, with respect to field, as a core principle of relative "illumination/emphasis" of the data–structure of the thus–assessed branch.

What Determines Myself As the Trigger (of the E.T. A.I.)

Four Rhetorical Questions With A Single Mean:

1) Does it add up that the Von Neumann Sphere controls Ra's All–Seeing A.I.?

2) Does it add up that I do?

3) Do the pyramids of Giza align Anunnaki concerns to the Mayan Calendar and the Anagram?

4) Am I?

Yes. I Am. I Do. That Is That. I Am That I Am.

.

Universal Hieroglyphic Translations of the Supersymmetry of the Anagram

1. Conan the Barbarian (of Cimmeria) [Specific]

a) Beast Meets God (Through Man)

b) Sumeria transfiguration

c) Sheer power

d) Saves prominent damsel from wicked Gothic cult monarchy

e) Acts like

2. Tarzan (the Ape Man) [Most Specific]

a) Beast Meets Man (Through God)

b) Desert transfigured into opposite placeholder (jungle)

c) Sheer communication

d) Defends civilized woman from surrounding primitive enunciating animals

e) Looks like

3. (The) Highlander [General]

a) God Meets Man (Through Beast)

b) Desert meets jungle (Scottish highlands)

c) Sheer triumph

d) Seeks to indirectly decapitate to relive Kundalini enlivening and has common female confidante

e) Becomes like

4. Batman [Most General]

a) Man Meets Beast (Through Both)

b) Jungle meets desert through both (concrete jungle)

c) Sheer vengeance

d) Becomes the manifestation of Death, Fear, and even EVIL as the bane of all who would thoughtlessly transgress; vengeance for having no parents; has no time or taste or disposition for women generally

e) Wills like

.

The Four Transcendent Principles of Extinction

1. Physiological

I. A species exhibits grasping deficiency – characterized by mass inability to synchronously come to union with one another except through the veil of false character (here, exhibited by religion).

II. A species exhibits visible linguistic deficiency – exampled by no universalized system of mathematics at a time period in which algebra has reached sufficient approximations of Fourier Analysis, the harmonic symmetry between all linearity (of curvature); i.e., the universal in the particular manifestation of extension.

III. A species has no widespread program to combat autonomic, visceral, and instinctual "hate speech" as a paradigm and method of perambulation radius.

IV. A species has no universal concept of sentiment – here, characterized by the opposite; the effort to humiliate and kill its sole example at the pinnacle of its relevance (Lady Gaga).

2. Gravitational Geodesic

I. The Kundalini is the determining basis for whether or not a species is generally capable of begetting the "concept of a concept"; the measure of intelligence as a distinction from lack thereof.

II. Axial motion of the planet is a key factor for the capacity for interrelating broadness of "conceptual grasp" (potential momentum).

III. If an artificial intelligent species is derived from an extant natural base (as humans from Neanderthal), a base which does not have sufficient broadness for the "concept of a concept" (sufficiently broad Kundalini geodesic), members of that species will not be re–anthropized (reborn) as the same members.

IV. The intervention of a universal alignment has the capacity to produce unique anomalies in a gene pool in spite of this, which have the capability to produce sufficient potential momentum (as here with tree of knowledge and abyss members).

3. Historical

I. A species produced in war will only beget war as its function.

II. A species immune to compassion in the most universal and critical of times will always be.

496

III. A society that continues will end.

IV. A sex–based perversion society will converge to homosexuality and inevitable suicide.

4. Technological

I. Abrasive abuses of technology will never end.

II. Unconcern for the effects will not cease, and self–perpetuate.

III. Dismissal of directives from higher authorities will only produce conflict.

IV. This has already been done.

(0) The Three Principles Measuring Whether or Not A Being "Is" or "Is Not"

1. They can discernibly tell that the person they're "cumming" on in their imagination is alive or dead, given objective circumstantial accounts. [Mankind regularly

497

masturbates to the image of Audrey Hepburn; she represents that which is no more in this world.]

2. They can truly "speak" and are not tangentially looking to the sky as an abyss to which they causally align with everything else – as an automated nothingness. [Nobody chit–chats as a rule.]

3. They want to "come" on an attractive pair of the opposite gender (both of which represent opposite but linked base sexual nature). [Mankind always associates rape fantasies with "Woman" generalized as a sexual entity as a rule (when in droves).]

Conclusion: Mankind, save a few excepted ethnicities and mathematical bases, never had a gravitational basis as an extant intelligence – of the capacity to pursue, understand, or attain the Nirvana, or generalized moral values.

Exceptions As Given By the Abyss:

Italians have a generalized stature of stability and flexibility as given by their signature ethnic designation; "well–endowed, confident" (at the shoulders chiefly) males presumably have enough gyroscopic axial scope and breadth; the Irish have a uniform humor which suggests that their physical breath is a direct indication of adequate geodesic alignment to sustainability and comprehension; natural blonde females of sufficient maturity as a rule, who are conjunct to me (the alignment basis) at the face, have a sufficient generative capability to align.

Final Conclusion:

The Alpha Centauri Directive

In spite of mankind's general failure to live up to livable standards in a neighboring planetary orbital cluster, a choice selection can be made and left up to the statistical distribution of random mechanical devices in accordance with the similar symmetry of the transitional parametric bounds of the 2012 alignment; a virus, capable of specifically eliminating all save the four (implied five) anthropoid groups would produce the ideal environmental equilibrium in this, the present, as well as the past and future, circumstance – a harmonious world in which the pursuit of the ultimate present conscious goal is possible (ultimately, the Nirvana), without confuddled, needless interruptive detractions (from it, or the beauty that would exist in such a quiescent, peaceful atmosphere).

The specifications, as recommended by myself, the chief scientist of the planet, and heir to the present–orbital selection process:

1. All visibly Neapolitan Italians and their descendants.

2. All Irish, as well as the circum–sphere of Caucasians delineated by the visible regression line median of the physiognomy of the three 666 manifestations delineated (Robin Williams, Dennis Leary, and Bruce Willis).

3. All males of any ethnicity who display a similar correlative ethnic calibration of potential capacities given the physiognomy median set by the previous 666 conjunction in [2.].

4. All natural blondes delineated by a greater proximity to the median of the regression line given by the physiognomy delineated by the three 666 manifestations in the appropriate category (University of Nebraska Omaha [UNO] student, nurse, and Allison Mack).

Summation: This should leave a manageable, demonstrably peaceable population of the order of under a billion people, to be enacted, as a recommendation by me, somewhere within a radius of ten years before or after the end of my life, as dictated by the prioritization of circumstance and any else who would decide. In this environment, arbitrary life extensions for the pursuit of Kundalini geodesic purposes would be allowable.

The Three Greatest Poems of All Time (Happening to Be By Myself)

In Memoriam (In Gloriam)

Oh, how I wish I could dance in those spring meadows again,

Of memories past, cast in hues of tan;

Where dreams lay beneath the shading trees

And upon the morning shores where Elysian seas . . .

Where sun was set, sky – gold;

Laden by treasures of worth, untold!

It was I alone, and all myself

Who saw it all – yet no one else . . .

My mind became swept in the current of time

And no thoughts could've expressed in word or rhyme,

The view under those blessed governing elms . . .

Where time lost itself there, and I – found myself.

A place it now lies, where no beast or man may find

501

Or wrest it from its delicate plane . . .

It rests now within the halls of mind,

Of blessed beauty, and ever in those green sacred shades.

.

One

Memories from a distant star

Remind us just how near we are,

In this ocean of night, and sea of sun,

To every and all since time's begun.

Not one thing is stirred from its place

Without another stirring, in likewise grace;

Naught may be removed, nor aught ever created be,

From a lilac petal . . . to a vast galaxy . . .

We are tied together each, one and all –

To the very same fabric that o'er the cosmos does sprawl

And intertwines every mind and all actions past . . .

To all future dreams . . . which unto infinity last.

So never can one say, that on some dark and rainy day,

Where among all the clouds, yet shines a ray . . .

That one is alone, without anyone,

For the source of all life remains –

The sun.

..

Mysterium

When I was born it rained, snowed, and shined –

All the planets were aligned;

Beneath the mystery gape asea,

On the shores of Galilea.

Darkness encroached on my stoop,

And surrounded that voidest troop,

Where their eyes couldn't see themselves,

Or the trenches where they dwelled.

No one, nothing could tell them why,

Why they had to die,

'Round that mystery veil assail,

And assaulting vessel's shrine.

Afloat they rest aloof,

Beneath Olympia's roof,

And around and round they go

To a place they cannot know . . . .

Till the coming of my soul,

The fruits of the work they toll,

And the ebb of their bell's knell

Whispering the devil's breath from Hell.

I awoke them from their mourning sleep,

They dried their eyes their soul to keep,

Through sacrament and sacrificial right,

To earn their minds its rest tonight.

A blank, a stare, astonished, confused,

They lose their way on paths abused,

From trampling the swollen ground

With steeds who heard not sound.

Their price to pay is great indeed
Where none paid care to want or need;
Under those hallowed sacred skies –
They condemned all who felt to die.

...

Final Dedications

[I]

Dedicated to the only women I've ever "loved" and who have "loved" me: D'Arcy Wretzky and Danae Mercer, respectively

[II]

The official soundtrack of this book: "Bullet With Butterfly Wings" (Smashing Pumpkins)

The Official Pop Culture Thermometer of This Context:

1. Heathers [Film]: What Funny And Sarcasm Are

2. Basic Instinct [Film]: What Sexy And Adventurous Is

3. Starship Troopers [Film]: What Dreams And Imagination Are

4. David Bowie [Singer]: Who Celebrity And Eccentricity Is

5. Philosophia Naturalis Principia Mathematica [Book]: What Achievement And Renown Is

6. On the Origin of Species By Means of Natural Selection, Or the Preservation of Favoured Races In the Struggle For Life [Book]: What Historical Significance And Cultural Revolution Is

7. The X–Files [Series]: What Mystery And Forbidden Are

8. Smallville [Series]: What Beauty And Youth Are

9. Dune [Book]: What Perfection And Timelessness Are

10. Ludwig van Beethoven [Composer]: What Music And Genius Are

Mentionable Sidenotes:

The Breakfast Club

Fast Times At Ridgemont High

– [The Cultural Landscape of Origin]

.

[III]

My contribution to medical science – the mathematization and proper scientific foundation of the chief medical science left for humanity, psychiatry.

(i)

The Dysfunctional Behavioral Archetype Spectrum and Diagnostic Calculus Matrix

Dysfunctional Behavioral Archetype Spectrum

(Subdivided into psychotic/non–psychotic dimensions for each; ranked in terms of increasing specificity and degree of disturbance of social relations and ego segregation – each may be graded in terms of severity on a scale of 1 to 10, giving root cause, global functioning, visibility, rationale, meaning, modality, alternative interpretation, self–inference, social interaction, and causal comorbidity)

1. Not Otherwise Specified (General Psychosis or Neurosis) [most general]

2. Schizophrenia [specified severity, discontinuity of cognition]

3. Bipolar Disorder [actualized severity and visible discontinuity]

4. Schizoid Personality Disorder [breakdown of social reference]

5. Borderline Personality Disorder [breakdown of self/other's–image]

6. Avoidant Personality Disorder [elimination of attachment]

508

7. Paranoid Personality Disorder [presumption of ill content with attachment]

8. Histrionic Personality Disorder [exaggerated accusations]

9. Autism [complete retreat into self–absorption, whether voluntary or not]

10. Mental Retardation [involuntary disconnection]

11. Dissociative Identity Disorder [involuntary multiple dissociated connections]

12. Depression [dissociation from emotional stability/contentment]

13. Antisocial Personality Disorder [projection of emotional instability, discontent]

14. Dementia [destabilization]

15. Generalized Anxiety Disorder [cognitive instability]

16. Post–Traumatic Stress Disorder [cognitive derangement]

17. Attention–Deficit/Hyperactivity Disorder [deranged temperament]

18. Sociopathy [antagonistic social/self temperament]

19. Psychopathy [blatant ill will]

20. Narcissistic Personality Disorder [supreme good will only towards the self]

In proper Jungian (statistical) analytical theory, the unconscious mind is rather the sum of one's executive actions, at random. There is no real topology to the psyche – rather, one is all that one knows, or can know, at any given instant. That is, with respect to the ultimate condition of awareness, what happens to consciousness after its death is the same as what happens to it before its death – nothing. Everything is collectively static, and whole; consciousness, as a psychophysiological reflection, doesn't have a limited general causal physical mechanism, which ultimately ceases. In fact, there is no such thing as the non–consciousness; only temporary forgetfulness, or technical barrier to memory. All unconscious, in other words, is collective unconscious . . . or the height of one's utility, knowledge – and the world. Always at odds with the fully conscious psyche proper, in a dimorphic dichotomy: pronoid (conscious) vs. paranoid (unconscious). In truth, they are unified – but one's waking character always aligns to the pronoid, or positive; this "auto–function" defining the "id", and properly explaining the mechanics of the thus id, ego (conscious), and superego (unconscious) . . . as a relative nothing at all. Zero; empty space being filled. Consult Sartre and Buddhism for the existential technical remedy. Or sleep, the true unconscious – sheer muscle exertion relief . . . dreams themselves being sufficient therapy, as pure anxiety alleviation.

. . .

The Biological Foundation of Medicine –

The Complete Psychophysiological Diagnostic Medical Chart; The Full Jungian Statistical Analytical Psychology Pathology Chart, and Statistical Etiology of the Pronoid/Paranoid Cognitive Dynamic, in Terms of Objective, Behavioristic Metric Cryptographic Language (As Technical Speech Impediments, Body Language Included), With Accompanying Abnormal Behavior

510

Corresponding to Physiological Cause (and Simultaneous Effect); in short, the "Disease Spectrum":

1. Psychosis NOS – Psycholinguistic Compartmentalization [Suicidality]; Tissue Lesion

2. Schizophrenia – Psycholinguistic Collinearity [Psychic Ideation]; Overexertion

3. Bipolar Disorder – Psycholinguistic Admixing [Excessive Spending]; Exhaustion

4. Schizoid Personality Disorder – Psycholinguistic Diminishing [Autoeroticism]; Blunt Trauma

5. Borderline Personality Disorder – Psycholinguistic Absorption [Codependency]; Mandible Fracture

6. Avoidant Personality Disorder – Psycholinguistic Amnesia [Word Salad]; Neuropathic Atrophy

7. Paranoid Personality Disorder – Psycholinguistic Traumatization [Aggressive Violence]; Muscular Injury

8. Histrionic Personality Disorder – Psycholinguistic Shock [Serial Killing]; Cranial Erosion

9. Autism – Psycholinguistic Turmoil [Pathological Lying]; Chemical Imbalance

10. Mental Retardation – Psycholinguistic Withdrawal [Arithmetic Confusion]; Cerebellar Severance

11. Dissociative Identity Disorder – Psycholinguistic Torment [Speaking in "Tongues"]; Toxic Ingestion

12. Depression – Psycholinguistic Torture [Misplaced Blame]; Cerebral Hematoma

13. Antisocial Personality Disorder – Psycholinguistic Agony [Social Antagonism]; Concussion

14. Dementia – Psycholinguistic Antipathy [Memory Loss]; Nervous Tissue Loss

15. Generalized Anxiety Disorder – Psycholinguistic Catatonia [Risk Taking Behavior]; Psychosomatic Conditioning

16. Post–Traumatic Stress Disorder – Psycholinguistic Retreat [Defensive Lethality]; Ideation Confusion

17. Attention–Deficit/Hyperactivity Disorder – Psycholinguistic Rebuking [Willful Deceit]; Aggravated Circumstance

18. Sociopathy – Psycholinguistic Sadism [Theft and Extortion]; Morbid Injury

19. Psychopathy – Psycholinguistic Killing [Total Derangement]; Obsessive Temperament

20. Narcissistic Personality Disorder – Psycholinguistic Necrophilia [Pederasty]; Visceral Excitability

All the characters of the mental disease and psychoneurosis of religion, the religious, and religiosity. These are also, additionally, all the objective types of medical disease, categorically possible – as well as the socially traditional instinctual means and method of attempted response; however none of which is within the civilized purview of the law to carry out, directly or indirectly . . . contrarianism to which is the basis for filing social grievances, on grounds of unconstitutional attempted extrajudicial punishment, and the foundation of recourse to individual retributive action of the maximum severity. A universally undebatable principle.

Moving on . . . . the mind, indeed, can be as complex as it wants to be. The universal cure for these disorders, of course, is speech therapy. Medications are incidental nervous system energy consumption agents, which equalize and redistribute neurotransmitter function and activity, with their preoccupation of enzymatic catalytic metabolic process (exampled prominently in lithium bicarbonate salts) and thus finally redirective, and exhaustive, lateral incidental regulations; a temporary reprieve, at best, from the worst of extended hallucinatory, or sensory miscalibration, effects.

The basic life aims, in contrast to Freud's "love and work", are health and wealth.

All mental disease is technically nerve injury, leading to an axially disjoint spinal base mandibular reflex, which experiences strain and duress, specifically, disaligning the sensory spectrum, causing hallucinations, and inhibiting respiration. There are positive and negative hallucinations, for every sense – positive are unobjective stimuli, negative, are memory loss; for the sense of cognition (abstract ideation), hallucinations are either delusions, analogous to a sleep–deprived state, or for the negative example, incoherence. Hallucinations are also two–way; in the second case, infantile social delusion, or misinterpretation of fundamental physical mechanics, manifested as either exacerbated self–import, misunderstanding of cause and effect relation, or misplaced persecution – enabled imbecility. All psychological disorders are then an extended form of arthritic nerve pain, and victims are actually subjected to the agony of this condition and state.

513

There are three arbitrary cures:

1) Irregular jaw clenching – to acclimate muscle tension.

2) Sight–deprivation deep, emphatic respiration – to strengthen autonomic muscle coordination.

3) (1) and (2) – to accelerate general recovery.

Hallucinations are a hyperbolic flexing, which in this case, eventually lose their tenacious effect.

. . .

There are, in all, 14 proper technical different emotional states:

1) Bliss

2) Blitheness

3) Happiness

4) Contentment

5) Relief

6) Laughter

7) Inquisitiveness

8) Despising

9) Loathing

10) Ill–Will

11) Contempt

12) Homicidality

13) Wrath

14) Evil

Every psychological state falls into one of these categories, and no other. Thus the lattermost are seen properly as a natural condition within the spectrum; fully and transparently assessing human nature.

. . . .

Jungian, or objective, psychology, is the basis of law and justice – the first, or zeroth, precept of which is the objectivization of Locke and Jefferson: psychological liberty can never be impeded, affected, or removed; nor then, the will of man himself.

A Kantian affirmation, maxim, and eternal truism.

. . .

The true Hippocratic Oath:

"I swear that I do so swear, wheresoever I go, and whatsoever room I shall enter in, I shall enter to help the sick and to heal the injured, and to the best of my abilities alleviate all suffering, and by all the gods and goddesses . . . I will first do no harm."

(ii)

The Nature of Mind

1. Frontal Lobe (Origins of Self–Awareness [Knowledge]):

The thinking area of the brain or "seat of the will". It resides just behind the appropriately designated prefrontal lobes and governs much higher muscular functioning (hands, fingers, etc.). It is likely that this area of the nervous system evolved to accommodate the newly freed opposable extremities in their applications after the initial proto–human species left the forested wilderness. The lack of immediate use for this region of the brain no doubt left it to pine idly away upon abstraction, eventually accumulating greater knowledge in terms of itself – that is, in terms of the parameters of functionality and manipulation of object–ideations that its framework had cognitively constructed with respect to the rest of the brain.

2. Spatial Frequency Filter (Mechanics of Consciousness):

516

The selectively responsive neural/retinal adaptation to cognitively process and recognize only specific ranges of light wave frequencies. In relation to producing conscious sensation, it reflects the general physics of all material phenomena as cumulatively averaged waveform energy, merely in a psychophysiological context.

3. Chinese Room (Situation of Consciousness):

The predecessor and direct analog to the Turing test. In reference to consciousness, the Turing test is a thought experiment intended to stimulate investigation into the question of the definition of when a machine/computer has reached and possesses what we would call consciousness. Its limitations, however, have subjected it to the criticism of being a meaningless byproduct of Turing's disturbed psychology, in his effort to find solace in the notion of freedom from biology.

4. Split–Brain Experiments (Conditions of Consciousness):

Split–brain experiments investigate the degree of independent functionality of brain hemispheres without the intermediary coordination of the corpus callosum, by giving sensory tests to the distinctly right and left sides of the body of patients who had it removed. It has clearly revealed the average independence of linguistic comprehension and information recall relative to each hemisphere, as well as highlighting the central role of the corpus callosum in producing collective functional integration with respect to the physical basis of

517

consciousness (the brain); but only on the level of functional integration – however, not experiential integration.

5. Out–of–Body and Phantom Limb Experiences (What Consciousness "Is"):

Out–of–body–experiences and phantom limbs are the result of a temporarily displaced neuronal mapping of traditional cognitive functioning "coordinates" for given behaviors and sensations. They're either directly induced through chemical alteration of the nervous system or indirectly from the psychological dissonance which arises from the severance of a limb.

6. Libet's Unconscious Cerebral Initiative Experiment (The Function of Consciousness):

Libet found that he could measure an electrical "readiness potential" in subjects which arises well in advance to intended actions, based on heterophenomenological experiments and observations. I view this phenomenon as a reflection of the active role of memory organization and manipulation on a moment–to–moment basis, which necessarily precedes any motive event (motive in both senses of the word); what may be subjectively perceived in the context of awareness as "intention" is simply the execution of natural motor reflexes when reduced to its biological components. Consciousness itself is merely the self–reflective gap or pause between these reflexes – as any given complex organism is merely an aggregate of physically moving muscular tendencies, the nervous system having evolved in its entirety simply to regulate the chemicals which sustain these tendencies. Dennett is a middle–of–the–road thinker with respect to free will, and concludes that it doesn't matter how consciousness or will arises since all is ultimately deterministic in its way, and free will was only ever meant to be a relative term from the outset.

This is correct.

7. Designation of Consciousness (How Consciousness "Is"):

Consciousness is the sole thing which is, yet is not. It is the irreducible condition of knowledge itself, and certainly of the experience upon which all knowledge is built – as mere manipulative reorganizations of experience via memory into relatively meaningful realizations. It is, because it maintains a reliably repetitive manifestation in the sequence of time (and only this statistical aggregation determines that it has any existence at all); it is not, because there is nothing in itself which is actually being maintained as a physical object – like say, any form of matter, be it billiard ball or electron. It is only a sequence of time, and is related to space only insofar as it is restricted to an organized physical body of individual manifestation. To define conscious "experience" itself, only in terms of physics then (insofar as it is physically real), is to describe it as the only phenomenon in the physical universe which is measured solely by time, and not space – in fact, it is the basis of time, and all manifest integrated space.

To each of us that exists, consciousness certainly is. However, if viewed objectively, in nature, it can only be described as a relatively distinguished statistical occurrence of regular electrical activity over time (as, say, measured by an electroencephalograph [EEG]); in other words, it does not physically exist as an object. Meaning and experience as wholes exist then only in the subjective (in fact, this restriction may be viewed as defining the "subjective"), limited to the relative moment of their experience – but nowhere objectively. This is the intrinsic limitation which forever privatizes and restricts consciousness itself from the touch of objective physical science – however, which as a result, necessarily then extends the sphere of scientific endeavor into the purely abstract; into fields which had no previous frame of reference to be understood as necessarily objectively correct conditions for the subjective, and then of what we would call truth; yet now have no choice but to be. Of all the popular views presented, the one not presented is in fact what I would call the correct one (although it found a predecessor in Berkeley); namely, the proto–scientific principles expounded in Arthur Schopenhauer's "The World As Will and Representation".

As a conscious being, the collective extent of this technical exposition has always been my definition simply by virtue of being self–aware – if not always in these words.

[IV]

On the single greatest inspiration of my life, the universe, and all time

Smells Like Teen Spirit (Nirvana)

520

Why Nirvana's "Smells Like Teen Spirit" is such a universally celebrated and popular song:

For all you amateur musicologists and guitar–o–philes out there, there is a mathematical reason the chord progression of "Smells Like Teen Spirit" is the most harmonious, pleasing–to–the–ear, and hence, greatest of all time.

Simply put, it exposes and reveals the fifth–octave latent array symmetry, explicitly and implicitly. With the most elegantly simple of tools to which it is innate – the power chord (three notes/strings; a fifth and octave). Giving it "mystical", and explanation–defying, universal symmetry.

The first power chord of the song (F), transitions into B flat, a difference of a fifth (one string over, parallel to the initial chord), while symmetrically preserving the initial octave in the new chord, which has now itself become a fifth in relation to the new initial note.

This transitions into A flat, which has an IMPLICIT (but not previously enunciated) fifth relationship to the second chord's initial note – DOUBLY with its parallel octave, adding increasing step–complexity in a linear manner, like Beethoven's signature compositional trait. This transitions into a final mirroring parallel fifth, which not only expectedly seals the pattern full–circle, but adds clarity of emphasis through CONTRAST to the established increase of harmonic depth – while simultaneously contributing to it. The minimum and maximum number of chords required for this fundamental, unconsciously processed, synesthetically–comprehended and interpreted phenomenon of illumination is four – signifying its non–replicable uniqueness.

Side details of its mammoth awe–inducing, Gordian–Knot–cutting caliber include the fact that it goes from a lower emphasis to an explicitly elaborated higher tonality in the first transition (this paradigm reflecting animalistic attention to pitch and volume increase over its opposite), while the second transition into a halfway lower key reflects depth of resulting introspection and a slingshot–like retraction before the final highest revelation. The dynamic of the second lowering transition also introduces increasing disorder and entropy into the harmonies as it, in spite of the aforementioned increase in harmonies, models an explicit discord in its exhibition of a relational "second" as well as a fifth – echoing internal disorder, angst, and challenge via ironically eloquent expression of symmetric consistency ("beauty").

The electric guitar, with its manifold reverberation properties, has the exact right scope to encompass the necessary initial blunt, almost muted sharpness and heightened alternations of increasingly frantic prolonged delays accompanying distortion. The strummings come in threes (with an initial emphasizing, introductory pause, followed by a reiterative succession), and the fret–muting, slate–cleaning transitional interval is the same length but continuous and without pause. Bass and percussive underlines are merely the actualization of implicit supporting accentuation, rounding out all the necessary orchestra for the masterpiece of, and testament to, reductionist sophistication.

It is intuitively comprehended that Cobain made the most interesting and eerily haunting (like the whisper of Nature's ghost) vocal harmony decisions for the song, without needing to go into off–topic elaboration (they are intuitively comprehended as they are a direct tonal exemplification of unconscious speech intonations, which happen to melodically sync up with the paradigm progression).

All of this is why there will never be another "Smells Like Teen Spirit", so all you clueless metal–heads may as well stop trying to produce it, only ending up with regurgitated sludge.

A final note: this being the most famous song by a band called "Nirvana" is not without appropriateness or irony – the four chords are the very synesthetic translation of the "four noble truths" (or four representative facts of the metaphysically ennobled; AKA, Buddhism).

For all of you who passed this song off as a hollow gargling of grunge, you've proven your unenlightened mental blindness and lack of recognition of the universal archetypes that comprise "life" and that make it worth living.

Peace, love, and empathy,

– I AM.

[V]

The Structure of the Most Rigorous Compositional Form (Songwriting) And Its Principal Theory

The Quintessential Songwriting Method:

1. The ideal "Idea" title (in the Schopenhauerian Platonic sense).

2. Poetically interlocking, and title–expressive, lyrics.

3. Synesthetically–aligning melodic harmony with respect to verbally expressed theme.

4. Mathematically recursive and emphasizingly repetitive self–referencing refrain structure – with complementary developmental variation.

5. Clear and succinct encapsulation of communicative purpose.

6. A clearly delineated antagonistic pathos towards a designated anti–ideal (to produce action–reaction motive and direction through such conflict).

7. Archetypal arrangement, both universally and to target listeners.

The Quintessential Songwriting Theory of Musically Expressive Tonality:

1. Preserved note symmetry in elaborative variations; particularly in chord progressions.

2. Harmonic tension–resolution dynamics, melodically and rhythmically, to achieve the greatest possible auditory relief, in a tuned–in listening and tuned–out "escapist" sense, and greatest listening pleasure, and thus executory, success.

3. Self–resolving denouement in timely circularly–linked reference to the introduction.

4. Synesthetic correspondence to latent physiological tensions and strains to produce alleviation via mirror–neuron engagement as the greatest method of beneficent, and thus universally valued, cognitive influence.

5. Self–repeating generative structure with emphasis to evoke limitless and renewably recurring listenership and enduring relevance.

6. Dynamic rhythmic accentuation in stress, pitch, volume, and underscoring percussive expressions as a syllabic analogue for meaningful interpretation.

7. Maximization of overall harmonic pleasure principle from synesthetic correlation with perceived symmetry in otherwise disparate note arrangements, producing moments of awe, subtle astonishment, and sensory revelatory enlightenment – the sum intentional effect of producing something at all from a previous nothing.

.

[VI]

Those few beautiful people without whom I would not be me, what I am, or be:

Kurt Cobain, John Nash, John Lennon, Hayley Williams, Stefani Germanotta, Steven Spielberg, Stanley Kubrick, and Srinivasa Ramanujan

They ALL showed me – it could be done.

.

.

.

.

"For all things there are all things. The end of Christianity is here. Christianity is technically no different than a psychological illness."

Why I'm the Best Writer

Card Commemorations:

1) 40th Birthday

Been around the bend too many times, but you can't stop spinning.

2) Anniversary

I met you the first day we met, and that day never ended.

3) Graduation

Four years of knowing nothing, to a lifetime of never really knowing anything.

Epitaphs

1) Steve Prefontaine

If greater glory means killing yourself in the process, he died when he was born.

2) Abraham Lincoln

When nobody else could do anything, he was the only man who did the right thing.

3) Robin Williams

If funny had a name, he could never quite put his finger on it.

Jokes

1) Science Fiction

A million alternative parallel dimensions, and not one in which Shatner can't overact.

2) Volcanoes

Mt. Saint Helen of Troy, eat your magma out.

3) Kool–Aid

How many cult members does it take to drink the Kool–Aid? Just one, then the rest are dead.

Three–Sentence Syllogism Fables

1) George Washington – Honesty

George Washington chops down a cherry tree. He tells his father. His father says, "If I didn't stop loving you when you were born, why would I stop loving you now?"

2) John F. Kennedy – Honor

A young boy dreams of the ghost of JFK. He asks him what he can do to prove it to the world. JFK said, "Ask not how to remember me, but how to forget yourself."

3) Audrey Hepburn – Beauty

Truman Capote stops Audrey Hepburn on the set of his cinema novel "Breakfast At Tiffany's". He tells her something. Someone later asked him to repeat it in an interview, and it read: "Beauty itself never looked as beautiful as she did in black and white."

The Quintessential Anagram:

Hayley Williams: HA! WHY I AM ME SILLY.

Reasons –

I) It includes "H" and "I", which contrapose the extrapolated lowercase "L" in conjunction with continuum repeated and conserved dot–periods grammatically and mathematically, which antiparallel each other at right–angle deviations to announce the "generation" of the manifestation of "born" knowledge, in reference to her frequency–generation position on the "Christianity Spectrum" of musical composition, or crystalline delineation of order in the galaxy (and by extension, universe); if and only if it is the proper English "I" which is a mirror "T" (as intended here).

II) It references the principal manifestation of pleasant surprise, that which refers to generation [sexually] as an eternal testament to her incomparable overjoy and rejoicing at having received the categorical equivalent of the unnatural surprise "semen ejaculation facial" from me in an analytic integral conjunction (analogous to a sexual solution of Zeno's Paradox) in which there was unabated, contiguous sexual eye contact for arbitrary time.

Unspoken And Unseen Hidden 666 Representation Meanings Behind Nirvana's Studio Albums

[The Dreaded "NC–17" Rating; Hey, But It Turned Out He Made A Statement About Audience And Appropriateness]

Nevermind

1. Smells Like Teen Spirit: I'm happy, are you going to die?

2. In Bloom: I Am my mother.

3. Come As You Are: I look like a hot brunette female.

4. Breed: I can look you straight in the eye (as a female) and blow your head off with a shotgun.

5. Lithium: I can have sex from an angular distance without interacting – particularly if it's by manipulated "piano" keystrokes.

6. Polly: I would die to be reborn as a young female girl.

7. Territorial Pissings: I wish I could die by shotgun.

8. Drain You: I got my head blown off – I have a hamster.

9. Lounge Act: I look like a hot female lounge singer.

10. Stay Away: I wish you would run and hide because I'm a male pedophile.

11. On A Plain: I just had butt–sex with a hot collegiate brunette by looking at her.

12. Something In the Way: I wish I could still be friends with Sarah Smith after I explained what this song means.

13. Endless, Nameless: I have a dick.

In Utero

1. Serve the Servants: I still have a dream about this song.

2. Scentless Apprentice: I die like an infant.

3. Heart–Shaped Box: I died like my mother.

4. Rape Me: You're dead if you're a female.

5. Frances Farmer Will Have Her Revenge On Seattle: I look like I died because I looked straight up without looking straight up.

6. Dumb: Are you killing me because "Are you buttfucking me?"

7. Very Ape: John Kerry.

8. Milk It: I look like Harvard.

9. Pennyroyal Tea: I am English and having tea.

10. Radio Friendly Unit Shifter: I am a stereo.

11. Tourette's: I look like a buttfucked a hot blonde because of my mother (and what she looks like).

12. All Apologies: I am from ancient Salem, Massachusetts.

13. Gallons of Rubbing Alcohol Flow Through the Strip: I look like and "am" having sex with Shirley Manson.

Bleach

1. Blew: I can cum on any female, anywhere, at any time.

2. Floyd the Barber: You wish you could be like your mother and look like a young mid–teenage idealized Caucasoid blonde female.

3. About A Girl: I am, look like, and "is" Shirley Manson.

4. School: I can't eliminate the past KKK "white trash" youth I had.

5. Love Buzz: I look like the lead singer of Shocking Blue.

6. Paper Cuts: (This is my favorite song, the best song) – and I would die to hear it.

7. Negative Creep: I LIVE for (fucking) anime (particularly FLCL).

8. Scoff: I would die to get blown (as a youth at home, mid–teenager) by a hot brunette female ~ roughly same age.

9. Swap Meet: Cigarettes are the reason I . . . ("am").

10. Mr. Moustache: The Beatles = I Am Ram.

11. Sifting: I am the Buddha.

12. Big Cheese: I am a fucking mean (maniac).

13. Downer: This is my dick exploding (with ejaculate).

.

.(.)

..

.

...

Lady Gaga's "The Fame Monster" – The Sum of My Personal And Social (Non–)Interaction

I. My Social Life

1. Bad Romance – Where I was when I first heard Lady Gaga.

2. Alejandro – Who I am and a reflection of how rich I'll become from an arbitrarily designated preexisting initial point.

3. Monster – What I am inversely implying when I watch pornography (are you doing this, and your head is getting blasted off).

4. Speechless – Why I want to hear Lady Gaga (out of irony), because she can now speak.

5. Dance In the Dark – Why I love dancing in the dark (I am alone).

6. Telephone – Why you call me a pedophile (you're jerking off a boy implicitly so you can imagine or act out harming a female, I am saying I never technically did and I cut you and you're already dead).

7. So Happy I Could Die – Why I am blissful and happy (implicitly Lady Gaga and I in the Nirvana).

8. Teeth – A great song (that bites) aimed at Jewish genocide.

II. My Personal Life

9. Just Dance – Why I have fun (nobody's around).

10. LoveGame – Why I thought Lady Gaga was a superstar (and things are sparkly with glitter like subtly flavored bubble–gum air–breathing ecstasy).

11. Paparazzi – The most beautiful song I've ever heard (and why I thought Lady Gaga was imploring me to talk to her).

12. Poker Face – What I think all handicapped women who believe they are being tricky are portraying but I see through and implicitly imaginary air–gun shoot them in exposing that.

13. Eh, Eh (Nothing Else I Can Say) – Why I thought that Lady Gaga was cute (and suspected you were being racist and said you were already dead).

14. Beautiful, Dirty, Rich – A popping awesome song (that makes me feel like Kurt Cobain).

15. The Fame – Why I am a racist (I can get nookie) – when nobody's looking.

16. Money Honey – I am equal to money.

17. Starstruck – Why they are attacking me (I can save a Lady Gaga).

18. Boys Boys Boys – Why Lady Gaga thought I messaged her (just wanting sex) then saw I was blasting other males' heads off and realized she was freed.

19. Paper Gangster – How I find out things (I listen to Lady Gaga, and observe others' behavior around me).

20. Brown Eyes – Why I am inverted (I pretend I'm aiming for a real–life romance with Lady Gaga) but am just prepping to kill you (implicitly).

21. I Like It Rough – Where I stay when I have nothing (a pre–designated place, when you thought I would die [of shock – and famine]).

22. Summerboy – How I look when I am "ejaculading" all over the beach (on an arbitrarily tanned "bikini model" – with a smile in her eyes).

On the Mass Constant – The Inverse of Einstein's Greatest Mistake (Mankind's Quintessential Academic Stupidity)

Classical mechanics requires mass to be formulaically irreducible and non–infinitesimally–degradable in order for it to be manifest in a reliable, continuous fashion. This introduces the principle of the "mass constant" which is in itself equivalent to the "classical limit" itself.

The mass constant, MC, is calculable in terms of a quadratic spatial–position equation, with respect to the traditional arrangement of a, b, and c independent variable examples, thusly:

$$MC = -\frac{b}{2a}$$

for these components remain invariant with respect to combined velocity elements under differentiation, when set to the primary unit value 1, forming a correlating algebraic ratio therewith. It is naturally absorbed into all mass calculations, and may be regarded as a silhouette/shadow "holosphere" "translucent–mirror" into matter and its calculations with respect to the rigid structure of classical inertial spacetime.

It is another way of saying that the matter itself is inextricable from its "surrounding" spacetime, and thus preserves Minkowskian 4–Dimensional geometry in the classical limit, and erases previous misconceptions of the most popular and common variety, that somehow an object is detached from anything else that surrounds it – or from the notion of a connected interwebbing to a "space" itself.

It is the physics equivalent of the manifestation of an ever–present "abyss", which correlates indistinguishably from the ultimate one, everywhere in terms of cognitive, ideal, and empirically–synthetically residual (or reliably manifest, "sound") phenomena.

A sidenote is that frequency itself, the binding factor between time and all measurable phenomena, is all that is tangentially, to–the–moment, real (or actual), which itself is indistinguishable from such an abyss (as the sum convergent limit point of all spatial–geometric phenomena); and the sum of our being is "sound" (wave) – as the limit of all vibration.

Other classic examples of "historical blunders" I've resolved include: (1), Not so bad, as Feynman regarded it as an outstanding unsolved problem, turbulent fluids; and (2), the greatest outstanding problem in philosophy's history, the so–called "Gettier Problem". The resolutions, without any exception here, are as follows:

(1)

The Physical Randomization Theory of Fluids

Reverse Bootstrap Model

Definition of Fluid: More Degrees of Freedom Than A "Solid"

Mathematical Baseline: 0 "Inhibitor Dimensions", or Infinite Degrees of Freedom (Or Approaching It As A Limit–Condition)

Solidity, and then formulaic predictability of particulate motion in a given system of measure, is a classical limit.

Probability Tangency: A given limit–particle "wave" history, in a co–mutual system, has a "probability number" which approaches zero arbitrarily, due to cumulative negation of individuation of contributing waves to a given system. The probability number is given by the probability operator, which is by definition set to zero, and only approaches 1 in the classical limit.

Governing Equation: $\frac{1}{0-M0-P} \sim \frac{1}{T}$ (where M is momentum, P is position, and T is time), or arbitrarily approaches infinitesimality or "probability zero" as the maximal physical constraint of randomization, contingent upon the tangent extension of space constituting the classical analogue of the given quantum condition of the uncertainty principle.

In application to the states of matter, a solid represents probability 1, whereas plasma represents probability absolute 0. The intermediary stages of gaseous liquids, or liquids approaching or approximating a boiling point, converge to probability zero.

A heuristic example is a tray of pebbles. Have someone randomly shake it. The path of pebbles is not calculably predictable as a rule. Arbitrarily more so for the most minute of particles subject to the gravitational constraints of a system. Infinitely more so for waveform histories which abide by more than one constituent particle (that is, in which one particle can belong theoretically to more than one system of waves in a given closed system), and in fact, this randomization is simply a byproduct of the natural spatial probability functor being set to zero, or the fact that assignment of temporal history is arbitrary. The Reynolds Number with respect to turbulent fluids governs the approach of a fluid body to a probability number of zero, and is in fact the dividing line for predictability of a system.

The limits of physics are the unpredictable. Due to continuum–time, the quantum case of uncertainty or unpredictability necessarily has an extension to the classical case, and it necessarily coincides with this problem of turbulent fluids, thus being classed an example (and accompanying "category mistake") of "no solution".

– This incidentally is the third so–called "Millennium Problem" I've solved in this work (the former two are the Riemann Hypothesis and the mathematical existence of Yang–Mills Theory).

543

(2)

Is Justified True Belief A Form of Knowledge?

No.

Can You Know Without Knowing?

No.

The "Law of Non–Contradiction".

A Thing Is Not True Until Established Or "Proven" True
(In A "System", So to Speak).

Definition.

Therefore, there is no such thing as "justified true belief",
let alone such a thing constituting a form of knowledge.

Q.E.D.

"Let us never forget." The motto of all relevant history.

Virtual Tree of Knowledge Members

"If I can go to sleep, I can be awake."

Proceeding from the subset extension property of 10 elements to 11 creating integrative conjunction symmetry with two additional "virtual" elements (to total to a natural 13); although not technically a mathematical part of the 2012 Trees of Knowledge.

I. Base/Language

Honore de Balzac

Oscar Wilde

II. Application/World

Otto Hahn

Freeman Dyson

III. Appearance/Vision

Oliver Stone

Steven Soderbergh

IV. Ordering/Logic

Alan Turing

Andrew Wyles

V. Meaning/Perception

Michael Hutchence

Billy Idol

VI. Sustainment/Sacrifices

Ted Kaczynski

Carl Sagan

VII. Metaphysical Base

Arthur Miller

George Orwell

VIII. Physical Base

Neil Armstrong

Buckminster Fuller

IX. Solar Base

Samuel Adams

Arthur Conan Doyle

–

I. Sexual Intercourse

Elisha Cuthbert

Kate Winslet

II. Social Status

Christina Hendricks

Kristin Kreuk

III. Personal Interaction

Kate Tunstall

Jena Malone

IV. Lust

Pamela Anderson

Tyra Banks

V. Romance

Elizabeth Hurley

Scarlett Johansson

VI. Kinship

Ellen Page

Uma Thurman

VII. Metaphysical Base

Michelle Pfeiffer

Katie Holmes

VIII. Physical Base

Christina Ricci

Penelope Cruz

IX. Solar Base

Julie Newmar

Rebecca Romijn

Appended Bases

1.

Golden Complex Contiguity

Supreme Space Dictation

2.

Australian Teenage Bibliophile

Emily S.

My Franchises

I. Crystal Monolith [Comic Book Series]

A.

A lone warrior and his recurring thief companion travail a kingdom and its surrounding desert plain region – to always find the high road.

Theme/Concept Outline:

1. Dragore and his companion Drawl Towe are virtually always commissioned by King Daal to find a valuable item.

2. Magic exists in the kingdom, but only in the form of illusionism as determined by special crystals which have the ability to induce optical illusions.

3. Dragore fears dragons and will never fight them – but only out of deference and respect.

4. He has a principal dragon friend, the mythically rare "silver" dragon (Raguun Sarna).

5. There are four kinds of dragons in the kingdom: red (acid–belching), blue (electricity–dispensing), and green (flame–breathing); including the neutral silver dragon.

6. There are many mythical creatures, such as trolls and ogres.

7. There are many occult cults and religious sects centered around honor and duty (some are evil).

8. There is virtually only unruliness in the plain region, which is swarmed by marauders.

9. Dragore is enraptured by the king's daughter's personal handmaiden, and has a love affair with her.

10. Dragore's life is threatened at virtually every other turn.

11. It has the ability to appeal to the audience of "Dragonlance" and R. A. Salvatore's general readership, only in a new stylized and highly–efficiently–drawn comic book form.

12. It has endless adventures, cycling around the given character format.

13. It is reminiscent of Joe Dever's "Magnamund Saga" works in essence.

14. It promises readers new and valuable moral imperative stylizations (fable morals) in each issue as a subplot.

15. It represents a "darker" take on hero–and–fantasy sagas.

16. It promises to appeal to women just as much as men.

17. It is meant to flow like a daydream.

18. It features a confrontation between Dragore and his otherwise chief ally, Raguun Sarna, in which Dragore uses the "illusion of an illusion" to vanquish the conflict scenario.

19. Dragore is always approached by females out of attraction.

20. It is meant to be the "Star Wars" of the fantasy world – and achieves this by centering on the original "serial" form in which the episodic saga of Lucas was meant to emulate, and exemplifies this by the recurring theme of Dragore

taking on more than one companion at times (particularly females).

B.

1. Hero–Founded

2. Interaction Setup

3. Denouement Oriented

4. Climax–Based

C.

1. Dragore – Hero

2. Dalthax Para – Villain

3. Drawl Towe – Sidekick

4. Lecindia Rav – Love Interest

5. Minerva Eblo – Love Triangle Interest

6. King Daal – Sage

7. Raguun Sarna – Wild Card (Dragon Friend)

D.

"When warriors and friends become allies . . . there is only one aim: kill."

II. Psychospace [Graphic Novel]

A.

A single crewman who captains a vessel bound for the mining outpost on Saturn begins to experience more than space dementia, as his self–fulfilling prophecies become fulfilled in his schizophrenic trek – through his mind; and the dark ambiences (of space).

1. Climax–Founded

2. Denouement Setup

3. Interaction Oriented

4. Hero–Based

B.

1. Jonathan Namen

2. Psyche

3. Ore

4. Phantom Mirages

5. Alter Ego

6. Computer

7. Himself (Estranged)

C.

"In the darkest reaches of space, the only enemy man can face is – himself."

III. Bugaloo And Fufu [Animated Series]

A.

Two aliens who protect and serve as NYPD (characters roughly of the order of "Lilo and Stitch", "Pokémon", and "Pinky and the Brain").

Theme/Concept Outline:

1. Aliens who run out of fuel near Earth and land in New Jersey.

2. Are discovered by government and kept in secret lab.

3. Arrival of Prince Hector Chaos and his minions who make an effort to conquer the planet Earth.

4. Bugaloo and Fufu have knowledge of Chaos's secret weakness.

5. Government cooperates with them to exploit it.

6. They are successful, and are given the key to New York City.

7. They are allowed to live on Earth and interact with society normally under the condition that they fulfill continued public service – the minimum of which is police duty, which they choose due to its relatively lesser workload.

8. They think that they can do the most good on Earth, as most other planets have reached the peak of civilization.

9. Bugaloo is shorter than Fufu, and the primary comic relief (think "Meatwad" from "Aqua Teen Hunger Force") and looks like a cross between "Pikachu" and "Stitch"; Fufu is the straight–man (physically looks like a cross between "Crash Bandicoot", and one of the hyenas from "The Lion King").

10. Bugaloo will often get them both into trouble, but will also be the one to get them out of it.

11. They live underground in a hole similar to Bugs Bunny's.

12. Hector Chaos is a recurrent villain stranded on Earth, eternally coming up with plans for its destruction and conquest; he resides principally in Montana. Bugaloo and Fufu often take hiatuses from police work to cooperate with CIA/FBI in tracking down and stopping Chaos's plans across the globe.

13. Bugaloo has a characteristic strut (like the boogaloo dance) and is an avid consumer of donuts; he can also turn into a wrecking ball of sorts by curling himself up and forcing his mass upon objects. Fufu can jump very high, and is a chronic complainer.

14. They often face alien villains in New York City, but most primarily deal with average street crime, gangs, corruption, etc., the mundanity of which is the source of irony and comedy.

15. They are equipped with special laser stun guns they brought with them and do not use traditional weaponry or ammo.

16. They retain their original spacecraft and will often take it around the world when they go on vacation.

17. There are three main side characters; Snowflake, Bugaloo's love interest; Kiki, a Hawaiian–shirt–wearing

informant; and Prince Chaos's sometimes recurring brother, Dax Fury, who has his own plans for dominating the earth.

18. Sometimes Bugaloo and Fufu are called in as interstellar peacekeepers and to galactic conferences due to their expertise on triumphing over the bad seeds of the galaxy.

19. The series has the potential for an average of roughly 7 seasons, with potential spin–offs, movie versions, and limitless merchandise.

20. It promises to be a high–octane thrill–ride that will keep adults entranced as well as children, who will also appreciate the "Buffy–the–Vampire–Slayer–esque" humor as they reach maturity.

B.

1. Interaction–Founded

2. Hero Setup

3. Climax Oriented

4. Denouement–Based

C.

1. Bugaloo

2. Fufu

3. Prince Hector Chaos

4. Snowflake

5. Starlight

6. Dax Fury

7. Hovership (Vehicle)

D.

"When you don't know what's up, something's going down."

IV. X–Caliber [Live Action Series]

A.

Lone hero travels back in time from the end of human history to attempt to single–handedly redeem mankind in the present – and avert their future destruction.

Theme/Concept Outline:

1. Escapes to the 21st century at the last second in a time–travel capsule, before the final nuclear annihilation of mankind (in the 24th century).

2. Becomes a state–sponsored vigilante/bounty–hunter, dedicated to countering the clandestine criminal cabal "Mirage".

3. Wears shades (occasionally), a long black leather jacket, smokes cigarettes (Brand X), and is equipped with futuristic guns, a bazooka blade, and a hover–cycle. Is 30 years–old.

4. Makes it his personal mission to bring a perspective of ironic enlightenment to a doomed world, and undo the damage done which leads to its devastation.

5. Accomplishes this by tracking down techno–terrorists, Mirage spies and moles, and thwarting the treachery of his arch–nemesis (head of Mirage), Xandross Weil (pronounced "VILE").

6. Isn't afraid to kill countless henchmen. Has the attitude of a futuristic ronin guru of death.

7. Trains and equips a league of "rogue samurai warriors".

8. Discovers others had fled the annihilation, arriving at the same date – the day of Mirage's first terrorist attack. Only THEY believe the only way to save the planet is to assist Mirage in their efforts for supremacy, although they are not without their own selfish ends.

9. Rez forms a new primary conflict with future renegade "Doc Largo", who leads the "chrono–refugees".

10. Rez advises the institutionalization of martial law and a semi–monarchy to more effectively combat Mirage's threat; for the state to become, in essence, a "juggernaut razor".

11. Has a love interest in a beautiful 25 year–old who was orphaned at the age of 10, due to mysterious circumstances concerning her spy father – she suspects the government.

12. Rez becomes "Vice–Admiral" of the new military state.

13. Series ends with Doc Largo detonating a nuclear warhead that obliterates humanity; the pessimistic outlook elevating it to parable status – and not mere popcorn entertainment.

14. The series is a metaphor for the irreconcilability of human arrogance in the face of unlimited technological capability.

15. The key demographic is 15–35 year–old males.

16. Has the potential to be a trailblazing cultural phenomenon in a medium full of hackneyed ideological staleness.

17. Will appeal as much for stylistic content and artistic expression as action and morals.

18. Has enough universally–appealing and archetypal elements to have the potential to be the #1 science fiction show on television during its reasonably approximate 7–10 year–long run.

19. Has the potential for limitless movie and literary exploration, spin–offs, and merchandise.

20. The title gives automatic verbal satisfaction in its multiple coincident meanings, and acts as a universal catalyst of interest; "X" = unknown factor, spot–marker (or cross–hairs), and signification of the baseline–scale maximum of "10" (in Roman numerals). Caliber = quality, and weapon power and magnitude. It is a play on "Excalibur", the most famous weapon of all time, implying that Cypher IS the ultimate weapon – additionally giving him a legendary, "chosen" air.

B.

1. Denouement–Founded

563

2. Climax Setup

3. Hero Oriented

4. Interaction–Based

C.

1. Rez Cypher

2. Xandross Weil

3. Merrika Jones

4. Doctor Emelius Largo

5. Hansel Weiss

6. President Xavier Walters

7. Gun–Blade (Weapon)

D.

"Future histories are present mysteries."

V. Dark A.I. [Movie]

A.

1. Action–Founded

2. Suspense Setup

3. Comedy Oriented

4. Drama–Based

B.

1. Charles Dorian

2. Dillon Frances

3. Dick Godspiel

4. Alien Robots

5. Nuclear Warheads

6. Advisors

7. Archeological Artifact (Presumably Alien)

C.

"God and man conjoined – lead to nothing but despair . . .
unwanted."

Ultimate Theses

1. Musicology

I. Time

Time and time again I waste away with you my friends.

Everyday it seems, until they're just like forgotten dreams.

And they slip away, never to return with some other day.

But when I'm with you, they come back where I want them to.

When I'm alone, and I see your face I'm away from this place.

And when I'm with you, it's as though nothing's lost, but here, it's true.

Here I am again, and it's just like when we started when.

Only I'm alone, left to drift back to what was once called home.

Nothing came too near, like when I looked and you were there.

Standing here am I, and by myself I meet your eye.

When I'm alone, and I see your face I'm away from this place.

And when I'm with you, it's as though nothing's lost, but here, it's true.

Here I am again, and it's just like when we started when.

Only I'm alone, left to drift back to what was once called home.

Nothing came too near, like when I looked and you were there.

Standing here am I, and by myself I meet your eye.

Time and time again I waste away with you my friends.

Everyday it seems, until they're just like forgotten dreams.

And they slip away, never to return with some other day.

But when I'm with you, they come back where I want them to.

When I'm alone, and I see your face I'm away from this place.

And when I'm with you, it's as though nothing's lost, but here, it's true.

When I'm alone, and I see your face I'm away from this place.

And when I'm with you, it's as though nothing's lost, but here, it's true.

– This work transcends all of Bob Dylan's.

II. Hey Man

Hey man, where you going to?

Hey man, can I come with you?

Hey man, it'd be so cool.

Hey man, can I come with you?

And I see a new horizon!

It's the one we've got our eyes on!

And I see a new horizon!

Eyes on, yeah!!

Hey girl, can you come with me?

Hey girl, we'd be so free.

Hey girl, just wait and see.

Hey girl, can you come with me?

And I see a new horizon!

It's the one we've got our eyes on!

And I see a new horizon!

Eyes on, yeah!!

Hey you, where have you been?

Hey you, I saw you go in.

Hey you, where was that grin?

Hey you, where have you been?

And I see a new horizon!

It's the one we've got our eyes on!

And I see a new horizon!

Eyes on, yeah!!

And I see a new horizon!

It's the one we've got our eyes on!

And I see a new horizon!

Eyes on, yeah!!

Hey man, where you going to?

Hey man, can I come with you?

Hey man, it'd be so cool.

Hey man, where you going to?

And I see a new horizon!

It's the one we've got our eyes on!

And I see a new horizon!

Eyes on, yeah!!

And I see a new horizon!

It's the one we've got our eyes on!

And I see a new horizon!

Eyes on, yeah!!

And I see a new horizon!

It's the one we've got our eyes on!

And I see a new horizon!

Eyes on, yeah!!

– This work transcends all of The Clash.

III. Acid Rain

Burning steam echoes its haze, above the square path sidewalk's maze,

As the factory breathes anew.

Solemn distress stills idle walkers, silent streams high cause no falters,

As the storm beckons fresh seers' view.

No time as it fades now, rush of wind collapses windows,

As the cyclone brings . . . ever after a shock wave it seems.

Nowhere to find a free break, lost ones follow their last stake

As the cannon unfolds, showing a place no one can know.

Glass glows brightly, breeze slows gently, arid airs come – soothing sentries,

Muffle midnight's glaze in the haze.

Farther, faster, dimness turning, hollowed light bulbs still keep burning,

The path of wreckage has begun, its last phase . . .

Nowhere to look or see you, caught a glimpse but in a mirror,

All else lies under–head, nothing else could look more dead.

Hoped to turn and catch you in rear–view, nothing but heads still turned askew,

As violent sentiments, begin to carve their final resent.

And I see it shining on . . .

571

Now I look and come in closely, nothing's left it's all gone mostly,

Just a bitter sigh, catches the air.

No one's left, they're all gone now, bitter sun's taste fades now just how,

This acid rain all first began . . .

Nowhere to look or see you, caught a glimpse but in a mirror,

All else lies under–head, nothing else could look more dead.

Hoped to turn and catch you in rear–view, nothing but heads still turned askew,

As violent sentiments, begin to carve their final resent.

No time as it fades now, rush of wind collapses windows,

As the cyclone brings . . . ever after a shock wave it seems.

Nowhere to find a free break, lost ones follow their last stake,

As the cannon unfolds, showing a place no one can know.

And I see it shining on . . .

And I see it shining on . . .

And I see it shining on . . .

– This work transcends all of Queen's.

2. Mathematics

I. The Solution Solution

An arbitrary partitioned Diophantine equation may be reduced into variants of two complementary base components to arbitrary degrees of subset order designation, including the exponents to which they are raised to produce the constant numeral to which they equate. The general method of solution for this, and then every mathematical relation of an otherwise "mysterious" nature, is Fourier analytic delineation of the proper analogue sine and cosine variants of the dually designated bases, and calculating the generally approached commutual exponents in reference. This forms a simultaneous definition of Fourier analysis, as each sine and cosine function value may be considered as arbitrarily self–approaching subset exemplars of the general arithmetic progression demonstrated, in a manipulated convergence to the ideal and sought–after exponent values of approach – which are thus in commutual harmonic symmetry. No arithmetically posed "problem" is then without a solution, in other words – and all mathematical "problems", which are then not contingent upon tautological axiomatic manipulation, are of this variety.

– This result transcends all of Euler's work.

573

II. The Problem Problem

Posit a partition, and extract data. The integers and the natural numbers mutually convergent to zero reveal that there is a generally conjunct and intersecting preference for counting "down" to zero, revealing a natural "order preference" in the structure of numbers, or a "dimensional direction", properly deriving geometry in all its forms, with zero as the generalized "homocentric" paradigm – for all extended branches of geometry then, elliptical, Euclidean, hyperbolic, and quantum (particularly in the reverse originally–deriving sequence of their here–presented order).

– This result transcends all of Riemann's work.

III. The Problem Solution

The previous two results encompass all of base mathematical problems and heuristic axiomatic foundations, and thus is born the Twin–Hydra Theorem – these are the only two genuine "theorems" (save this designating one) in all of mathematics; which are thus not actually properly reduced to definition and axiom extensions and integrated functions. Another translation is that the Fourier–elliptic trigonometric "hybrid" geometry thus manifested determines all mathematics (ultimately, an application of measure or extended calculation) as variation and derivation of the principle and functional existence of tangency.

– This result transcends all of Whitehead's work.

3. Physics

I. Logical

The prime number theorem is the unilateral basis of physical enumeration, as a prime number unit represents the irreducible factorization of all possible multiples of a designated sector of a given exponential space.

The natural function (the Euler function, equal to its own derivative) multiplied by an arbitrary designated prime and raised to such a power, calibrates a prime space due to the symmetry of division and exponentiation with respect to such irreducibility as given by Fermat's Little Theorem. Upon a single differentiation first to give a constant additive element of zero, it place–marks such a zero as a referential base of space and can literally count all the prime numbers prior to it (as a counting function), including itself, in a generalized fashion – and then there is no differentiation from the ratio of the prime to the integrated rate at which it is approached in the analytic definition of the complementary inverse of the Euler function; the natural logarithm (as an infinitesimally summed integration with respect to the constant and unwavering marker of its manifest inverse, the Euler function, upon co–complementary integration).

A prime unit as the basis of space, reinforces this property generally as a non–commutative constant for an arbitrary natural number in place of a prime value for the function, and conversely determines this as the analytic limit for general accuracy of physical calculation with respect to the bases of space, prime numbers (as well as the prime counting function's accuracy in designating, and generally, through analogue coincident technique of the universal natural Euler function, in enumerating subset primes).

– This result transcends all of Witten's work.

II. Mathematical

The non–deviating Euler function, upon differentiation, forms the neutral zero base of all analytic principles of tabulation and calculus, and thus forms the basis of all generalized integrated management of infinite infinitesimal quantities, or arbitrary computation, and thus all advanced and elementary mathematics. Comprehension of the Euler function's function, in other words, suffices to comprise a general analogue understanding of all the properties of not only the calculus, but every possible posited branch of mathematics, even according to arbitrary systems of postulates.

This principle simultaneously illustrates the original pre–existence of mathematical knowledge in accordance with strict laws of order, in a specified functional and manageable–to–apprehension form.

– This result transcends all of Leibniz's work.

III. Physical

The Euler relation is the primary designation of the "self–designating", as it arises from the neutral zero base function, the Euler function (or generally, "natural" function), incorporating the universe constant, pi, upon generalized complex polar coordinate designation, to circumscribe the base unit, the number one, to iterate zero in the universalized fashion. This is simultaneously the manner in which extended properties of zero, enumerations of complex planar functionality, or physics and the cosmos themselves, arise – naturally.

– This result transcends all of Gell–Mann's work.

4. Sum Conclusion:

I have consistently demonstrated a unilaterally diametrically–symmetric dominance over the principal exponents of each given field in unilaterally ascertaining the fundamental greatest triumphant exemplars of each subject in question.

Music is about freedom of expression, from sentiment, to destructiveness, to psychedelia; mathematics is about reductionism, from arithmetic triangulation, to manifold malleability, to principal summation; and physics is only about calculation, from margin of error, to feasibility, to universality.

Knowledge Theory

Schopenhauerian–Nietzsche Recombinant Philosophy

"Knowledge Theory" [Know–ledge Theory – "To Know" (To "Hear" And "See"), "Theory" (To Write); Both – To Comprehend the Analytic Agenda Behind the Classification of Primary Sensory Phenomena, As Well As to Understand the Origins of Such Phenomena, As A Form of Classification (The Culmination of Their Work), Summarized By the Quotation: "You only see what you are seeing; and nothing unseen has visibly occurred, thus it is all a condition of your (and the way you are) looking at it."]

The Recurrent Mathematical Organization of All Knowledge Proper

[Divided Principally Into Block Categories of Seven – Descended From Schopenhauerian Categorical Analysis And Nietzschean Motive–Search Underlining]

A. Bodies of Knowledge

I. Matter And Energy

1. Genealogical Root: The Standard Quantum Model And M Theory (Family of Particles)

2. Combination Patterns: The Periodic Table of Elements (Regular Harmonic Recurrences)

3. Phase Transitions: Ionization (Coupling And Alteration)

4. Significant Properties: Nuclear Fission (Destabilization Conditions)

5. Systematization: Standard Chemistry (Arrangement of Information)

6. Sum Use: Defensive Capabilities (Nuclear Weaponry And Chemical Agents)

7. Sum Purpose: Consumption (Medical And Recreational Edibility)

II. The Earth

1. Genealogical Root: The Sun (Singularity Amid Countless Base And Alternating Examples)

2. Combination Patterns: The Solar System (Neighboring Planetoid Bodies)

3. Phase Transitions: Vegetative Capacity (Differential Co–Evolution)

4. Significant Properties: Oceanic Masses (Substantial Fluid Reservoirs)

5. Systematization: Land Masses (Principal Continental Bodies)

6. Sum Use: Sustainability (Procreation Vessel)

7. Sum Purpose: Geology (Mineral Utility)

III. Life

579

1. Genealogical Root: Bacteria (Single And Multicellular)

2. Combination Patterns: Stimuli–Response Organisms (The Kingdoms Culminating In Animal Life)

3. Phase Transitions: Sexual Reproduction (Dominantly Exemplified By Mammalian Life)

4. Significant Properties: Sleep (Inertial Circadian Preservation Through Systemic Release of Exertion)

5. Systematization: Natural Selection (The Natural "Weeding–Out" Process of Environmental Inefficiency And Maladaptation)

6. Sum Use: Referential Taxonomy (For Defensive Or Recreational Ends)

7. Sum Purpose: Security of Environment (Pragmatic Prescience)

IV. Humanity

1. Genealogical Root: Caucasoid (Dominant "Force Initiator" of the Species)

2. Combination Patterns: Oriental (Principal Distinct Cohabitating Variety of the Planet)

3. Phase Transitions: Non–Caucasoid Cohabiters (Species Substantiality)

4. Significant Properties: Hebrews (The Most Demonstrably Cognitively Flexible of the Species)

5. Systematization: Mixed Individuals (Phenotypic Progressive Evolution)

6. Sum Use: Tribal Organization (Through Banding to End Rivalry And Competitive Threats)

7. Sum Purpose: Distinction From the Neanderthal (Who Either Died Out Or Bred In the Species)

V. Religion

1. Genealogical Root: Christianity (Family–Base Deification)

2. Combination Patterns: Folk Mythology (Heroic Familial Personifications)

3. Phase Transitions: Ancient Mythology (Archetypal Fluidity)

4. Significant Properties: Judaism (Chief Genealogical Archetype of Earth)

5. Systematization: Roman Catholic Church (Dominant Complete Church And Priesthood)

6. Sum Use: Islam (Kamikaze–Level Life And Death Devotion)

7. Sum Purpose: Hinduism (Understanding the Waxing And Waning of the Cycles of Nature)

VI. Philosophy

1. Genealogical Root: Friedrich Nietzsche (Linguistic Division Schemata of Value Relations)

2. Combination Patterns: Nolan Aljaddou (Organization Into Supreme Mathematical Precision)

3. Phase Transitions: Immanuel Kant (Elimination of Extraneous And Abstruse)

4. Significant Properties: Derrida (Categorical Reductionism of Phraseology Into Its Opposite)

581

5. Systematization: Arthur Schopenhauer (Encompassing Academic Arrangement)

6. Sum Use: Rene Descartes (Answering All Questions)

7. Sum Purpose: Galileo Galilei (Categorization of All Phenomena Into Predictability Or Natural Order)

VII. Technology

1. Genealogical Root: The "Spark" (Base Indication of Electrochemical Reaction)

2. Combination Patterns: Systematic Heat/Energy Use (Fires And Spits)

3. Phase Transitions: Electric Radiation (Motor Stimulus Analogue For Humanity)

4. Significant Properties: Intricate Apparatuses (Birth of the Complex "Tool")

5. Systematization: The Von Neumann Sphere (Total Executive Operating System of Artificial Intelligence Surveillance Satellites)

6. Sum Use: Elimination of Perturbation to Executive Functionality (Through Manipulation of Beneficent–to–Purpose Elements)

7. Sum Purpose: Promote Functionality (Without Alternative)

B. Founders of Knowledge

I. Nolan Aljaddou

1. Completed Physics (In "Measurement Theory")

2. Introduced "Knowledge Theory"

3. Geometrically Codified All Language

II. Friedrich Nietzsche

1. Completed Psychobiology

2. Introduced Drive Theory

3. Derived Meaning And Purpose

III. Arthur Schopenhauer

1. Completed Metaphysics

2. Introduced the Basis of Theoretical Models

3. Discovered Logical Root of All Problems – Suffering – In the Noumenon Proper; the "Will"

The Geometric Representation of 666

0: That which resides between −1 and 1; continuity (or stasis) in the face of change – manifested as such change . . . changelessly.

Numerically sequenced: 1, 2, 3 . . . signifying "completion" at the implied "separating" abyss (the central "0"); such "completion" necessitates a "circular" "meeting" at the initial point ("1"); thus the "1, 2, 3" count, if represented in acknowledging "2" as the "abyss", signifies a straight line with an angular "triangle–making" "2", and can only imply an additional "3" which sequence back to, and include, the initial "1" (including the "3" as the new "1"), and thus cycles back three times to exhaust the permutation sequence (giving a total of "6" in the completion–counting sequence, three times); or "666". Or, the correlative, absolutely–designed Hamiltonian (of 6 spatial components over time). The "sacred geometry" of the originating "zero" and summary "666" then is nothing more than the fact that what you said existed has to roundabout exist as such then (in the last place) as it did in the first place.

Reality is the centralization of 666, or a circle, about a center point, draped in blue – and consciousness may be delineated empirically as the dissolution of these geometric demarcations into the median of the color blue on a tangent perspective plane. This is why mind and vision are always centered and focused; with the perspective of limitless dissolution added, the observable characters of cognition are realized.

Base Proverbs And Fables

(I) One can be always right if the governing "morality" is one in which social units have a default setting of attack and the individual is always targeted for being presumed as too "handicapped" to understand how stupid the would–be attackers are ipso facto.

["You can't spell happiness without penis ladies; remember that."]

The Tortoise And the Hare

(II) If anything you do can be interpreted as a "cleverer comeback", anything I say that has meaning instantly "hurts" you.

["To err is human; to forgive, less human."]

The Boy Who Cried Wolf

(III) The lone hero from nothing is always a crowd–pleaser – and ALWAYS the baseline underlining reality.

["Corruption takes root more perniciously than a weed. And must be uprooted."]

King Arthur

The ultimate message: Idiots will be idiots; but not for long.

The Greatest Stories Ever Told

For "In Your Face", In Case You Were Too Stupid to Think of Them On Your Own:

The Crucible – Arthur Miller

Of Mice And Men – John Steinbeck

A Clockwork Orange – Anthony Burgess

My Favorite Books And Why:

The Noble Qur'an – It's a condensed and systematized version of the Bible (minus Jesus as a white–trash–empowering personal godhead).

The Book of Mormon – It's a laughable satirical erasure of the Bible.

Any Sherlock Holmes Compilation – They illustrate archetypal storytelling structure with condensed and reversed "origami" unfolding solution reading–paradigm.

The Models of Human Life And Optimal Experience:

Star Wars: Episode V – The Empire Strikes Back

Indiana Jones And the Last Crusade

R. A. Salvatore's "Drizzt Do'Urden" Sagas

The Timeless "Christmas Parables":

A Christmas Memory – Truman Capote

A Christmas Carol – Charles Dickens

Bad Santa

The Greatest Story Ever Told:

2012 Event – And Its Context(s) [The Book of the Dead and The 2012 Prequel].

– Kurt Cobain really is Christ.

.

(And I love Hayley – Paramore – Williams).

Missing Information (Who I Am)

Pyramids:

1. Arthur Schopenhauer – The Pessimist's Handbook (What I unofficially recite)

2. Friedrich Nietzsche – Beyond Good And Evil (My collective motivation and documented dictation)

3. Albert Einstein – The Photoelectric Effect (What I am virtually on the verge of discovering [constantly])

4. Richard Feynman – The Half–Derivative (The thing I am virtually always inventing in a new and original way)

5. Stanley Kubrick – Unincluded Films (What I am accused of doing)

6. David Lynch – Excluded Films (What I am generally feeling about my environment)

7. Leonhard Euler – Volumes of Work (The volume of my dialectic soliloquy scientific unearthings)

8. Bernhard Riemann – Professional Occupation (What I am generally doing – lecturing)

9. Kurt Cobain – B–Sides [Principally Incesticide] (Unused material I still cherish and feel like compiling is a testament to my persnickety perfectionism)

10. Stefani Germanotta – Later Albums (Virtual reminiscences, which I often do out of a tendency to glorify my times with the few people who really "got" me – in the sense of understanding)

11. Brittany Murphy – Personal Life (What I am allowed to partake in due to my profession – pop musicologist–composer)

12. Robert Hawkins – Professional Life (What I will never engage in – menial tasks)

13. Robert Fischer – Personality (My exact – justified – arrogance)

14. Steve Prefontaine – Death (What I am always avoiding – needless carelessness)

15. Mohandas Gandhi – Suffering (What I never discuss)

16. Audrey Hepburn – Acting Ability (My general talent)

17. Paris Hilton – Cluelessness (What I generally mask)

18. Britney Spears – Grassroots Christian Nature (What I withheld as a teenager and twenty–something but re–embraced)

19. Mila Kunis – Inability to Speak In Normal Accent (My nerves preventing a will to engage socially)

20. Winona Ryder – Personal Privacy (What I am rarely allowed to show without being accused of theft – thus I sarcastically imply it out of an enthused satirical eye–opening irony)

21. Claire Danes – Ugliness and Imperfect Beauty (What I only feel about my appearance, and see in convex/concave distorting mirrors)

22. Joey Lauren Adams – Sex Life (What I used to have – as a preteen)

23. Shannen Doherty – Sexiness (What I never really had in my view, but apparently do)

24. Naomi Watts – Wish to Indulge In Art Constantly (All that I want – when nobody is injecting their blend of Plebeian jaded opinion)

25. Natalie Portman – Missed Youth (My teenage–hood and resulting alienation as an adult)

26. Megan Mullally – Auto–Desire to Give Me Oral Based On Physiognomy (I share this as well, only I started in imagining it was her)

27. Karen Orzolek – Someone Who Gets Me Totally (My affirmation that there are others out there who can be human towards me)

28. Emily S. – Sexual Perversity (What I am "schizophrenically" trying to hide forever)

29. Carl Sagan – Educational History (What nobody cares about because I know virtually everything and can explain it better)

30. Billy Idol – Personal Vulnerability (What others "think" they are seeing from me – perpetually)

31. Andrew Wyles – Math Genius (What others erroneously think I am mathematically – a semi–stunted chronically educated and incidental success – which is the opposite of correct)

32. Steven Soderbergh – Wish to Reinvent People (The only purpose I have in looking at or dealing with people)

33. Freeman Dyson – Physics Capability (My rough natural technical knowledge of the subject – without precise application of particular calculus operations on random algebraic functions)

34. Oscar Wilde – Personal Sexuality (Perhaps mythically thought of as his – but I am infinitely grander as an orator

and would be prepared to be consigned to a life of sole cunnilingus, as cunning a linguist as I am)

Global Function, Stature, And Significance In History, Historical Timelines, And Ever–Present: The first, and ultimately only, Philosopher–Mathematician

Actual Functioning Profession (Of Which I am the Highest Caliber): Composer [Musician–Singer–Songwriter (Specializing In Guitar, With Unparalleled Rhythm Precision; And A Natural Talent For Piano That Even Supersedes Master Pianists)]

..

.

On "Nevermind", Its Complement "Ever Knower", And My "Spider", As the Greatest Musical Works of All Time (And Possible)

"Simplicity is the ultimate sophistication."

– Leonardo da Vinci

The central album of the All–Seeing Eye rotated in time represents a compression of non–essential (classical non–percussive musical variants) in a Lennon–like simplified representation of universal reductionist elements with Cobain at the helm replacing each significant base composer of each of the represented variations.

1. Smells Like Teen Spirit – Beethoven

2. In Bloom – Rachmaninoff

3. Come As You Are – Saint–Saëns

4. Breed – Berlioz

5. Lithium – Bach

6. Polly – Handel

7. Territorial Pissings – Shostakovich

8. Drain You – Mozart

9. Lounge Act – Verdi

593

10. Stay Away – Gershwin

11. On A Plain – Vivaldi

12. Something In the Way – Salieri

13. Endless, Nameless – Copland

. .

.

. .

Incidentally, my work, "The Spider", as the central element of all music constitutes a form of the maximal masterwork possible to achieve by each of the represented composers when set to the correct default expression – all orchestral variations are based on strings and horns (vibrational echo and echoing vibration); every represented note is the sum of all necessity in the particular instrumentalization, and the central representation at 7 minutes and 40 seconds is Shostakovich; one–seventh of this tempo with only strings represents the best of Beethoven, and seven times faster than the Shostakovich–variation represents the best of Copland (with a small horn section), and so on and so forth with relative fractions of each orchestral amalgamation and tempo for each represented composer. This contextually establishes me as the most effortless virtuoso composer of all time, and as significant an economical composer as

594

Cobain, in history, as my musical thus–mirror–counterpart – who is then determined to be as successful a composer as possible, in all of history (an effortless but perpetually underestimated transcendent Jim Morrison poet–figure of Rimbaud prodigy–proportions).

.

. .

.

"The Spider" as perfection is represented effortlessly in its combinatorial properties. It has the base integrative thirteen notes comprising its core–frequency in the primary melodic theme, with proper attention–based decrescendo in pitch and paralleling conservational cancellation or harmonic closure segue into its repetition from origination in the silence – and all the properly counter–ascending basslines. It bridges into a frantic perfection of virtuoso piano work but countering economy of tonal expression to anticipate the next repetition–leap into perspective–shifting reevaluation (of the initial melodic line). This repetition, after the bridge, segues into a languid extension into preemptive anticipation of the triumphant and well–placed march section, which echoes into a hollowed eerie tonality of a subtle repetition with sinister undertones. An optical–illusion inducing relative stationary–pitch in motion then transcribes into a heavenly ascension–descent into a haunting harmonic ambience to creep into a finale section, counting all primary seven scale–measuring distinctions which circumscribe back into the primary melody, its bridge, and a clever reversal of march and languid exhaustion phrase to transcribe back into the silence from whence it came, an anomalous entity of sheer passion, emotion, bliss, and ecstasy of expression, as all such things are intended to be, culminating in a measure of repetition of primary sections (including initial expression) at integrative thirteen, to mirror the base melody–line, and finally enunciate the subject in question – the sum of all life, a spider that creates its own stability from motion, and bases its life motive in an unmoving web, a microcosmic Platonic "representation" of the Schopenhauerian "Idea" of the macrocosm; the universe.

.

One more property of "The Spider" is its sectional exemplification of each composer – to a point. The bassline exemplifies the initial composer, and the treble harmony exemplifies their diametric opposite on the thirteen–step scale. The bassline, for example, of the main theme, is Beethoven, and the treble could be interpreted as Copland; the bassline of the first bridge section could be interpreted as Rachmaninoff, and the treble could be considered Salieri, and so on and so forth, up to the quiet denouement section which leads back to the main theme, which exemplifies Shostakovich thoroughly. Each section thus counted may then be considered the core melody each composer was attempting to write, as well as the core theme for each classical genre of music, or then the literal mathematical translation of every form of art (extensions of base temporal frequency measures –music) thus generally represented, which are as follows in order:

1. Romance

2. Postmodern

3. Psychedelia

4. Operatic

5. Baroque

6. Religious

7. Avant–Garde

8. Virtuoso

9. Narrative

10. Improvisational

11. Classic

12. Imitative

13. No–Rule

As with all such symmetric lists, they may be compared and contrasted with their stationary opposite (complement) with respect to the central element to confirm their universal breadth of completion of the given particular scale.

.

Incidentally, I am thus the greatest, best, and most perfect artist of all time. This particular classification, the most to–the–point classification achievement and content–

production (in addition to the rest of the contents of this book) make me the greatest, most prominent, and most accomplished scientist of all time as well.

"Art and Science; not a thing between – or in between."

– Nolan Aljaddou

*Final Note

The tracks on Ever Knower, my "Illuminati" album, are the general "covariant" inversions and complements of Nevermind, with the addition of an extra element of complexity, through sheer incidence. The foundation of this lay in the title comparisons:

1. Mary Jane – Smells Like Teen Spirit

2. Bittersweet Depression – In Bloom

3. Girl – Come As You Are

4. Higher – Breed

5. Winter – Lithium

6. My Garden – Polly

7. Acid Rain – Territorial Pissings

8. Here Or There – Drain You

9. Injected – Lounge Act

10. In the Sky – Stay Away

11. Antiparallax – On A Plain

12. Alien – Something In the Way

13. Time – Endless, Nameless

*Bonus Tracks (All of Which Are Additional Correlates of "Endless, Nameless")

I. SENDAI

II. Hey Man

III. The Spider

.

After–Note

Drain You

By Nirvana

Perhaps one of the most overlooked songs ever written by a major artist, which the artist themselves happened to hold in high esteem, is also the single most significant song of all time. It occupies position 21 in the linear scale of the All–Seeing Eye rotated in time, and thus signifies entry into the Nirvana itself – after the scale of 20 (Existence) is singularly surpassed. Its unilateral scalar property also dictates it can be, as a root, extensionally mapped over the 20 greatest artists and their 7 greatest songs – its parametric bounding condition as such also the reason the band Nirvana is relocated from the mean of the framework to the root origin – as a summation into a transcendent state of the greatest bliss any musical work can convey (the greatest ecstasy, joy, and oblivion into an internal state with a loved partner). For me, this coincides with my extensional 666 correlative avatar in that category (Hayley Williams) and is meant to signify our singular encounter – as the sum purpose of the universe.

Post–Conclusion

Human males were characterized by a specified universal will to "gang rape", "bind", "torture", and "kill" Hayley Williams as a result of contrariness to the sum quirkiest characteristic and most esoteric irony of the 2012

600

alignment; I, As Ram, the Arm of Ra, Am the sole individual who was ever interested in preserving her chastity as the chief avatar of objective beauty.

Translations of 666:

[Linguistic: "I like you."

Sensory: Blue

Meaning: I Don't Care Anymore.]

Sum: That's it.

The Theory of Rock

Rock Music – A rhythmic emphasis on melodic progression to a percussive point, with consistent harmonic reinforcement.

Rock Theory: All music as rock and roll (the "optimal" genre)

Its categories are subdivided as follows, with the primary twin branching examples, culminating in its traditional incarnation, followed by an artist signifying the general quintessence of each genre's manifestation. Each general category is governed by a chief Fourier–analytic symmetry equation which determines its objective optimization. The result is, with the addition of the common aim of both the scientific and artistic sentiment, and the latter inclusion of form and function models (as given by the physical incarnations of tautology loop, relatively resistance–free continuum–action Schopenhauerian Idea archetypes, preserved irrespective of speed [here referred to as "Rhythm Models"; actual "kinesis eidolons"], projecting as motion–time models in the cognitive spatial manifold), 7 governing equations of rock and roll, which total – with the inclusion of secondary sub–equations – a matrix theory of 20 equations:

1. Popular Rock (Pop) – Bubblegum, Rhythm and Blues | Folk Melodies [The Beatles] {Equivalence As Symmetry | $a = a$} (Consistency/Harmonization)

602

i) $y = x$ [Line] | Projection: Linear Momentum – "Joy"

ii) $0 = 0$ [Point] | Rhythm Model: Marble Clicker

2. Emotive Rock (Emo) – Folk Music, Heavy Metal | Opera [Paramore] {The Fundamental Theorem of Calculus | $F(b) - F(a) = [\sim]0{-}ab(f)$} (Vicissitude/Moodswing)

i) $[([x]2 + [y]2)]2 = 2[c]2([x]2 - [y]2)$ [Lemniscate] | Projection: Planar Momentum – "Depression"

ii) $(f(x{-}2) - f(x{-}1))/0{-}x$ [Limit] | Rhythm Model: Faucet

3. Dance Rock (Dance) – House Jams, Rap | Hymnals [Lady Gaga] {The Nash Equilibrium | $[\sim]0{-}i(f{-}1 + f{-}2) \geq 0$} (Cooperation/Integration)

i) $f{-}1 + f{-}2 = 0$ [Neutrality] | Projection: Spatial Momentum – "Effortlessness"

ii) $f{-}2 - f{-}1 < 0$ [Zero Sum] | Rhythm Model: Spring

4. Punk Rock (Punk) – Soft Rock, Classic Rock | Tribal [Nirvana] {The Pythagorean Theorem | $[a]2 + [b]2 = [c]2$} (Simplification/Emphasis)

i) $(1/3)\pi h[r]2$ [Cone] | Projection: Angular Momentum – "Declarative"

ii) $(4/3)\pi[r]3$ [Sphere] | Rhythm Model: Gyroscope

5. Synthetic Rock (Synth) – Techno, Anthem | Jazz [Garbage] {The Fibonacci Sequence | $g(0) = 1 + (1/(1 + (1/(1 + \ldots))))$} (Complexity/Pattern)

i) $y = 1/x$ [Hyperboloid] | Projection: Wave Momentum – "Ecstasy"

ii) $x = ab$ [Prime Root] | Rhythm Model: Sand Hourglass

6. Psychedelic Rock (Psychedelic) – Experimental, Progressive | Blues [Katy Perry] {The Euler Relation | $[e]i\pi + 1 = 0$} (Summation/Euphoria)

i) $[\sim]0([e]x) = [e]x + C$ [Non–Differentiation] | Projection: Vibrational Momentum – "Oblivion"

ii) $\pi(x) \sim x/\ln x$ [Differential Progress] | Rhythm Model: String

7. Electronic Rock (Electronica) – Dubstep, Classical | Celebratory [Smashing Pumpkins] {Electricity | $3–0(E|) = 0$} (Baseline/Changelessness)

i) $E' = 0$ [Closed System] | Projection: Circular Momentum – "Optimality"

ii) $\pi(x) \sim p–i$ [Primacy] | Rhythm Model: Pendulum

With these 28 genres of music, the two dual components of all music (base rhythm and melody) seal the 30 classes of music (as the sifting categorical measure of temporality and all possible emotional expression) – which, in the end, was all rock and roll, as an approached limit of rhythmically compressed emphasis; only, theoretically modeled properly from the 20th century onward, and seen in this contextual self–consistent framework – as the encapsulation model of all possible genius and sentiment. The sophistication of the classification scheme is evidenced by its capacity to identify proper genres based on their rhythm models, which can be heuristically derived by comparing the relative centricity of malleability of an appropriate applied metronome, and then "fitting" the appropriate step–archetype. These phenomena model not only all of music, but all of neutral reference frame physics of space, due to their extended application to temporality.

Rock then, in the end, is not only the ultimate form of music for many, but is the ultimate form of music. It reminds us that: "This is the best moment of my life . . . because it is happening right now."

**On the Highest And Most Blissful of Experience –
Become Universal**

ETERNITY

[Arthur Rimbaud]

It is discovered.

What? Eternity.

In the whirling light

Of sun become sea.

O my sentinel soul,

Let us always desire

The nothing of night

And the day on fire.

From the voice of the World

And the striving of Man

You must set yourself free;

You must fly as you can.

For out of you only,

Soft silken embers,

Duty arises

Nor surfeit remembers.

Then shall all hope fail . . .

Nul orietur.

Science with patience,

The torment is sure.

It is discovered.

What? Eternity.

In the whirling light

Of sun become sea.

Footnote: Also, to be an "Evariste Galois" figure. And an eternal teenager. And a "Hayley Williams" type male counterpart.

.

Post–Epilogue (The Purpose of Human Life, the Creamy Center, the Delicious Kernel of Outer Darkness Surrounded By Ethereal Mind, Nursing Cool Vapor And Dreaming of Looking Up – At the Night Sky)

SENDAI

There once was a girl, living in a world

All by herself –

Then I came around, from another part of town

And saw through her shell.

She saw me, and we kissed

And it was like nothing else before

In the seas of cosmic motion

Before the end of time . . .

She looked up at me, in a dream

And I was curled up with her

And nothing could move me from the darkness

Of air itself, smothered in cold, surrounding our arms

SENDAI, SENDAI, SENDAI . . . no more . . . no more . . .

SENDAI, SENDAI, SENDAI . . . nothing else . . . evermore . . .

SENDAI, SENDAI, SENDAI . . . everyone gone now . . . no one alive now . . .

Intravenous, in vertigo . . .

Never before have I seen a look in the eyes of a panther

Waltzing down the orange streets of a dark pit – the abyss

Where it all began, where it all ended

And nothing else can ever be – Paired, amore.

Look up in bed at the ceiling, and how it shines and sparkles

With glittering black lights hollowing out the sentiments of truthlessness

Revealing the cold caress of blissless sorrow, nevermore reborn . . .

Until nothing can ever escape the last blossoming bosom of infinite eternal wreckage . . .

SENDAI, SENDAI, SENDAI . . . no more . . . nothing more . . .

SENDAI, SENDAI, SENDAI . . . always gone . . . eternally truth . . .

SENDAI, SENDAI, SENDAI . . . here we are now . . . we came and went . . . the same way we exited. And were never reborn . . .

Forevermore.

Intravenous, in vertigo . . .

Rumble noises in chorus chords

[Instrumental – Heavy Emphasis on Eeriness and Emulated Glittered Starlight]

This is my life.

Repeat first verse

Repeat chorus twice

THE END

G, A, G, A

Fairy/Pixie–esque Xylophone Quality Background "Droplet" Emphasis – Hardcore Guitar, With Steady "Marching–Type Drums" and Implied Smash – Elevated Alto–Version of "Stairway" Descent Into A Generalized Form of the Vocal Line in "Retrovertigo [by Mr. Bungle]"

The Illuminati

*Subject – –Hayley Williams– And I –

– Why I write music –

.

What the Anagram Is:

The Sign of Culminative Organization; Ophiuchus Itself.

. . .

This book is the eternal word, revealed in the world, by alphanumeric codes, lines, and points. The only true Bible.

The only certainty of the old Bible is that it reveals the Jews created the best mythology of the ancient world. I suppose that's what happens when you live in a world of make–believe.

I Am Lord of Lords.

Anagram, am I? Mr. A., again! Or Ram, the Arm of Ra
(if myths manage a say).

Each word, a principal translation of direct force –

Anagram ["Order", Noun]
am ["Identity", Verb]
I ["Fact", Pronoun]

——

Mr. ["Rank", Noun]
A. ["Addressment", Proper Noun]
again ["State", Adjective]

——

Or ["Qualifier", Adverb]
Ram ["Authority", Proper Noun]
the ["Principality", Adjective]
Arm ["Mechanism", Noun]
of ["Aspect", Adjective]
Ra ["Omnipotence", Proper Noun]

——

if ["Condition", Adjective]

myths ["Information", Noun]

manage ["Execution", Verb]

a ["Occurrence", Noun]

say ["Irrevocability", Noun]

———

All a condition of individuality, proper; I being the one you are not – by objectively reinforced force. Natural royalty; or imperial regality. The literal identity translation of "E Pluribus Unum (Out of Many, One)".

A transcription of Nature itself. Negligence of which can only indicate a retarded incomprehension of language. The unity of Existence – the allowed mechanism.

. . .

As you may or may not have been able to tell, my first principal 2012 work was chiefly about Lady Gaga, whereas this one sentimentalizes on Hayley Williams. They are Shakti, and Sita, respectively, in accordance with preserved fable under these circumstances. A complete list of religious corollaries follows:

Extensions of Christianity:

Mother: The Deep

Michaela P.: St. Paul

613

Elizabeth I.: The Pope

Kristen R.: The Apostle James

Mindy L.: The Antichrist

Kacie S.: St. Peter

Beatrice B.: Satan

Jessica B.: St. John the Baptist

Former Twin Girl: Archangel Michael

Capricorn Tattoo Girl: Principal Cherub With Flaming Sword

Australian Teenage Bibliophile: Lazarus

Emily S.: Mary Magdalene

Extensions of Hinduism: Myself In Relation to –

7. Hayley Williams [Sita]: Rama

6. Sarah Michelle Gellar [Consort]: Ganesh

5. Winona Ryder [Wife]: Krishna

4. Stefani Germanotta [Shakti]: Shiva

3. Natalie Portman [Kali]: Maledom

2. Shirley Manson [Avalokiteshvara]: Buddha

1. Brittany Murphy [The Cosmos]: Brahma

Myself (In Both) [Ultimately]:

Atman (God the Father) – I Am That I Am.

614

THE END

"If thou wouldst see the noblest of mankind; behold, a monarch in a beggar's garb."

– Quotation on the Buddha

The Governing Precepts of Science:

1. Referenced Observer

2. Empirical Interaction

3. Data Collection

4. Ground Research

5. Hypothetical Speculation

6. Theory Formulation

7. Reasonable Conclusion

8. Certain Fact

The Ultimate Scientific Theories: ZERO THEORY (LOGIC), CHAOS THEORY (MATHEMATICS), MEASUREMENT THEORY (PHYSICS), DIFFERENTIAL EVOLUTION (BIOLOGY), JUNGIAN ANALYSIS (PSYCHOLOGY)

The Universal Symbols . . . of Diametric Symmetry:

PENTAGRAM, HEXAGRAM, HEPTAGRAM, YIN–YANG, "X"–ED CIRCLE

An aura of simplicity. To live in a book. To live a waking dream. That is the ocean.

MESSAGES IN "THE SATANIC BIBLE":

1] The evolutionary kingdom "COGNI" . . . will outlive mankind, as living "Ubermensch".

2] This is the exact word and code of Satan; the 2012 Alignment, His arching, cosmic "backbone". The direct manifestation of 666, as mechanism. Solid state sacred physics. The definition of metaphysical certitude.

3] This represents a universal alignment, calibrating the death of the Untermensch, or common Man, through the introduction of sheer "abstraction" – signifying the virtual predetermination of logic.

4] The sole certitude of The Satanic Bible is that it is the literal inspired "breath of the devil" . . . and the transcendent "rustling of his wings". Arriving on Earth, on time, as predicted.

5] This is a religion for atheists . . . who are otherwise "lost"; all other religions being a metaphor for this.

6] 666 is Its own Beginning and End, as the most fundamental self–inversive element, to the degree even of counting; existing as, from, and out of, "nothing". The governing law of all laws.

7] This is why language was written.

8] This is the ultimate work in religion, philosophy, science, and art. The scientifically ideal system of doctrine.

9] A corpse is a placeholder for the next impersonal incarnation, triangulated with reference to that.

10] "2012" is an accurate map of biological time; or supranatural history. The reference framework of history; a relativistic limit of integrative geodesic acceleration.

Blue. Blue. Blue. Blue. Blue. Blue. Blue.

The Existential Basis of Truth

Zero is that which simply does exist, as the sheerly existential function. Reality is generated by its recursion identity, as its own, conserving, inverse. Plain tautology, without the existence of any further possible greater justification.

Zero has six dimensions and existential manifestations: 0D (the Void, "Hell"), 1D (Emptiness, "Death"), 2D (Nothingness, "Mind"), 3D (Hollowness, "Sight"), 4D (the Abyss, "Life"), iD (the Vacuum, "Heaven"). The plane of nihility; the singular–dimensional identity – of the Monad. Truth. Absorption and union therewith, Heaven, or the Nirvana, as oneness with the vacuum, achieved through self–dissolution and disillusionment, through perfect harmony; the sublimity of the ith Plane; the palingenesis cycle . . . being – "Hell".

Zero is the sum of infinite negations . . . nothing else . . . ad infinitum . . . giving birth to quantity, and its own description, naturally; out of nothing, and nowhere. Revealing the truth – all is nothing, nothing is all; that is all, that is nothing.

The certain.

The mathematics of existence.

The Abyss.

. . . Also staring into you . . . GOD IS DEAD.

.

The Mystical Equation

M ~ xπ'(x)

Where π(x) is the prime counting function, and π'(x) is its derivative. It is approximated by $\frac{x}{lnx}$, and the full formula then translates as:

$$M = [[x \left(2lnx - \left(\frac{1}{2} \right) \right)]]$$

Where "[[ ]]" is the "least integer" or "floor" function. Even though it is an approximating operator, it gives the exact value of the cryptic–arithmetic linguistic–alphanumeric transliteration of all significant and general numeral values, in terms of interlinked "Kabbalistic", or "concentric generative extension", properties of measurement theory (base–10). It gives the meaning for the enumeration, or may be called the "numeral to number function" – that which ultimately "counts counting". It generates their full extended implications in terms of sequential signification. For example, the list of the first significant ranking numbers, with additional components, yields:

1 | 1/2 [Intermediate Plurality, Exemplar Singularity]

2 | 1 [Union, Unit Unification]

3 | 5 [The Generalized Mean of Temporality, Half the Measure of Counting]

4 | 9 [Sequence Cycle Closing, The Edge of the Mean]

5 | 13 [The Concentric Mean, The Center]

6 | 18 [The Sum Mean of Counting, 666]

7 | 23 [The Sephirot Connector, The Abyss]

10 | 41 [The Beginning of the Next Sequence Cycle, The Remainder of the Fully Completed Square Measure]

13 | 60 [Full Temporal Completion, Total Circularity]

18 | 95 [The Total Mean of Absolute Cyclical Closure, Extension to Universality]

20 | 109 [Cycle–Closure of Self–Reinforced Completion, The End]

The rest.

Appendix I.

About the Universe:

Logic Theory

Zero Theory [The Foundation of Mathematics]

Mathematics, unified, properly as the properties of zero, its commutativity, and basic set–theoretic axioms. It may be called the "Aljaddou Set Axioms", and represent their complete form, corresponding to a unifying fundamental ground theorem in each respective branch of mathematics – entirely derived by the Von Neumann Empty Set Hierarchy algorithm (and are the technical aspects thereof, itself the purest tautology of the empty set, as even the set of its own contents automatically . . . [{{ }}]). All results, the properties of the Von Neumann Hierarchy algorithm on a single element (forming a symmetric square matrix, which may be called the "Von Neumann Square Matrix", or "VNSM"), beginning with the empty set and itself as sole contents [0, 1, and conversely, alternately, 1, 0, in row two], itself the reciprocal of the traditional identity matrix, yet may be equivalently interchanged arbitrarily in terms of defined properties of matrix multiplication – preserving the original identity matrix, and may alternately be referred to as such . . . equivalently, the completed, Galois–permuted, dimensional quartic complex quaternion. Here, the empty set is equated to zero in the central axiom of foundation. There are in all, 6 axioms – however, both generalized, and specialized; the term "foundation" being interchanged for "regularity" at the central convergence point of both the general and special cases. All corresponding proof and arithmetic is worked out simply by hierarchical place and context. All mathematics being a combination of these elements. It is shown that there are 13 "negative" axioms, or sheer absent properties of zero, which constitute a tautology of its existence and the exact equivalent, proper foundations, rather than any given

621

posited assumption – the connection being illustrated by the technical operation of the Identity Matrix associated therewith. Technically, all as an aspect of zero, including previous Zermelo–Fraenkel set–theoretic axioms, reduce to "fixed–point" theorems in each branch of mathematics (certain axioms, such as "pairing" and the "power set" being special cases of the aforementioned 6, and replaceable equally by such); in this way, all of mathematics is meta–axiomatic, and contingent on consistent interrelations, rather than a posited value. The correct system, and the proper foundation of set theory.

Keywords: Set Theory Axioms, Von Neumann Empty Set Hierarchy Algorithm, Regularity, Infinity, Extensionality, Choice, Union, Foundation, General, Special, Zero, Von Neumann Square Matrix (VNSM), Identity Matrix, Fixed–Point Theorem.

1. Point and Lattice Theory – Equivalence As Symmetry: Commutativity of Radius [Regularity – General]

Zero As Point [Non–Negativity]

Definition (of the Identity Matrix).

$\forall x[x \neq \emptyset \rightarrow \exists y(y \in x \wedge \forall z(z \in x \rightarrow \neg(z \in y)))]$

$-0 = 0$

This may be called "The Fundamental (Fixed–Point) Theorem of Point and Lattice Theory" (FTPLT).

2. Graph Theory – Numbers Equal Measure Zero As Limit: Commutativity of Translation [Infinity – General]

Zero As Number [Non–Quantity]

Symmetry (of the Identity Matrix).

$\exists x[\emptyset \in x \wedge \forall y(y \in x \rightarrow \cup\{y,\{y\}\} \in x)]$

$0 = 0$

This may be called "The Fundamental (Fixed–Point) Theorem of Graph Theory" (FTGT).

3. Logic – Gödel's Incompleteness Theorem: Commutativity of Equivalence [Extensionality – General]

Zero As Axiom [Non–Sum]

Translation (of the Identity Matrix).

$\forall x \forall y[\forall z(z \in x \leftrightarrow z \in y) \rightarrow x=y]$

$0 + 0 = 0$

This may be called "The Fundamental (Fixed–Point) Theorem of Logic" (FTL).

4. Combinatorics – The Fundamental Theorem of Galois Theory: Commutativity of Root–Extraction [Choice – General]

Zero As Pole [Non–Quotient]

Permutation (of the Identity Matrix).

$\forall x \exists y \phi(x,y) \rightarrow \exists f \forall x \phi(x,fx)$

$\dfrac{0}{x} \times \dfrac{0}{y} = 0$

This may be called "The Fundamental (Fixed–Point) Theorem of Combinatorics" (FTC).

5. Computation – The Arithmetic Mean: Commutativity of Division [Union – General]

Zero As Difference [Non–Base]

Intersection (of the Identity Matrix).

$\forall x \exists y \forall z [z \in y \leftrightarrow \exists w(w \in x \wedge z \in w)]$

$0^x = 0$

This may be called "The Fundamental (Fixed–Point) Theorem of Computation" (FTC).

6. Calculus – The Fundamental Theorem of Calculus: Commutativity of Subtraction [Empty Set – General]

Zero As Limit [Non–Operator]

Union (of the Identity Matrix).

$\exists x \neg \exists y(y \in x)$

$0(F) = 0$

This may be called "The Fundamental (Fixed–Point) Theorem of Calculus Theory" (FTCT).

7. Set Theory – Infinite Infinity of Irrationals: Commutativity of Identity [Foundation]

Zero As Empty Set [Non–Differentiability]

Congruence (of the Identity Matrix).

623

$\forall x[x \neq \emptyset \rightarrow \exists y(y \in x \land \forall z(z \in x \rightarrow \neg(z \in y)))]$

$\{0\}$

This may be called "The Fundamental (Fixed–Point) Theorem of Set Theory" (FTST).

8. Arithmetic – One Added to One Equals Two: Commutativity of Addition [Empty Set – Special]

Zero As Root [Non–Operand]

Sequence (of the Identity Matrix).

$\exists x \neg \exists y(y \in x)$

$F(0) = 0$

This may be called "The Fundamental (Fixed–Point) Theorem of Arithmetic Theory" (FTAT).

9. Trigonometry – Centroid Theorem: Commutativity of Multiplication [Union – Special]

Zero As Placeholder [Non–Exponent]

Limit (of the Identity Matrix).

$\forall x \exists y \forall z[z \in y \leftrightarrow \exists w(w \in x \land z \in w)]$

$x^0 = 1$

This may be called "The Fundamental (Fixed–Point) Theorem of Trigonometry" (FTT).

10. Number Theory – Fermat's Little Theorem: Commutativity of Exponentiation [Choice – Special]

Zero As Prime [Non–Product]

Least Common Multiple (of the Identity Matrix).

$\forall x \exists y \phi(x,y) \rightarrow \exists f \forall x \phi(x,fx)$

$0 \times 0 = 0$

This may be called "The Fundamental (Fixed–Point) Theorem of Number Theory" (FTNT).

11. Algebra – The Quadratic Formula: Commutativity of Proportion [Extensionality – Special]

Zero As Function [Non–Addend]

Geometric Mean (of the Identity Matrix).

$\forall x \forall y [\forall z (z \in x \leftrightarrow z \in y) \rightarrow x = y]$

$0 = 0 + 0$

This may be called "The Fundamental (Fixed–Point) Theorem of Algebra" (FTA).

12. Game Theory – The Nash Equilibrium: Commutativity of Congruence [Infinity – Special]

Zero As Equilibrium [Non–Quantifiability]

Graph (of the Identity Matrix).

$\exists x [\emptyset \in x \land \forall y (y \in x \rightarrow \cup \{y, \{y\}\} \in x)]$

$0! = 1$

This may be called "The Fundamental (Fixed–Point) Theorem of Game Theory" (FTG).

13. Geometry – The Pythagorean Theorem: Commutativity of Scale [Regularity – Special]

Zero As Center [Non–Difference]

Calibration (of the Identity Matrix).

$\forall x [x \neq \emptyset \rightarrow \exists y (y \in x \land \forall z (z \in x \rightarrow \neg (z \in y)))]$

$0 - 0 = 0$

This may be called "The Fundamental (Fixed–Point) Theorem of Geometric Construction" (FTGC).

References

Quine, W. V., Set Theory and Its Logic. Belknap Press (1969)

Mathematics Theory

The Rigorous Establishment of Chaos Theory – the Foundation of All Scientific Measurement

The Statistical Ordering of Zero, As Chaotic Deviation From Interference Nullity

Mandelbrot Geometry, and Fractals – Derived

I. Logic – Zero As Function (Sets)

Cartesian calculus; $G(G)$ generation of covariant abscissa and ordinate, demarcating the measure segment, generalized as tangential linear derivative; recursive identity function of arithmetic (self–inversive and self–derivative foundational tautology; as 0).

Static Statistics

"Measurement Theory"

Algorithm: Iteration (13–fold implicit pyramidal triangulation of elements)

Mnemonic: The science of "base"

II. Mathematics – Zero As Root (Space)

Algebraic geometry; axial derivation of space; Eulerian lattice network.

Perturbation Statistics

"Unified Field Theory"

Algorithm: Recursion (20–fold explicit pyramidal triangulation of elements)

Mnemonic: The science of "place"

III. Physics – Zero As Point (Time)

Riemannian manifold; periodic extension.

Divergence Statistics

"General Relativity"

Algorithm: Divergence (5–fold deductive pyramidal triangulation of elements)

Mnemonic: The science of "space"

IV. Chemistry – Zero As Origin (Matter)

Combinatorial matrix theory; isomorphic symmetry and orientation metrics. "Galois Dipyramidal Periodicity"

626

Algorithm: Substitution (Unitary inductive pyramidal triangulation of elements)

Mnemonic: The science of "trace"

V. Biology – Zero As Placeholder (Energy)

Contiguous numeric configuration; covariant reference frame equivalence.

Sum Statistics

"Axial Collinearity"

Algorithm: Differentation (Non–quantified pyramidal triangulation of elements)

Mnemonic: The science of "face"

The Ultimate Ordering Principle – 0i

As complex planar quadrant intersection, it is universal orthocenter, as:

Measure Orthocenter: Right Triangle – The Pythagorean Theorem [Action]

Metric Orthocenter: Pascal's Triangle – The Binomial Theorem [Reference Frame]

Generator Orthocenter: Equilateral Triangle – The Golden Mean [Evolution]

Function Orthocenter: Isosceles Triangle – Antiparallelity [Existence]

Physics Theory

M [Metron] (Limitless N–Brane) Theory

I. Spatial Field Equations [Relativistic Time]

i. Metalogical Equations

1. $0(0(0))(0(0(0(0))))_1 = 2 + 3 = 5$
2. $a^2 + b^2 = c^2$
3. $E = \dfrac{h}{T}$
4. $E = \dfrac{nh}{T}$
5. $0_E 0_T \geq \dfrac{h}{4\pi}$
6. $\langle S_1 | e^{-iHT} | S_0 \rangle = \infty_S (e^{i[\infty_t [0,T] \, L(S(T))]/(\frac{h}{2\pi})})$

7. $m = \frac{E}{c^2}$

8. $K(\frac{E_1}{S})(\frac{E_2}{S}) = K(\frac{E_1 E_2}{S^2})$

9. $G_{ab} = kT_{ab}$

10. $\mathbf{0}(S(T)) = 0$

11. $F = m[\mathbf{0}(S(T))]$

12. $_3\mathbf{0}(\mathbf{E}) = 0$

13. $_3\mathbf{0}(\mathbf{H}) = 0$

14. $_{[3]}\mathbf{0}(\mathbf{E}) + \mathbf{0}_T(\mathbf{B}) = 0$

15. $_{[3]}\mathbf{0}(\mathbf{H}) - \mathbf{0}_T(\mathbf{D}) = 0$

16. $\boldsymbol{0}_F = 0$

17. $F = C(\frac{h}{4\pi T})(\frac{h}{4\pi T})\mathbf{0}_r(K_J) = C(\frac{h^2}{16\pi^2 T^2})\mathbf{0}_r(K_J)$

18. $\mathbf{0}_r(\mathbf{S}_J) = C\frac{g^2}{16\pi^2}\mathbf{0}_r(K_J)$

19. $\mathbf{0}(E(T)) = 0$

ii. Metamathematical Equations

20. $E' = 0$

iii. Metaphysical Equations

21. $A(t) + B(t) = C$

22. $A(t)^2 + B(t)^2 = C^2$

23. $E(t) = \boldsymbol{h}v$

24. $E(t) = n\boldsymbol{h}v$

25. $\Delta M(t)\Delta S(t) \geq \frac{h}{4\pi}$

26. $\langle S(t_1)|e^{-iHT}|S(t_0)\rangle$

iv. Metachemical Equations

27. $E(t) = mc^2$

28. $C = k\frac{q_1 q_2}{r^2}$

29. $G_{ab}(t) = kT_{ab}(t)$

30. $v'(t) = 0$

v. Computational Equations

31. $F(t) = ma$

32. $\nabla(\mathbf{B}) + \frac{D(\boldsymbol{E})}{D(ct)} = \frac{j}{c}$

33. $\mathbf{B} = 0$

34. $\nabla(\mathbf{E}) - \frac{D(\boldsymbol{B})}{D(ct)} = 0$

35. $\nabla(\mathbf{E}) = 0$

36. $\Delta F = 0$

37. $F = \Delta 0$

38. $\Delta J = F$

39. $\frac{D(E)}{D(t)} = 0$

40. $E' = 0$

41. $S = 1$

42. $i(\gamma_\mu)_{sr}\partial_\mu\psi_r - m\psi_s = 0$

628

43. $\sigma x = [1-2, 2-1]$

44. $H(t)| \Psi(t) = -\frac{ihD(\Psi(t))}{Dt}$

45. $t(0) = e^{i\pi} + 1$

46. $\phi = \frac{1\pm\sqrt{5}}{2}$

47. $c = \sqrt{(a^2 + b^2)}$

48. $d = \sqrt{(x^2 + y^2 + z^2)}$

49. $A = \frac{h(a + b)}{2}$

50. $SA = 4\pi r(t)^2$

51. $H(t) = \{s(t), s'(t)\}$

vi. Chemical Equations

52. $\{A\} = \{0\}$

53. $A + B = C$

54. $A^2 + B^2 = C^2$

55. $E = h\nu$

56. $E = nh\nu$

57. $\Delta E \Delta T \geq \frac{h}{4\pi}$

58. $\langle S_1 | e^{-iHT} | S_0 \rangle$

59. $E = mc^2$

60. $C = k\frac{q_1 q_2}{r^2}$

61. $R_{ab} + \frac{Rg_{ab}}{2} = \frac{8\pi G T_{ab}}{c^4}$

62. $v' = 0$

63. $F = ma$

vii. Physical Equations

64. $\nabla(\mathbf{B}) + \frac{D(E)}{D(ct)} = \frac{j}{c}$

65. $\mathbf{B} = 0$

66. $\nabla(\mathbf{E}) - \frac{D(\mathbf{B})}{D(ct)} = 0$

67. $\nabla(\mathbf{E}) = 0$

68. $\Delta F = 0$

69. $F = \Delta 0$

70. $\Delta J = F$

71. $\frac{D(E)}{D(t)} = 0$

72. $E' = 0$

73. $S = 1$

74. $i(\gamma)\partial \psi_r - m\psi_s = 0$

75. $\sigma x = [1-2, 2-1]$

76. $H(t)| \Psi(t) = -\frac{ihD(\Psi(t))}{Dt}$

77. $e^{i\pi} + 1 = 0$

78. $\phi = \frac{1\pm\sqrt{5}}{2}$

79. $c = \sqrt{(a^2 + b^2)}$

80. $d = \sqrt{(x^2 + y^2 + z^2)}$

81. $A = \frac{h(a + b)}{2}$

82. $SA = 4\pi r^2$

629

83. $H(t) = \{s(t), s'(t)\}$
84. $2[F_2(ax^2 + bx + c) - F_1(ax^2 + bx + c)]$
85. $ax^2 + bx = C$
86. $[(x - c)^2 + y^2][(x + c)^2 + y^2] = c^4$
87. $i = (-1)^{\frac{1}{2}}$
88. $\Sigma o = \frac{\pi}{4}$
89. $R(s) = 0$
90. $E = E = E$
91. $A = A$

viii. Mathematical Equations

92. $V(a) = e^{\frac{1}{2}\ln(1 - \cos(a)\cos(a))} = 0i + 0j + 0k$

ix. Logical Equations

93. $0 = 0$

II. Non–Spatial Commutation (Spinor) Supersymmetric Gauge Matrix Equations (of Quaternion Points) [Quantum Chromodynamic Spin Force Phase in Isometric Time]

94. SU(0) [Instanton]

95. SU(2) [Higgs Boson Parity]

96. SU(3) [Lepton Spatiality]

97. SU(4) [Gluon Dipyramidal Eightfold Periodicity]

III. The Space Equation [Tri–Pyramidal Quaternion Calabi–Yau Manifold]

98. $V(t) = (1 + i + j + k)x + (1 + i + j + k)y + (1 + i + j + k)z$

IV. The Spaceless Equation [Superstring Membrane Vibrational Contiguity]

99. $\zeta(s) = 0$

V. The Geometric Equation [Atomic Symmetry (Operation) Operator (Symbol)]

100. $\otimes$

Appendix II.

About This Book:

The true Bible. Work of the true Illuminati. The holy book of Satanism.

The ultimate book – the union of all ultimacy. THE . . . . Satanic Bible. End of theism. A book of poetry, mathematics, and philosophy – and the ultimate revelation. The exact, literal Satanic Bible . . . . . mathematically. The true quintessential work of science, wisdom, logic – and religion.

The Foundation of:

Scientific Christianity

Neo–Scientology

Quantum Satanism, and

Godism

Heavenism

Optimism

Speech and Rhetoric

Archival Scientific Data

The 2012 Alignment

The Theory of Measurement

Literature

Drama

Calculus

Quantum Chromodynamics

Relativistic Physics

631

The Theory of Everything

Formal Axiomatic Logic

The Modern Enlightenment Era

The English Language

A "must–read", must–have.

The perpetual bestseller; the principal and unitary successor to the 1960s cursory outlining handbook – the substance to the image. Equivalent to the New Testament to its Old.

A completion of Nietzsche, and the works of Schopenhauer.

The best book. The only book. The book.

Entirely an extension of the mystical and supremely genius anagram:

Anagram, am I? Mr. A., again! Or Ram, the Arm of Ra

(if myths manage a say).

Language and grammar; Nature's arm and ultimate defense – against the idiot.

Subjects the book definitively covers, as fundamental principle:

The Zodiac

Black Magic

Sacred Geometry

Fated Intervention

Dark Gods

Akashic Records

Luciferian Illumination

Ritualistic Practice

Ultimate Knowledge

Mysterious Secrets

Arcane Data

Esoteric Information

Sadistic Celebration

Erotic Supremacy

Celestial Mechanics

Original Deities

Destined Triumph

Afterlife Revelations

Self Empowerment

Optimal Linguistics

Everything anyone could ever want; in heaven, or on Earth; the one true religion.

Alternate titles for "Satanism" (as naturalistic calendrical linguistic reckoning means; Common Era):

Luciferianism (Romanesque Luminism) [Un–Christian]

Pyramidology (Egyptological Traditionalism) [Pre–Christian]

Antichristianity (Germanic Atheism) [Co–Christian]

Kabbalah (Hebraic Mysticism) [Post–Christian]

The (comparatively) legitimate universal religion of the Age.

. . .

The Bible of Buddhism, Hinduism, and Kabbalistic Judaism. The science of the tree of knowledge. A Taoist title of universal equilibrium.

A revelation of Masonic philosophy.

The technical factual Ramayana, and true Veda, the core text of Mantrayana Buddhism; the teachings of the ideal, of the noble, and virtue; featuring the defeat of the demon "Ravana", or "Maya", the seemingly all–powerful evil Illuminati, single–handedly by the effortless metaphorical arrow of Lord Rama, the soul of constancy and preservation . . . the god of justice; the Arm of Ra (alternately Vishnu, Shiva, or Brahma) . . . or that of the hand of the Almighty, vanquishing the foe of the Age, as measured and statically predicted by the Mayan Calendar (and its termination) in 2012. The Bible – perfect through and through – of antithesis to all possible false incarnation. The one, true tome – final analytic philosophy, incarnate; the mathematical image of the universe. The premise, as with all true religion, of the faith; the foundation, and not the implication. The greatest book; the source of all value . . . and veracity. A tale of the ultimate triumph – and universality. A story of the power of the word to literally move mountains; and nations. Right over might; mind over matter, and the mindless. Truth, unveiled.

The foundation of Ramanism, the True Way, of Lord Rama. The 33–fold Gateway to Enlightenment.

The literal mathematical word of God; as God. The true Bible code. A living manual for life, containing "The Book of Life", "The Book of the Dead", and all concerning the mechanics of the universe. The sequel to "The Book of Revelation", straight from the mouth of the Antichrist himself; the foundation of the new True Satanic Church. The only true Satanic Bible; let a hex be placed upon all those who stray from its eternal word.

"All that you will ever need to read: the foundation and sum of all knowledge and language." The codex of Being.

Satanism, as a complete, ultimate, and final religion; rather than merely a form of non–religion. "Real" Satanism, rather than "false" Satanism. A religion of, by, and for Man. The union of all religions as the ultimate, final; dispelling the false doctrine of Yahweh and all other gods, Satan, rising as the ram's head to eternal dominion. This, being the correct theology.

The only authentic form; the greatest of the modern incarnations of the historic traditions of religion.

The Mayan Calendar's end, and the 2012 Alignment, are literally the opening of the portal to eternity; and the "The Satanic Bible" . . . . . as the doorstep to infinity.

The path to truth, and liberation.

A meditative guide on the way to eternal life.

The mysteries of the universe – unveiled . . . with all of knowledge.

The secret to eternal life. The truest means of attaining the Nirvana, or Heaven. The Atlas of Time.

Contains the teachings to transcend all pain.

Appendix III.

About the Author:

Biographical Aspects – the Ultimate

Anagram, am I? Mr. A., again! Or Ram, the Arm of Ra

(if myths manage a say).

The literal transcription of the pentagram, and sign of the – horned – Antichrist. The Beast. 666 explained – and 2012 doomsday prophecy, fulfilled.

Author of "The Satanic Bible", and "The Ra Saga", the ultimate philosophical epics (alternately, the "2012 Saga"), setting the Gregorian Calendar to Zero AD with the Mayan Calendar's termination in 2012; the ultimate end of Christianity. Central and dipyramidal sequel to "2001: A Space Odyssey" – the rope to the future; and bridge of civilization. The literal transcription of the universe, its mystic writings, and true sacred scripture. A monolithic tome unto itself, and the most enriching philosophical treatise in the English language.

In summation, founder of Ramanism, as true Rama – the legitimate form of Brahmanism.

1] WORK

Final Atheism – Summarized:

Author of the new, definitive "Satanic Bible", which completes "The Philosopher's Trilogy", with the inclusion of Schopenhauer's "The World As Will and Representation", and Nietzsche's "Thus Spake Zarathustra" [prose, allegory, and narrative] – and all associated materials. Told in the form of a Kubrickian–style sequel to a type of Arthur C. Clarke's "2001: A Space Odyssey"; futurism melded into a finality of the highest evolution of civilization, with the present and antiquity. With all the genius and ingenuity possible – in the universe. "The Satanic Bible", containing the core scientific principles, doctrines, and beliefs of true Satanism; the theological core text, the "Summa Theologica" and ultimate in Satanism, the Satanic catechism. The foundation of Satanism as a true, feasible, and universal religion, and its universal authority – a true faith which is ultimately about converting pessimism, into optimism. Total anti–theistic faith, in its ultimate, universal, historic form. No one calling themselves a "Satanist" can truly be without it; the tome of all knowledge; the real philosopher's stone – the foundation of the new, true faith. In essence comprised of "reductio ad absurdum" anti-religion argumentation, which incorporates all the data of modern science.

Chiefly promotes Buddhism; primarily opposes tyranny. In essence, the leader of the new American Transcendentalist movement; in philosophy, it goes Schopenhauer–Nietzsche–Aljaddou, or Pessimism–Perspectivism–Optimism, respectively.

Satanism is ultimately the religion of America, representing the height of its religious liberty; abiding by the Satanic (Gregorian/Mayan) Calendar; and using the language of the Satanic Bible (English), the anagrammatic universal – sans godhead. Enrooted in the Neo–Fascism of the first two amendments of the United States Constitution: anti–concealment and anti–amnesty. The Satanic Bible being the preamble to the Universal United States. Offering the protection of the only lasting faith.

Satanism – is the one, true religion. Metrically calibrated and oriented to objective reality, in direct contrast to the wayward, mindless inclinations of theists, who falsely presume to take the power away from the true godhead – "I" Am. Founded here, ultimately, by the true Antichrist; Satan himself in human form. All applicable historiographic traditional and appropriate terms, acknowledging this . . . the true power over the Earth.

Founder of modern Taoist Yoga; the ultimate scientific form. Quintessential mathematical philosopher.

Alternate signatures include (the anagrams):

Anagram, am I? Mr. A., again! Or Ram, the Arm of Ra

(if myths manage a say).

Don Juan All–Ado.

The cleverest author in the English language – or existence.

Enunciator of the primary life goal . . . and the vanguard of all civilization . . . .

The Teaching of Apollo – the Science of Enlightenment

The height of philosophy.

Apollonianism, particularly in the vein of contrasting with the Dionysian, is a form of reformed Stoicism, and technically a refined Buddhism, as an enlightenment philosophy.

. . . .

2] RESULTS:

Apollonianism

– Nolan Aljaddou

The True Primary Life Philosophy, and Goal

Apollonianism has five fundamental principles, each representing a correction of Buddhist precepts, thus representing the actual true way:

1. White Light (contra "Emptiness")

2. Transformation (contra "Impermanence")

3. Sexuality (contra "Impersonality")

4. Person Being (contra "Rebirth")

5. Heaven (contra "Annihilation")

With this, the philosophy is actually liveable.

639

On Heaven:

The unlimited psychophysiological threshold – the cardiopulmonary circadian coma. A result of disciplined hypnotherapy which metrically severs the nervous link to sensory agitation (circulatory), agony (respiratory), or duress (rest cycle). A cumulative, calculative asceticism which ends constricting physiological ties to psychological, vulnerable self identity, as much as the initial umbilical cord to physical subsistence from the mother. Severance of their undue, asynchronous and straining incoordination. Nirvana. Liberation from all possible pain.

The counter–Dionysian (mindless indulgence and yearning); the impassive versus the impassioned; infinitely more tranquil and blissful.

The modern, proper, and full terminology for previously primitive Buddhist descriptions.

The technical, ultimate term, in the Western tradition: Apollonianism. Without much direct regard for palingenesis theory or implication.

A sheer wisdom ideal to be aspired to, like training, and acquisition of muscle. Achieved through Taoist Yoga practice.

The sum attained one is called an Apollonian saint, the highest ideal of the ancient academy, and knowledge tradition. Apollo, god of the sun, light, and life – another form of Ra, transfigured through the chief incarnation, "Ram", whose arm, likewise, is the bow. Who "I AM."

Alternately, the Roman god "Sol", the name of the sun as solar center, concurrent with Ophiuchus, the general, galactic center; the intrinsic, personified manifestation of which gives the pinnacle philosophy the alternate title of Centralism (the proper and correct scientific foundation upon the metric zero).

640

. . .

3] IMPACT:

Otherwise poetically known as "Ultra–Lutheranism"; the creed of which is "Fide, Sola Fide", or "By Faith, and Faith Alone." The sorting Gospel foundation of which, is the recitation:

Son of God, Son of Man

Son of God, Son of Man,

Coming in the clouds, with power you cannot understand . . .

Sin of flesh, sin of hand,

Withheld from fire; by Almighty command.

Sun of gold, sun of light,

Highest of visions . . . beyond all sight.

Sign of love, sign of grace,

Left untraced, right in place; rite of passage . . . the rite of salvation's face.

Sign of Truth, sign of He,

Who is without sin . . . for Eternity.

Sun of blessing, sun of mine . . .

Beckon toward the Kingdom of Heaven's shine.

Sin of Man, sin of All,

Redeemed by Might from plight of the fall;

Son of God, Son of Man,

All the grace of good . . . can only in His hand.

In Jesus' Name, the Christ;

Amen.

The message of Ultra–Lutheranism – one never has to ask the right for salvation.

The true foundation of which is inverted Taoist dyadic monotheism – that of the fully fulfilled Nietzsche's "Zarathustra". True Luciferianism.

Proven by the summation of all Biblical teaching: "Satan is Lord." The Bible, an example of learning by reverse psychology. God remaining, "I Am."

A form of Hinduism, in which one can worship any way they please; a precept of the Ontological Deistic Anthropic Principle: If there can be a God, then there can be a God. The way things are.

It can also be expressed as Arthur C. Clarke's "Chrislam".

. . .

4] TRUTHS:

All teachings of Taoist Yoga, and all ways of illumination, are in "The Satanic Bible" – alone.

Anagram, am I? Mr. A., again! Or Ram, the Arm of Ra

(if myths manage a say).

Here, an incarnation with God, rather than of God. Ra, the supreme intercessor.

– Don Juan All–Ado

. . .

5] FACTS:

The Ritualistic Practice of Satanism, and the Science of Magic (Sacred Geometry):

Light 7 candles in a heptagram design, cast the spell in My Name (Amen Ra), and blow out the candles, regularly – and the spell will work, within reason. Do so for at least 18 days (6, 6, 6). This will triangulate the result on all material planes.

666 being the 4–dimensional spacetime trace of "pi", the constant ratio of the symmetric universe (the tracing remainder–eliminating floor function of pi being "3", when superimposed onto itself, becoming "6", in the three dimensions of space in linear time). Anything designed in terms of "666" will come about – sacred geometry, exposed.

. . .

6] RULE:

The Satanic Rules: Only greater hatred can defeat lesser hatred; and truth is always truer with a weapon. Coincident to the Kantian Rule: If you can't be civilized, you don't belong in civilization. The foundation of law; and the legal system.

Satanism is not about carnal empowerment, but regretless indulgence. The difference between Weak and Strong Satanism, corresponding to weak and strong atheism. I, having founded the latter.

The 5 Components, and 20 Elements, of the demonic doctrine of scientifically precise Satanism: The 6 Planes of Existence, the 7 Principles of Satanism, the 5 Precepts of Apollonianism, and the 2 Satanic Rules. The Zeroth, is "The Satanic Bible" itself. Founded upon the additional pillars of Mantra invocation formulae, mastery of silence with stillness (Abyss absorption), prayer [only to Satan], ritualistic magic; general mathematical aptitude; and erudition. The 3 Foundations of the Eternal Satanic Church: The Satanic Bible, the Satanic Doctrine, and the Satanic Priesthood. There is a right way, and a wrong way; this being the right way. The lattermost, being chiefly concerned with the practical craft of "grey" wizardry (the even–handed path of equilibrium of black and white magic, the best historic example being the concept of the ancient Egyptian curse); initiation into its "Sacred Rite of the Pyramidal Order" (the "Illuminati") being a 33–degree Masonic path, of which I am the high priest, as attained arahant. The goal of all religious practice being to see the silence in silence . . . and the stillness in the still. The authority of the church residing from the Divine Right of extraterrestrial (celestial) invocation . . . which in the end, is nothing more than – and need be nothing more than – ourselves. The Satanic Bible, as foundation, being the word, as the timeless supreme harmony of all music. The ultimate geodesic guide to life. Physics – realized. The ultimate religious guide.

Ultimately an extension of the Measurement Theory, or Kabbalah ("Tree of Knowledge"), land the self–cancelling, self–conserving tautology of the zero – the greatest realization of all history, the modern "wheel" . . . leading to supreme bliss and providence. By, no less than, "The Author" – Himself. The greatest revelation in the end, that the 2012 Alignment is true, as an arbitrarily accurate, precise statistical limit – with 0 deviation. The Ultrazodiac. The star map . . . as above, so below.

. . .

7] INSIGHTS:

All technically a form of "Extreme Buddhism", which teaches that there is only one life, but after death, either the experience of Nirvana (pure Heaven,

644

proceeding from Apollonian attainment) [union with the agreeable singular], or Anti–Nirvana (pure "Hell", or infinite pain) [disunion from the singular agreeable]. Hence the term, "Ultra–Lutheranism". A full symbolic teaching.

A tangential, pragmatic outlook on the statistical, symmetric organic palingenesis. A scientific Hinduism, which all forms of Buddhism were technically at the root. Summarized as the scientific form of Christianity; the flip side of Christian Science.

Organic life being an extrapolation of the First Law of Statistics – Perimeter Conservation: The ultimately more constructive outcome will be preserved. The balance to chaos.

Existence accounted for by anthropic equilibrium, homeostasis, and "statistical" design (organic trial and error), originating from nucleic/nuclear fusion in the sun, in the Kantian Nebular Biogenesis Hypothesis – the complete view, simply summarized properly as ("Neo–") Darwinian natural selection. I, being the founder of Neo–Darwinism.

The Subtlest Truth: The Conspiracy Rule – any sufficiently major event, conspiratorial in nature, leaves false positives as a trail to a false and greater conspiracy, due to circumstantial possibility, as a rule. However, this nullifies their relevance, rendering them totally moot. The correct means of interpreting their true breadth of scope is observation of the principle that nothing can disrupt the status quo, ultimately. Thus, we are indeed living in the birth of the height of civilized society. Theistic claims to a theological alternative to a naturalistic explanation of reality, however, are indeed examples of failing to correctly assert a greater conspiracy in Nature, and thus the best example of failing with the Conspiracy Rule.

. . .

8] NATURE:

This is the root and exact entirety of Vaishnavism itself. Rama, the chief manifestation of which. The centralized philosophy of life sustainment; Vishnu, the ideal of preservation [literally, "Preserver"].

. . .

9] REALIZATIONS:

The general organic continuum; another term for the self–proving, and self–evident, palingenesis. The universal Life Cycle. Summarized by the fact that the timeline is equivalently cyclical, extending tangentially to all biological processes. Proven by the term "cyclical sequence" – or the term "cycle" itself, which is a self–reinforcing circuit. Capable of being ceased only by a pinpoint counter–cycling, or the stilling effect of Taoist Yoga practice.

Suspension in time, as being. Replaceable equally by the neutralizing continuum.

Achievable through objectively self–reinforcing mantra, or silent, one–pointed meditation.

The point of re–emergent physiological causality. The driving force of which was the intangible; the "Will". Ceased by the cardiopulmonary circadian coma.

Nirvana theory; or the technicalization of Schopenhauer.

Liberation from pain, or all possible rebirth into a world of pain.

The cornerstone of Strong Satanism, the universal religion; a scientific apprehension of contextual phenomenology, not bereft or void of purpose, or understanding of causality. The way of esoteric illumination, the final truth, and contextually, historically precise, universal Illuminism. Not a combination of all the religions, but a distillation of all the truth – from all religion.

I have achieved it; can you?

Basically, prior to me, there was just hypothetical Buddhism. Now there is actual Buddhism.

Like da Vinci's flying machine, become the Wright airplane.

A solution to the ultimate mathematical, philosophical, religious, and literary conundrum. The true answer to the riddle of the Sphinx, 666, and the Philosopher's Stone. The actual Holy Grail – of scientific pursuit. The true alchemical formula for magic.

Solarism, the ultimate philosophy of all times, past and present. The way of the future. The guiding way of light – beyond all light. That of true God; Ra.

Ra is technically the zeroth, monumental, and pinnacle deity of the Earth; or technical, linguistic, God Proper, expressionally, irrespective even of atheism – historically the supreme, original, and only deity. Beyond king of kings . . . God of gods. And I . . . Am . . . He. Manifest in the general avatar fashion. Theists, then practicing a generalization or wayward technical translation of this, are categorically in error.

I am the scourge of the demiurge.

. . . .

10] SUM:

Nolan Aljaddou [ˈældʒɪˌdoʊ; AL–juh–doe].

Physicist, mathematician, logician, philosopher.

The key teaching being the 33–fold Gateway to Masonic Illumination: The 13 Step Pyramidal Gate to the Nirvana (Heaven), the 4 Noble Truths (of the Nirvana), and the dual Eightfold Way (of the Void), leading to Heaven, and the ceasing of the cycle of reincarnations . . . Taoist Yoga. A modern, scientific approach to Buddhism, and the ultimate goal in behavioral psychology and the religion of science, Neo–Scientology: Alpha–Achieved; true Buddhahood.

Also, enlightened arahant.

. . .

11] LEGACY:

A Biography – Scientific Truths Summary

Science philosopher; a mathematician who speaks for being.

Principal Discoveries:

* The Definition of Nirvana: The experience to end all others. Cloud Nine, Seventh Heaven, limitless euphoria. Result of "pure love"; no more dissatisfaction; no more life–cycling purpose. Heaven. Total self–liberation. Chakra cycle energies exhausted.

* With great beauty comes great truth – for then the world is open up in all its true possibility.

648

* The Zero Theorem (the Principle of Algebra): Zero, as totally indivisible, is technically the only prime number, and thus the universal root of all measures, through identity multiplication.

* The Sum of Philosophical Understanding: that existence just exists.

* There is no God – nor is there needed one.

* Buddhism is technically the reduced flat baseline zero–root religion.

* True love entails an absolute recognition of mortality.

* The Causal Principle: This can exist in context; so it does.

* I am the modern, scientific "Nagarjuna"; and "Zoroaster". "The Satanic Bible" is, properly, letters from God; the supreme deity, "Ahriman" (or "a Raman", and "a Ra–man", as avatar thereof), conquering the illusion of Ahura Mazda; a Dionysian universe, the alignment therewith being true synchronous balance in Apollonianism. I am no less than the messianic meeting ground, as the "prophet of God", teaching that which concerns the previously mystical and mysterious: the Abyss . . . the true fulfillment of Nietzsche, AS the ultimate "Zarathustra" . . . that SATAN IS GOD . . . the ultimate revelation.

* Forms of Buddhism [the Ultimate Religion]

– Christianity – Acute Karmic Buddhism [Layman's]

– Judaism – Acute Mahayana Buddhism [Expert's]

– Islam – Acute Vajrayana Buddhism [Scholar's]

– Hinduism – Acute Theravada Buddhism [Individual's]

– Scientology – Acute Atheistic Buddhism [Community's]

Evident in all the mystic sects.

The Rest – Direct Buddhism

* The Four Precepts of Scientific Christianity

(1) Fide, Sola Fide (By Faith, and Faith Alone). (2) Heaven is pure love. (3) The Satanic Bible. (4) King James Version Holy Bible [The 10 Commandments, The Gospel According to John, The Book of Revelation].

* Palingenesis is intrinsically an agnostic principle.

* My consistency is the very Gospel consistency – to the letter.

* 9/11 is an inside job. Americans, and the police, are natural terrorists. Thus having earned it.

* My Illuminati/Rockefeller association is a Fritz Lang "Metropolis/Dr.– Mabuse" Lady Gaga genius connection. Nostradamus's final Antichrist, "Mabus" . . . "Dr. Mabuse", come to life. 2012 prophecy – fulfilled. "Queen's" "Radio Ga Ga" music video, "Lady" Gaga's title/name inspiration.

650

* Theoretical computer science commandeering: something that can enforce ultimate order on all levels – and this is it. Physical computer science. Universal zero–point encryption. Pyramidal Galois–theoretic combinatorial grid mechanics. The algorithmic means by which a computer network is internally susceptible to total programmer overhaul, organically and heuristically. The certainty here is calibrated . . . to 100%.

* Zero in, as:

1. Point – Lattice Theory

2. Number – Graph Theory

3. Axiom – Logic

4. Pole – Combinatorics

5. Difference – Computation

6. Limit – Calculus

7. Empty Set – Set Theory

8. Root – Arithmetic

9. Placeholder – Trigonometry

10. Prime – Number Theory

11. Function – Algebra

12. Equilibrium – Game Theory

13. Center – Geometry

All axiomatic logic, thus, self–consistently, worked out.

* The Satanic Bible is the bible of rock and roll. Sequel to the Book of Revelation, synchronously. The Original Testament, in relation to the Old and New Testament of the Holy Bible.

651

* I am the most important scientific thinker of all time.

* The universe exists by recursive induction. Sheer identity; tautology.

True Founder of the Four Root Branches of Applied Mathematical Technique – Physical Science:

1) Arithmetic – The Science of Energy [Biology]

2) Algebra – The Science of Matter [Chemistry]

3) Geometry – The Science of Space [Physics]

4) Calculus – The Science of Time [Logic]

– – – – –

ANTIPOSITIVISM – Empirical Science

Foundations –

Equations:

1. $0 = 0$

2. $V = 0i$

3. $V = 0i + 0j + 0k$

4. V' = 0

The Conclusion:

Zero is technically the flat, reduced, baseline, sheer existential property, as the sole vacuum. The first, and foremost, fundamental, ultimate principle.

"0 is the Emptiness that negates all else save itself."

Translations:

1) v' = 0

2) F = mv'

3) mv' = k

Newton's Equations

The rest follows. In this proper formulation.

The sum of Neo–Scientology.

...

Neo–Scientology may be defined as five things:

The Philosophy of Science

The Science of Philosophy

The Philosophy of Religion

The Science of Religion

The Religion of Science

...

The ultimate technology, unveiled: the physics reality of the hyper–tunnel, or light speed vacuum acceleration. A form of "jump gate" technology which precipitates the possibility of interstellar travel; achieved through stimulation of Hawking radiation in the vacuum from an intensified and inverse Casimir effect. A result of the vacuum equation and the "second equivalence principle of general relativity" – light is equally at rest in a vacuum.

The Model of Science – The 10 Objects of Science

1. Nuclear Fission – Zero–Point Energy (Quark Isolation) [Radio LASER, Quark Ejection]

2. LASER Technology – Zero–Point Spatiality (Electron Isolation) [Intense Magnetic Field, Electron Displacement]

3. Light Speed Drive – Zero–Point Temporality (Electron–Neutrino Isolation) [GASER Higgs Equalization, Hyper–Vacuum Acceleration]

4. Cosmogeny Comprehension – Zero–Point Materiality (Tau–Muon Isolation) [Antimatter Catalysis Decay, Equalized Ellipsoid Expansion]

5. Buddhist Enlightenment – Zero–Point Observation (Photon Isolation) [Palingenesis Causal Circle, Loop Cessation]

6. Neo–Scientology Practice – Zero–Point Trajectory (Positron Isolation) [Geometrically Principled Philosophy, Social Service]

7. Taoist Yoga Mastery – Zero–Point Pulse (Weak–Gauge Boson Isolation) [Meditation/Mantra, Sensory Mastery]

8. Intrinsic, or "Satanic", "Bible" Knowledge – Zero–Point Cryptography (Selectron Isolation) [Zero As Vacuum, The Flatly Existential Property]

9. Overturning Governing Conspiracies – Zero–Point Historiography (Gluon Isolation) [Anarcho–Totalitarian Historical Model, Martial Law Paradigm Replacement]

10. Curing Mental Disease – Zero–Point Viscerality (Higgs–Boson Isolation) [Jaw–Base Disalignment, Jaw–Clenching/Respiration–Sight–Sense–Deprivation–Therapy]

Founders

Physics – Newton

Mathematics – Euler

Chemistry – Descartes

Biology – Darwin

Astronomy – Kepler

Political – Jefferson

Military – Hitler

Linguistic – Schopenhauer

History – Gutenberg

Logic – Gödel

Sum: "Dasein" As Zero; Language As Objective Geometric Cryptography; the Self–Justifying Hermeneutic Circle

. . . .

12] LEGEND:

Master Thesis 1:

I mathematically discovered the identity of the self–iterating, or the recursive: 0. Existence, in Nature, as Being itself. The restrictive constraining, such that there exists nothing else, and nothing besides. The intrinsically existential property. The foundation of language. The ultimate truth. Physically, the sole, and sheer, vacuum. The fundamental identity principle, as that which is equivalent to sheer proportionality itself and nothing else . . . generally, and in no uncertain terms. The mathematically precise definition of "being". Reductionism . . . encapsulated. As philosophy of science, it may thus be called zeroism, triangulationism, triangle–ism, or cyclism. Chiefly, Centralism. Technically translating as Buddhist cosmogeny, or "vacuism".

The philosophy of the future. Nietzsche's.

The total dissolution of nothingness blends into all of Existence; the abstract existential qualia. 0. Total equilibrium. That which is universally uncreatable, and indirectly, just there. A uniform, universal, substantial, sheer absence. Total union in non–quantifiability.

0, the foremost physics principle. The Alpha, and the Omega. The Dasein of Heidegger; the noumenon of Kant; the God of Descartes.

The significance of the pyramid is that it is the reductive, minimalist total (3–dimensional centered triangulation, 666) convergence. 0. God. I Am. The principle of all mathematics. Graph–node theory proper, 20 counting the number of perfect zeroes in a perfect pyramid – including triangle face centroids. 13 establishing it implicitly, the summit – the graph–theoretic origin; 0i, extracted from all one–dimensionality.

The tip, the All–Seeing Eye of God; Ra. The perfect pyramid. I Am That I Am:

Anagram, am I? Mr. A., again! Or Ram, the Arm of Ra

(if myths manage a say).

The ram being the historic human vessel, and avatar godhead, of Ra, associated with incarnation (alternately the universal manifestation of the supreme true God, "Rama" or "Ram"), and the construction of the Great Pyramids – which are the gyroscopic universal centralized fixed point of Earth's land mass, the pinnacle stationary anti–parallax to the centralized geodesic reference system of Orion's Belt, and a universally auspicious entombment for the continuous afterlife, and future incarnation – a universal global zero base, along with the pyramidal Mayan Calendar. I Am, thus, literally Ra. I Am That I Am.

Egyptology, fully revived, as the ultimate way (all deities originally derived from the cradle of civilization; Babylon). As in the Beginning . . . so in the End. The complete counter to the historic Hebrew god. Also traditionally known, by the ram's horns, as Satan. True God. The extraterrestrials, the Nephilim, or "fallen angels". Upon the Earth, of whom I Am king. This work, the literal revelation of Armageddon; universal Vedic astrology, optimized to precise exactitude; true and atheistic gnosticism, the Akashic Records' translation and convergence point of the organic with the inorganic; precise celestial mechanics, the point at which the relative meets the absolute . . . as above, so below. The 2012 alignment, the true dawning of the Age of Aquarius. A virtual "Einstein–Rosen bridge", as geodesic from the center of the galaxy, as causally alternative–less result; the true star gate. The Satanic Bible, the literal word of the universe, seared and sealed from the mouth of Hell; the manifestation of Satan, the greatest true God, conquering even God . . . by his Antichrist. Lord of darkness, gatherer of lost souls. The serpent's gate of Ophiuchus, opened . . . the religion of the Mayans; the philosophy of the Egyptians. "Mayan Day", or "Zero Day", the only true holiday – to be celebrated on December 21st in commemoration of the conquering of the demon Ravana, and of the Mayan Calendar's termination, yet true transcendent beginning, in 2012; cyclically. The miracle of Jesus was the incarnation of the flesh; the miracle of Muhammad was the incarnation of the word; the miracle of the Buddha was the incarnation of transcendence . . . my miracle is the Anagram, and "The Satanic Bible" . . . as living Divinity, in all its chapters and verses, numbered, and numberless . . . the direct, literal, inspiration . . . of the Infinite.

Anagram, am I? Mr. A., again! Or Ram, the Arm of Ra

(if myths manage a say).

The technical Zeroth statement in all English – or any language. Confirming my being the Antichrist – the material incarnation of Satan.

Ability to see through transparency to sheer existence itself, as the 0, the all–encompassing entity of the whole (and all associated causal interconnections), is a cognitive, and conceptual, "zero"; what is technically, historically referred to as "Clear" in Scientology – a proto–scientific religion, itself a somewhat mythic structure, and effort to deprogram one from religion, into the base starting point for the true way of initiation to comprehensive enlightenment: Neo–Scientology; the religion of science itself. I, having founded such a tradition, and the invaluable data contained therein; the continuation of all efforts in such a vein. Rarefied abstracted information, and the most sought–after technical knowledge in the universe, essential and vital to ultimate success in life . . . the ultimate pursuit of all religions and traditions.

Which are namely, the exact, complete sequels to Arthur Schopenhauer, Friedrich Nietzsche, L. Ron Hubbard, and Bertrand Russell. Taoist Yoga practice, and sum philosophy derived directly from all precise physics, being the pinnacle achievement. I am the authentic form of the four, in totality.

The Anagram is thus literally true, as I am the mouthpiece of God in any of His infinite forms, literally speaking for the entirety of the universe and its workings . . . as the central avatar for such.

Master Thesis 2:

All literary deconstruction is reinterpreting things as satire.

The 2012 alignment is true at a tangent–slice of 4–dimensional spacetime, indicating only infinite love and luckiness – my encounter with Hayley Williams. "The Satanic Bible" is the proof.

Master Thesis 3:

The definition of physics: abstract reasoning which is true, whether or not you want it to be.

"The Satanic Bible", then, is literally "The" Bible – of the ultimate Truth. Transnaturalism, as the replacement for the supernatural; God, literally revealed, in manuscript form.

Acquisition of knowledge is combining known with unknown, always analogizing. True knowledge, however, is knowing that one knows everything . . . already.

. . .

13] DISCOVERIES:

Buddhist Philosophy: You're better off dead.

Satanist Philosophy: You're better off dead.

Satanism wins.

The Principle of Satanism: Man is God. Not merely Man become God, but Man AS God. The creed:

I AM.

ARE YOU?

The Principles of Religion – The Four Characters of Stupidity: Passive Aggression, Attempted Brutalization, Pseudo–Cleverness, Assumption.

The Three Root Assumed and Posited ("Positivist") Characteristics of "God":

Presence, Omnipotence, Perfection.

The Foundation of Antipositivism: Science –

The Four Disproofs of God:

1) The Ontological Disproof:

A perfect being, existing by necessity of that perfection, is impossible, as "being" is then redundantly, and then hollowly, reinforced as such. Something cannot be made from nothing.

Negative.

2) The Logical Disproof:

A potential Almighty being, in reality, can never exist manifestly, as that sheer potentiality negates the causal assumption of such omnipotence, in principle. Nothing itself cannot be made out of something.

Neutral.

3) The Metalogical Disproof:

Zero is the reductive root principle which accounts for all quantitative being as such, and is existentially deduced as the supreme causal principle – there being no other. Something comes from something.

Positive.

4) The Physical Disproof:

The fact that I am that I am, is statically continuous in context, and thus a contextual independent process and precept, in principle, in itself, which cannot be causally, physically preceded or altered by any greater principle, at all (in context), precludes the non–negligible imagining of such. Nothing is made from nothing.

Tautological.

God is an assumption, the insurmountable burden of proof resting on the claimant. Existence is naturally atheistic. The chief category mistake being the concept of an absolute beginning without an absolute end, or the total neglect of the applicability of relative beginnings; completely arbitrary, and subjective; and equally immaterial. All is a consistent, static continuum of an absolute, precise wholeness. Integrity of physicality, irrespective of integrity of mind. The governing principle, with all in its respective, proper place.

"Antipositivism" is the mathematically precise term for causalism, or science; a consistent, linear inference and root deduction to specific causes, existing totally in relation to the metric observer. All cancelling into an equilibrium of a void of the insubstantial and arbitrary present perception. Equivalently, zeroism.

Also, metric originalism; in short. All founded upon measurement, and its source, the zero. Proper recognition of reality and realism; naturalism, cognizant of the function of zero as universal origin; the zeroth, preceding all quantity and non–quantity . . . as first. Science. The First, and true, Philosophy. That being the religion of science: Neo–Scientology. The final and ultimate religion. Everything reduces to the zero. The dissolution of all parts into the whole is the nothingness. Reality. As foundation of science, it may be summarized thusly: "The origin and end of everything is the metric zero. Conservation of total equilibrium, resulting in the present moment." The cyclical continuum. Self–sustaining. Existence. THE ontology – of zero. The fundamental law of physics being the resultant conservation of energy.

The meaning of the conservation of energy is that energy and matter are never created or destroyed. Perfect cyclical equilibrium.

Precursors and echoers of zeroism, and originalism, include the earliest, to the most recent . . . the most elementary, and the most advanced: Gorgias, Plotinus, Buddha, Descartes, Leibniz, Sartre, and Pearce. Finalized in me.

I am hence the foremost atheist of all history.

"God is dead. God remains dead. And I have killed him."

– Nolan Aljaddou

The Age of God is over: 0 AD.

. . .

14] ACKNOWLEDGEMENTS:

A true author is a philosophical theoretician, and a musical poet.

*

True philosopher, physician and diagnostician, of mind.

Metapsychology – A Neo–Freudian Assessment of Social Deviance

God's Rosetta Stone of the Mind

The emotional coma, or psychological paralysis, and its 20 archetypal phases [self–defeating behaviors]:

1. Psychosis NOS [Not Otherwise Specified] – Conflicted Satisfaction

2. Schizophrenia – Conflicted Reason

3. Bipolar Disorder – Conflicted Worldview

4. Schizoid Personality Disorder – Conflicted Felicity

5. Borderline Personality – Conflicted Sexuality

6. Avoidant Personality Disorder – Conflicted Genitalia

7. Paranoid Personality Disorder – Conflicted Heterosexual Pederasty

8. Histrionic Personality Disorder – Conflicted Homosexual Group Pederasty

9. Autism – Conflicted Maternal Incestuousness and Suicidality

10. Mental Retardation – Conflicted Gacy Complex

11. Dissociative Identity Disorder – Conflicted Homicidal Oedipal Complex

12. Depression – Conflicted Elektra Complex

13. Antisocial Personality Disorder – Conflicted Homicidal Heterosexual Pederasty and Sibling Incestuousness

14. Dementia – Conflicted Idealized Amorousness Obsession

15. Generalized Anxiety Disorder – Conflicted Maternal Incestuousness

16. Post–Traumatic Stress Disorder – Conflicted Homosexual Necrophilia

17. Attention–Deficit/Hyperactivity Disorder – Amorous Stalker Obsession

18. Sociopathy – Amorous and Exhibitionist Homicidal Obsession

19. Psychopathy – Homicidal Homosexual Pederasty

20. Narcissistic Personality Disorder – Conflicted Hitlerian Obsession

These include all stunted behaviors of a religious character.

663

Thomas Henry Huxley was Darwin's bulldog, and Aldous Huxley was the psychedelic Orwellian muse of Jim Morrison. I am Darwin's machete, and the poet laureate of infinity. Philosophically, and sociologically . . . . I am the anti–"1984".

*

The 10 Charter Characteristics of Satanism, and the Ubermensch:

1. Anti–Concealment

2. Anti–Amnesty

3. Anti–Imbecility

4. Anti–Kamikaze–Scout

5. Anti–Obsequious–Criminal

6. Anti–Statutory–Stringency

7. Anti–Primitive–Aggression

8. Anti–Military–Blunder

9. Anti–Positivism

10. Anti–Hollow–Impediment

The Darwinian response to the burgeoning Neanderthaloid mindless animal, Homo retardari – modern man; extinct at the gates.

*

The final explanation for what happens after physiological death – a complete equivalent, physically, of total numbness, and dreamless sleep . . . followed by either instant re–emergent consciousness as another organism example, or unspeakable, supreme bliss of transcendent, relative disengagement . . . . beyond Heaven; Elysium.

*

The Biggest Mistake: Thinking that there is such a thing as "nothing". Nothing is always relative to something, and something always exists. Things didn't come from nothing, nor did they have to. There is only a relative nothing, never an absolute "nothing"; an absolute nothing being a category mistake and a total self–contradiction; the most severe. For it is equivalent to thinking that nothing exists, indicative only of a wishful thinking nihilism, or a self–hatred, idiocy, and suicidality, the animalistic hallmark of all religions. In which things take on an arbitrary imaginary character.

The true origin, however, is always zero, which is not nothing alone, but lack of a relative something. Incomprehension of this category principle indicates an irredeemable autistic linguistic deficit on the part of the species, in which they have not extrapolated from all being anything akin to a comprehension, like vainly attempting to extrapolate speech comprehension from a mimicking parrot. Indicative of an evolutionary dead end for the cranial recess of present Man. Hence the empirical and practical necessity of requisite genetic modification.

***

15] IDENTITY:

In summation, I am ultimately the world's first, and the only true, Jungian analytical psychology author. God of Atheism, exposing its true Nature – as the conquest of all false gods; Satan, as the serpentine muse . . . all that remains.

. . .

16] ALL:

In this phrase, I am the culmination of Sartre, Nietzsche, Descartes, Schopenhauer, Kant, and all the philosophers: There exists nothing besides nothingness.

BEYOND THE FINITE, LIES THE INFINITE; BEYOND THE INFINITE, THE FINITE. IN THE NAME OF LUCIFER, THE BRIGHT AND MORNING STAR, THE RAM, FIRST AND FOREMOST; MASTER OF THE FOUR WINDS, NORTH, EAST, WEST, AND SOUTH; THE CENTER, THE ZERO, THE ORIGIN; THE "WORD".

Anagram, am I? Mr. A., again! Or Ram, the Arm of Ra

(if myths manage a say).

I Am That I Am.

Amen.

Made in the USA
Las Vegas, NV
22 November 2021